ASHES OF OUR FATHERS

GABRIEL GAVIN

Ashes of Our Fathers

Inside the Fall of Nagorno-Karabakh

HURST & COMPANY, LONDON

First published in the United Kingdom in 2025 by
C. Hurst & Co. (Publishers) Ltd.,
New Wing, Somerset House, Strand, London, WC2R 1LA
© Gabriel Gavin, 2025
All rights reserved.

Distributed in the United States, Canada and Latin America by
Oxford University Press, 198 Madison Avenue, New York, NY 10016,
United States of America.

The right of Gabriel Gavin to be identified as the author of
this publication is asserted by him in accordance with the
Copyright, Designs and Patents Act, 1988.

A Cataloguing-in-Publication data record for this book
is available from the British Library.

ISBN: 9781911723578

This book is printed using paper from registered sustainable
and managed sources.

www.hurstpublishers.com

Printed and bound in Great Britain by Bell & Bain Ltd, Glasgow

CONTENTS

Map	vii
Timeline of Key Events	ix
Author's Note	xi
Introduction	1

PART ONE
A CONFLICT UNFROZEN, 2020

1. The Beginning of the End	25
2. From One War to Another	49

PART TWO
THE FALL OF NAGORNO-KARABAKH, 2022–3

3. "It's Started"	75
4. Jerusalem of the Caucasus	105
5. A Tale of Two Armenias	125
6. Blockade	151
7. Exodus	191

PART THREE
THE AFTERMATH

8. The World Watches On	223
9. A Nation United	251
10. A Nation No More	271
Acknowledgements	293
List of Illustrations	295
Notes	297
Select Bibliography	311
Index	317

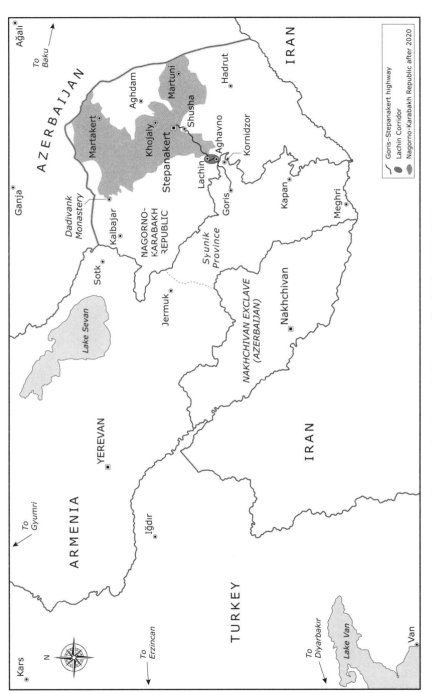

Armenia, Azerbaijan & Nagorno-Karabakh, 1992–2023

TIMELINE OF KEY EVENTS

1917–18: Collapse of the Russian Empire; Azerbaijan & Armenia declare independent republics. Nagorno-Karabakh's Armenian population declares independence.

1919: Azerbaijan launches campaign to reassert control over Nagorno-Karabakh, as ethnic violence rages; Armenian quarter of Shusha/Shushi destroyed.

1920–23: Red Army conquers Armenia and Azerbaijan, creating Soviet Socialist Republics; Nagorno-Karabakh becomes an autonomous region of the Azerbaijani SSR.

1988–94: Collapse of the USSR & outbreak of First Nagorno-Karabakh War; Armenians capture Shusha.

1991: Nagorno-Karabakh Republic proclaimed; independence unilaterally declared.

2020: *Sept–Nov:* Second Nagorno-Karabakh War; Azerbaijan captures Shushi. Russian peacekeepers installed post-ceasefire.

2022: *Sept:* Azerbaijan's Two Day War on Armenia. *Dec:* Lachin Corridor occupied; blockade of Nagorno-Karabakh begins.

2023: *Sept:* Azerbaijan launches final assault on Nagorno-Karabakh, conquering the region (One Day War). Stepanakert falls to Azerbaijan; mass exodus of Karabakh Armenians.

AUTHOR'S NOTE

This book is based on dozens of interviews with officials, soldiers, activists, experts and ordinary people over the course of more than three years. In order to protect their identities, the names of some people have been changed, or in other cases I have omitted the last names of those I have spoken to. In the case of civil servants and diplomats, many were granted anonymity to be able to speak candidly.

Language is a battleground in the South Caucasus. It is a longstanding tradition for those covering the region to refer to the place names used by the majority of those living there. Where territory has changed hands, as it so often does in this story, I have generally tried to reflect that in toponyms. For example, the capital of Armenian Nagorno-Karabakh, Stepanakert, becomes Khankendi after being conquered by Azerbaijan in 2023. The holy city known to Armenians as Shushi becomes Shusha once taken back by Azerbaijani troops during the 2020 war.

This is intended only to reflect reality on the ground, rather than endorse one side's claim over another.

For the book's map, which readers may find helpful throughout, I have used the names which appear most often in the text, for ease of use. Thus Aghavno is marked, as most of the book takes place prior to its handover to Azerbaijan, after which it becomes Zabukh in the text.

INTRODUCTION

In a decade defined by war, chaos and violence against civilians, the destruction of Nagorno-Karabakh is destined to be no more than a historical footnote. In a way, that's no surprise—this has always been one of Eurasia's forgotten conflicts. For three decades, few have taken much notice of the bloodshed, the tragedy and the hatred bubbling away in this corner of the South Caucasus. So, it was only to be expected that the exodus of Nagorno-Karabakh's entire population in September 2023 wasn't met with the headlines and the outrage that have accompanied other humanitarian catastrophes in Eastern Europe and the Middle East. But the fate of the hundreds of thousands of Armenians and Azerbaijanis caught up in the longest-running standoff in the former Soviet Union matters, and it reveals a lot about the world we now live in, one that's getting less and less safe, and where there are fewer and fewer consequences for those responsible. Without learning lessons from Nagorno-Karabakh, the violence, desperation, misplaced faith and shattered hope both sides have endured will soon be seen far further afield. It likely already is.

In March 2022, I packed an overnight bag and went to the central bus station in the Armenian capital, Yerevan, hoping for a ride to the border city of Goris. At a shack on the edge of the frosty square, I ordered an anaemic-looking kebab and waited for a *marshrutka*, the cramped minibuses that zip along side streets and highways throughout the former Soviet Union. But when the van shuddered into the lot, the man behind the wheel waved a hand to point out that it was full. Instead, I found Tigran, a thirty-two-year-old handyman moonlighting as a taxi driver for some extra cash.

"I can take you," he said. "But it won't be cheap. It's a five-hour drive—I can do it in four, but I'll have to make the trip back afterwards, and it's going to be snowing in the mountains."

As we watched a gas station attendant fill up the tank with pressurised LPG, a cheaper alternative to petrol that only occasionally causes explosions, I told him I was heading down to cover the conflict. Just a few days before, three Armenian soldiers had been killed in an apparent drone strike just across the border in the breakaway region of Nagorno-Karabakh, as Azerbaijani forces moved to take control of strategic high ground.

"Don't worry about the money. Just pay for the gas," Tigran said, beaming as he reached over to hug me. "It's so good you are here."

We drove on, arguing about my right to pay full price for his time, while Tigran flicked through photos on his phone with one hand, navigating the car around potholes and stray cows with the other. Just a year-and-a-half earlier, he'd been in Nagorno-Karabakh as a volunteer soldier, dressed in fatigues and brandishing an AK-74 rifle that looked older than he was.

"We were dropped off in the woods by a truck," he explained, pointing to a picture of four or five men standing around a campfire. "We had no orders except to defend the position. We didn't have a radio and we had to call around to find out what was going on."

When it came time to retreat, they did so on foot—begging speeding trucks and ambulances to stop and pick them up as they whizzed past.

INTRODUCTION

"He's dead now," my new friend said, zooming in on the face of one of his former comrades. "It was hell, but I'd go back tomorrow if I had to." In the glove compartment was his little red military service book, stamped once when he was conscripted at eighteen and a second time when he arrived at the commissariat to volunteer in the 2020 war. There was plenty of space for a third, fourth or even fifth stamp.

Tigran's story isn't unique. A few months later, on the other side of the border, I was standing on a hillside in what was now an Azerbaijani-controlled part of Nagorno-Karabakh looking down across the front lines with a young translator, Anar, who was explaining how disappointed he'd been that he wasn't called up for service to fight in that same war, while his brothers and friends were.

"But you have two young children," I asked, "weren't you afraid that if you went off to fight you might not come back?"

"No," he said, without even having to think. "If I died a *shahid*—a martyr—my family would want for nothing. Even if the government didn't look after them, our relatives, our entire village would."

This rugged landscape south of the vast Caucasus mountain range has played host to over a century of animosity and, like Tigran and Anar, every living generation of Armenians and Azerbaijanis has known violence, hardship and mutual hatred. In the autumn of 2023, decades of bloodshed reached a colossal crescendo. But war hasn't always been the default state for the two main ethnic groups who call this part of the world home. Throughout much of history, they lived side by side—not as modern nation states with governments and armies, but as disenfranchised peoples on the periphery of great empires. The Silk Road, traipsed by merchants carrying treasures like porcelain and spices from the east, passed through these mountains, making whoever controlled them astonishingly wealthy and powerful. As a result, the land was fought over and ruled through the centuries by Arabs, Mongols, Turkmen tribes, the Seljuk Turks from the east, the Persians from the south and the Ottomans from the west.

But, by the 1800s, a new invader was crossing the mountains from the north and, one by one, kingdoms and *khanates* were forced to bend the knee to the advancing Russian Empire. Storming fortified cliffside villages, coercing local leaders into answering to the tsar and even liquidating entire rebellious clans and ethnic groups, the Russians wrested the entire Caucasus from both those who had inherited it, and those who hoped to conquer it for themselves. In an epic account of those battles, court intrigue and massacres from 1720 to 1860, British explorer John Baddeley wrote that while Moscow had the manpower and the resources, their ambitions were often dashed at the hands of foes who had something almost as powerful. "It may be said without exaggeration that the mountains made the men; and the men in return fought with passionate courage and energy in defence of their beloved mountains."[1]

Baddeley was writing about the warlike clans of the North Caucasus, in regions like Chechnya, Dagestan, Ingushetia, Kabardino-Balkaria and Adygea, which bore the brunt of the military campaigns, rebellions, genocides and repression. By contrast, at the time, the south was far easier for the Russians to subdue. The Christian Georgians and Armenians, and the Turkic Azeris, had suffered under Persian rule and frequent wars with the Ottomans. But while the tsars and military governors may not have treated them as harshly as their neighbours, there was little doubt that while they may have their own individual pasts, their future now lay in being ruled from Moscow—and disloyalty would be punished severely.

The Armenians trace their ancestry back to the ancient kingdoms that ranged intermittently across what is now eastern Turkey and the South Caucasus since antiquity, priding them-

INTRODUCTION

selves on being the world's oldest Christian nation after King Tiridates III converted in 301 CE. Their language, with its curled alphabet and sing-song pronunciation, is like no other alive today. But the Armenians now live on only a fraction of the land they once inhabited. As the Ottoman Empire sought to consolidate its multi-ethnic territories and fight a Russian advance in 1915, hundreds of thousands of Ottoman Armenians were massacred or forced onto death marches towards the Syrian Desert, a genocide recognised by the United States, the European Parliament and at least thirty other countries.

The systematic erasure of these communities, from urban centres of learning to isolated farming communities, emptied modern-day Turkey of almost all its Armenians. Those "Western" Armenians who survived formed a vast diaspora stretching from Jerusalem, Syria and Lebanon to France, Belgium, California and Argentina. The "Eastern" Armenians in what was by then part of the Russian Empire were comparatively spared, and the land they lived on became what are now the Republics of Armenia, Georgia and Azerbaijan. As a result, while the true number of Armenians around the world is unknown, the Armenian government estimates that of a global population of at least 7,000,000, only around 2,770,000 live in the Republic of Armenia.[2]

Almost all Armenian surnames end in *-yan* or *-ian*, meaning "of." In most cases this refers to some distant relative who started their own branch of the family tree: Simon gave rise to the Simonyans, Martiros to the Martirosyans and so on. Others are tied to a historic family profession—Kartashyan (or Kardashian, as it would be known in the Western Armenian version of the language) means stonemason. Among Western Armenians are also family names that take their roots from the Turkish language, a relic of Armenian life under the Ottoman Empire—for example, Ekmekjian, meaning bread maker, or Tufenkjian for those descended from a gunsmith.

ASHES OF OUR FATHERS

Azeris are predominantly Shia Muslims, descended at least in part from the Seljuk Turks who swept across Central Asia and the Caucasus from the eleventh century, assimilating and converting local tribes as they did. Much like the Armenians, they too have a nation that crosses international borders, sharing ancestry, culture and traditions with Turkic ethnic groups from Istanbul to Siberia. Their language is more-or-less mutually intelligible to people across that vast territory—albeit with its own distinct letters, words and phrases. Intermixing was common with minority groups like the Lezgins and Avars (originally from Dagestan); the Iranic-speaking Talysh people who inhabit the south of the country; Kurds; Tats; and so-called Mountain Jews. In the kaleidoscopic racial and linguistic maps put together by the Russian Empire and the Soviet Union, Azeris were often labelled "Tatars," an umbrella term that lumped together all Turkic-speakers ranging from Crimea to the Altay mountains in Central Asia. While most Azerbaijanis are ethnic Azeris, the country also has a wide array of ethnic-minority citizens who serve in the army and in public office.

Many Azerbaijani names bear the marks of forced assimilation into the Russian world that historically dominated the region. While the root of a surname is most often Turkic, the typical Turkish -oğlu, meaning "son of," is replaced with the Russian equivalent, -ov or -ev. Someone named Mammad, the Azeri-language equivalent of Mohammed, would have given his name to generations of men whose last name was Mammadov and women named Mammadova, matching the Russian language's gender rules. Ali's descendants would be Aliyevs and Aliyevas. Again, though, the echoes of history resound through the phonebook—some Azerbaijanis retain noble Persian surnames like Alizadeh and Hajizadeh as a memento of centuries under the rule of Iranian empires.

Long before Moscow elites marked out what are now the fortified, sealed off and closely guarded borders between the two

INTRODUCTION

countries, the region's mountain passes, high-altitude plateaus, river valleys and wooded plains were a patchwork of villages, some ethnically Armenian, some ethnically Azeri, some Kurdish, some Yazidi, while cities were multicultural meeting places. The wild hinterland at the very edge of the Kremlin's reach captured the imagination of Russian poets and writers as a strange land of brutal bandits and unintelligible tongues, of blood feuds and bridal kidnappings, where snow-covered villages met dusty desert plains. It was something distinctly un-Russian, yet instinctively seen by Russians as part of their world; and, more importantly, a crossroads between Europe and Asia that had to be held at all costs.

In 1917, the Russian Empire that controlled much of the South Caucasus collapsed. As the Bolsheviks stormed the Winter Palace in St. Petersburg and the tsar was deposed, the Civil War moved south. Armenia and Azerbaijan, like neighbouring Georgia, declared their independence, and swiftly went to war with each other over territory, before being re-conquered over the next two years by the Red Army and their local Communist allies in a brutal campaign that saw them absorbed at bayonet-point into the USSR. With the Soviets came the Great Terror of 1936–38, which saw thousands of Armenians, Georgians and Azeris rounded up and executed as part of the paranoid rule of dictator Josef Stalin—himself born in Georgia. Hundreds of thousands more were deported to frigid corners of Russia, forced to labour for the state in inhumane conditions.

But the South Caucasus again, to some degree, escaped the fate of the people of the North Caucasus, just above the mountain range that separates the two. There, Chechens, Ingush, Karachays, Kalmyks and other minority groups seen as hostile to Stalin's rule were hunted down and deported en masse, often to Central Asia. While they were allowed to return over a decade later, the sheer brutality of that experience, and the death en route or in exile of so many people who had longed to return home, haunts Russia's North Caucasians to this day.

For the generations growing up as part of the USSR, the differences between Armenians, Azeris and other local minorities were made to seem less important than at any other point in history, with race and religion at least officially written off as relics of a bygone era. In the name of building communism, ancestral villages were emptied out, and their inhabitants moved into towns and cities to work in the colossal new industrial complexes and collective farms. Churches and mosques closed their doors as part of a policy of state atheism, while children learned Russian as a lingua franca in schools.

Hundreds of thousands of Armenians lived in the Azerbaijani Soviet Socialist Republic (SSR)—including an estimated quarter of a million in the capital, Baku—while over 100,000 Azeris lived in the Armenian SSR, where they had once been an effective majority in Yerevan.[3] Their official borders were nothing more than marks on a map inside a massive union state. And when the Soviet Union found itself thrust into the Second World War, Armenians, Azerbaijanis and Georgians died side by side in the name of defeating fascism.

That isn't to say there weren't tensions between different ethnic groups: as chronicled in Krista Goff's book *Nested Nationalism* (2020), discrimination and systemic policies designed to forcibly assimilate minorities into the majorities inside each of the Soviet republics were widespread. No state, no matter how repressive, can eliminate the xenophobia and bigotry that Armenians in Azerbaijan and Azeris in Armenia experienced and inflicted on each other. But the heavy hand of the state meant they rarely bubbled over into outright conflict, and the tension between the two groups during the Soviet era came nowhere close to what would follow.

Once again, trouble in Russia would mean abject chaos at the far reaches of its empire. By the late 1980s, the Soviet Union was

INTRODUCTION

sick, limping towards its tumultuous end. The USSR's hegemony was founded on the secret Molotov-Ribbentrop Pact that allowed Stalin to partition Eastern Europe and take for himself the Baltic nations of Latvia, Lithuania and Estonia; it was fuelled by the exploitation of resources across Russia and Central Asia; and propped up by fear and repression. The cracks were finally beginning to show. President Mikhail Gorbachev's last-ditch efforts at liberalisation with his policies of *glasnost* and *perestroika* (1985–91) had introduced just enough democracy and freedom of speech for those opposed to the regime to talk openly of ending it. In Russia, Belarus, Kazakhstan, Tajikistan and far further afield, local elites and Communist Party chiefs came to the conclusion that they could steal their countries' resources more freely if they were no longer being watched over by ideologues in the Kremlin. What for many ordinary people had been a chance at freedom and democracy gave way in many parts of the former Soviet Union, sooner or later, to more endemic corruption and more authoritarianism.

While the fall of the USSR defined a generation, and continues to fuel conflicts from Ukraine to Uzbekistan, in the South Caucasus it quickly gave rise to one of the longest running conflicts in the post-Soviet world, one that would touch almost everyone living there. Armenians and Azerbaijanis blame each other for starting the war that came next, as old divisions and competing nationalisms began to emerge from between the cracks in the crumbling Soviet state. The mountainous region of Nagorno-Karabakh—majority-Armenian, but drawn into the borders of Soviet Azerbaijan by Communist authorities—became a lightning rod for tensions.

As a name, Karabakh is believed to derive from the Turkic word *kara*, meaning black, and the Persian *bagh*, meaning garden. Historically, the term applies to a tranche of rich, dark, fertile earth that spans western Azerbaijan and southern Armenia, around 4,400 square kilometres of which is specifically referred to as part of *Nagorniy* Karabakh—Russian for mountainous. No fewer than three languages came together in the name of a place where ethnic groups and cultural traditions were intertwined. Towards the end of the Soviet period, around three quarters of the population in the territory was Armenian and the remaining quarter Azerbaijani, with both sides seeing it as an historic homeland. But, because of decisions taken by the Communist authorities, Nagorno-Karabakh had been administered as an Autonomous Oblast of the Azerbaijani SSR, and the impending breakup of the entire Soviet Union would put the region entirely inside the suddenly very real borders of a newly independent Azerbaijan—an outcome that Armenians, who had long campaigned for control over it, were set on preventing.

In his autopsy of the fall of the Soviet Union, historian Vladislav M. Zubok chronicles how the dispute morphed into a bitter ethnic conflict inside Azerbaijan, amid claims Azeris were being forced from their homes in Armenia as part of growing violence against minorities on both sides of the divide:

> In February 1988, within a week, one million Armenians were out in the streets of Yerevan, demanding the transfer of the region to Armenia. The rally was peaceful, but the response to this demand in Azerbaijan was violent: a bloody pogrom in Sumgait, a working-class area near Baku, took the lives of thirty people. The Azeri police did not intervene.[4]

While Gorbachev dithered, a humanitarian catastrophe unfolded. Ethnic violence exploded, and a mass two-way exodus began—of Azeris from Soviet Armenia and Armenians from Soviet Azerbaijan—with hundreds of thousands of people fleeing both republics amid the growing threat of attacks. Neighbour turned on neighbour, students on teachers, old family friends on each other. Mixed Armenian-Azeri couples tried to work out where

INTRODUCTION

they'd be safer. The ugliness of the scenes was matched only by the silence from the Kremlin—no state of emergency was declared, and the Russian military contingent sent to keep the peace did almost nothing. A controversial 1991 referendum held in Nagorno-Karabakh, but boycotted by the minority Azeri population, saw 99.98 per cent of ballots cast in favour of total independence.[5] Nobody on the outside considered it legitimate, but it was enough for the local Armenian leadership to double down on their plans to secede from Azerbaijan. Together, the Soviet Red Army and local Soviet Azerbaijani authorities launched Operation Ring, officially to disarm militant Armenian groups, but in practice deporting over 10,000 Armenian civilians from Nagorno-Karabakh and other areas of the Azerbaijani SSR.

As the Soviet collapse picked up pace, as the world that people knew disintegrated, the conflict merged into a full-blown war. Emerging for the first time in centuries as a country, the Armenians were better organised and bound by both national identity and fear of the consequences if they lost, having seen their countrymen expelled from their homes as ethnic violence flared. And so, tens of thousands of Azeris living in Nagorno-Karabakh, and more than half a million in the areas around it, were in turn forced to flee their towns and villages as Armenian fighters gained ground, often fighting house-to-house or launching sneak attacks on enemy lines overnight. The remaining Russian troops stationed in the region sold off their rifles and armoured personnel carriers to the highest bidders before being sent back home to a country on the brink of bankruptcy. Across Nagorno-Karabakh and surrounding areas, villages were torched, houses were looted, desperate people walked through the frosty mountains to find safety, and thousands of civilians were killed, their bodies left to rot on the rocky hillsides.

The First Nagorno-Karabakh War (1988–1994) was a decisive Armenian victory. It put the region's Armenians in effective control of not only their capital Stepanakert and the surrounding towns and villages, but also a huge expanse of territory that hadn't been part of Soviet Azerbaijan's original Nagorno-Karabakh oblast, which was what the Armenians had originally set out to secure. Settlements, even major cities like Aghdam, that had been almost entirely Azeri-inhabited were emptied out. Seven districts around the region were occupied—five of them squeezed between Nagorno-Karabakh and Armenia proper, and two to the east, serving as a so-called "buffer zone" in case of future skirmishes. A heavily fortified line of contact divided the internationally-recognised territory of Azerbaijan from the unrecognised Nagorno-Karabakh Republic, which had unilaterally declared its independence despite Azerbaijan vowing not to give it up and pointing to the violation of its borders.

However, Azerbaijan was in no place to do anything about it. The war brought the newly-independent country to its knees. A generation of Karabakh Azerbaijanis, men, women and children, would live for decades in limbo—in cramped barracks, tenements and even tents. The American journalist Thomas Goltz, who chronicled the desperate last stand of Azerbaijani troops in Nagorno-Karabakh and the murder of their citizens who fled too late, wrote in his diary that "Azerbaijan looked like it was about to fall apart, and not too many people seemed to care... It was being held up as a classic example of a 'failed state,' a place marked by such an appalling level of chaos, confusion and self-destruction that it almost did not deserve to exist."[6]

Apart from Turkey, with which Azerbaijanis are linked by deep cultural, linguistic and political ties, the country had virtually no allies on the world stage. Pleas to the international community for help, appeals to the principle of territorial integrity, demands for investigations into war crimes—all fell on deaf ears. The Russians were more interested in maintaining a grip on what had been the Soviet Union's only land border with NATO, the

INTRODUCTION

watchtowers and fences that divided Armenia and Turkey. They struck a friendly agreement with Yerevan to deploy Russian border guards from the FSB, the successor to the KGB, along the frontier of the new Republic of Armenia. Nobody wanted to back Azerbaijan, the losing side in a bitter ethnic conflict, and four UN resolutions demanding respect for Baku's territorial integrity went ignored.

Fewer still wanted to answer the awkward questions about the status of Nagorno-Karabakh. Armenia had never formally annexed the territory, fearing international condemnation for the land grab. According to its local leaders it was a sovereign state, but even Yerevan didn't formally recognise its independence, leaving it in limbo. In 1991, Armenia had signed an agreement to respect the borders of other former Soviet Republics, including Azerbaijan, as part of the Alma-Ata Protocols—named after the city in Kazakhstan where their leaders met, now known as Almaty. And yet, despite its insistence it was independent, Nagorno-Karabakh was still effectively seen as an extension of Armenia itself. Karabakh Armenians were issued passports by the Republic of Armenia, and more often than not the two states functioned as one. Nagorno-Karabakh, as far as its residents and politicians were concerned, wasn't just Armenian—it was Armenia.

It's an ill-fated irony that one of the only Armenians concerned that the status quo wouldn't hold was the country's first post-Soviet president, who had played no small part in supporting the war. Levon Ter-Petrosyan was unusual for the leader of a former Eastern Bloc state. For one, he was a Western Armenian diasporan, descended from a family that had fled the massacres in Turkey, and born in the Syrian city of Aleppo, the *Ter-* denoting that he hailed from a priestly family. And even more unlikely, he was an intellectual—a linguist who had spent years researching Aramaic, the ancient language of the Assyrian people. His parents had moved to the Soviet Union in the wake of the

Second World War, when he was just two years old, to be with their people. Other Eastern Bloc states would be led into the post-Communist age by former Communist Party apparatchiks like Belarus's Alexander Lukashenko or one-time KGB officers like Russia's Vladimir Putin. But in Armenia, those left holding the reigns, at least initially, were idealists.

Known for smoking cigarettes through a little holder to keep his fingers clean at meetings and rallies, LTP, as Ter-Petrosyan is universally known, had risen to the top of the Karabakh Committee, the group set up in 1988 to demand Armenian control over Nagorno-Karabakh. For his rabble-rousing, he and his fellow activists had spent six months in Moscow's notorious Seaman's Silence prison—the same one that would later hold Putin's opponents: oligarch Mikhail Khodorkovsky, murdered businessman Sergey Magnitsky, and opposition leader Alexey Navalny, who would later die behind bars.

With the First Nagorno-Karabakh War over, and the future of Armenian control over the region seemingly assured, LTP wanted to do a deal to normalise its status. In 1997, he wrote an article in which he warned: "The only option for solving the Karabakh issue is compromise, which does not mean the victory of one side and the defeat of the other, but a possible agreement reached in the name of conflict resolution. Let me be clear to those saying there is an alternative to compromise: the alternative to compromise is war."[7]

Instead of a frozen conflict and the ever-present threat of escalation, he planned to hand back the bulk of the occupied districts around the former Nagorno-Karabakh Autonomous Oblast, allowing hundreds of thousands of Karabakh Azerbaijani refugees to return home. In exchange, he hoped, Armenia and Azerbaijan would strike a peace agreement, Turkey would reopen its border with Armenia and end an economic blockade that was causing crisis and impoverishment in his young country, while interna-

INTRODUCTION

tional peacekeepers would be given a mandate to deploy to Nagorno-Karabakh and prevent future violence.

This extraordinary climbdown found a supporter in Azerbaijan's president, a former KGB chief and ex-Soviet Politburo member with immense public popularity named Heydar Aliyev. Aliyev was born in the Azerbaijani exclave of Nakhchivan, on the border with Turkey, but his family came from a village in what is now Armenia's southernmost province, Syunik. Together, despite their former Soviet-era roles as dissident and enforcer, the two leaders had agreed to try to keep a handle on the violence before Nagorno-Karabakh became a complete war zone. And, once it was too late, they both saw good reason to ensure it returned to peace. But, after a bloody conflict that had filled the streets with refugees and the graveyards with young men, few Armenians were prepared for compromise. Ter-Petrosyan was forced from office by hardliners in his own administration, ultimately to be replaced by the charismatic war hero who had served as president of the Nagorno-Karabakh Republic, Robert Kocharyan.

A former Communist Party official, the macho Kocharyan had joined the Karabakh movement as well, but saw LTP's willingness to give up territorial gains, without receiving the maximum in return, as a weakness rather than a strength. In his view, LTP was a traitor, who wanted to give away soil that Armenians had spilled blood for. Kocharyan couldn't have that, and would soon take the top job—ending all hopes of a negotiated settlement and installing an uncompromising, oligarch-backed government to rule in both Yerevan and Stepanakert. Strength, not surrender, would be government policy.

LTP is a tragic figure, all the more so because he seemed to grasp what Kocharyan did not—that Azerbaijan would not stay beaten forever. Sitting atop vast oil and gas reserves, the spurned Aliyev was able to negotiate a deal with Western energy firms to harness the country's natural resources and refill its coffers.

Having himself taken power in the wake of palace coups and street protests inside an increasingly destabilised Azerbaijan, Aliyev concentrated all focus on the need for unity in the face of a constant Armenian threat, giving him licence to squeeze out opponents and consolidate power in his own hands. Strength, above all else, was what was needed. With almost four times the population of Armenia and massive fossil fuel revenues flowing in, the arithmetic of the conflict soon swung in Azerbaijan's favour—by 2020, there were ten million Azerbaijanis in Azerbaijan, and just 2.8 million Armenians living in Armenia.[8]

It's impossible to say how many wars have been fought between the two countries in the thirty years since the fall of the Soviet Union. Regular skirmishes have rattled around the region since at least 2016, as the "frozen conflict" began to heat up, but many defy clear definition. How many teenage boys have to be killed for an isolated clash to become a war? How much territory has to be taken? There was the First Nagorno-Karabakh War of the 1990s, then the Second Nagorno-Karabakh War of 2020 (the one Tigran fought in, also known as the 44 Day War); there was an offensive in 2021, a Two Day War in 2022 and a One Day War in 2023, with countless killings, ambushes, landmine explosions and attacks and counterattacks in between. It's little wonder that Tigran the taxi driver kept his military service card in his glove compartment.

The bitter history of Nagorno-Karabakh has been covered over the past three decades by researchers, notably Tom de Waal in his 2003 book *Black Garden* and Laurence Broers in *Armenia and Azerbaijan: Anatomy of a Rivalry* (2019). This book does not aim to go over old ground. Instead, it looks to get to the bottom of how, just four years after the 2020 war, a frozen conflict that many had thought would drag on forever was brought to an abrupt and very final end. It traces how this patch of land, fought over and lived on by so many generations of Armenians and

INTRODUCTION

Azerbaijanis, ultimately fell silent. It aims to tell the stories of the people who were responsible for catastrophe after catastrophe, and of those who have paid the price. Where I have a bias, it is in favour of all those who have suffered and against all those who, in the region and far beyond it, stood by and allowed that suffering to happen.

Striving for neutrality in the South Caucasus has always reminded me of an old joke about a rabbi visiting Northern Ireland at the height of the sectarian Troubles. Almost immediately, the rabbi is accosted in the street by some youths, who demand to know if he is a Protestant or a Catholic. He replies that he is Jewish. The boys look puzzled, talk among themselves for a few moments, and again demand: "But are you a Protestant Jew or a Catholic Jew?" Covering the Nagorno-Karabakh conflict has been much the same. Whenever you out yourself as a journalist, most Armenians and Azerbaijanis immediately begin wondering whose side you're on—when, almost by definition, you can't be on either. But you can hardly blame them. The conflict that has dominated their everyday life has gone largely ignored by international media; their tragedies undocumented. And, even where there has been coverage, it's usually been with overt support to one side or the other.

Nagorno-Karabakh tests the very concept of impartiality—in the 1990s and now, outsiders have failed to take meaningful action out of fear they would be labelled pro-Azerbaijani or pro-Armenian. Most journalists, analysts and diplomats, quite understandably, have ended up simply parroting the talking points of both sides in equal measure, concluding that Armenians and Azerbaijanis are simply as bad as each other. However, neutrality doesn't lie in drawing an equivalence regardless of the situation, but in interrogating the positions of the players with the same critical lens. Being a good referee doesn't demand you ensure competing teams always draw, but that you treat them fairly. Describing reality isn't taking sides, even when one side refuses to acknowledge that reality—as has often been the case in Yerevan and Baku.

In the late 1980s, the great Soviet writer and war reporter Vasily Grossman travelled to Armenia. Just a few years before, the KGB had confiscated his manuscript for his magnum opus, *Life and Fate*, a dispatch from the front lines of the Second World War. His career lay in ruins and he was increasingly incontinent, suffering with the early symptoms of the stomach cancer that would soon kill him. In the memoir he wrote on his travels, *An Armenian Sketchbook*, Grossman recounts visiting a village with a popular local writer, known only as Martirosyan:

> Nearly everyone there had read his novel; they had become so deeply involved, grown so close to the main characters, that they wanted the author to change their fates. They wanted him to return one leg to someone who had lost both legs in an accident. They also wanted him to bring several dead people back to life. They addressed him as if he were a god, the almighty master of the world where the people he has created live out their lives.[9]

There is a note of envy in these words. Journalists like Grossman, unlike novelists like Martirosyan, don't get the chance to create worlds afresh. Instead of the god-like powers to reattach a limb or reverse a death, they must simply focus on painting the most accurate picture of the one they find themselves in, no matter how unjust it is—and the scenes Grossman had witnessed during the Second World War and in the repressive Soviet Union were deeply unjust. He had been blacklisted simply for reporting them.

The world I am writing about in this book is the one that I have seen myself, or heard about through the hundreds of people I have spoken to, not the one I would like it to be. There will always be those who, reading of an Azerbaijani soldier who lost a leg, consider it a sign of bias that I have not mentioned an Armenian soldier who lost an arm, or vice versa. For these omis-

INTRODUCTION

sions, I can only apologise in advance, and caution that this book does not, could not ever, give the full story. There are tens of millions of tiny tragedies, unnoticed and unaccounted for, that make up the overall picture of this conflict. I have tried to provide the reader with the clearest snapshot I can. Nor do I wish to draw a false equivalence between tragedies, or to find justification for one in the face of another; I will leave it to readers to decide when an eye for an eye amounts to justice, and when it only results in collective blindness.

The politics of language, however, is unavoidable. While Azerbaijanis and Armenians both have different names for individual towns and cities, even choosing how to identify the region where the conflict has played out is political. For Azerbaijanis, the concept of Nagorno-Karabakh ceased to exist with the fall of the Soviet Union, and the entire area falls under the Karabakh Economic Region, including the territory that was held by what they saw as an illegal, armed separatist entity. This strain of thought has been championed by the government since 2020, despite Baku's consistent use of "Nagorno-Karabakh" before then. While many Armenians insist that it should be referred to as Artsakh, I've found many of the region's own inhabitants simply refer to it as Karabakh, and themselves as Karabakhtsis. Indeed, throughout its history, the short-lived state used both Artsakh and the Nagorno-Karabakh Republic simultaneously. For simplicity's sake, I have generally chosen to use Nagorno-Karabakh, both for the territory that was once Soviet Azerbaijan's Nagorno-Karabakh Autonomous Oblast, and also for the wider area of Azerbaijan—the so-called buffer zone—that was controlled until 2023 by the unrecognised Armenian Nagorno-Karabakh Republic.

Despite their misgivings about the media, people like Tigran in Armenia, Anar in Azerbaijan and dozens of their countrymen put the kettle on, poured a cup of tea, lit a cigarette and told me their stories. Many did so because they hoped that if the world knew about what was going on, the cycles of violence and silence might come to an end. For a long time, I believed that too—far faster than I'd imagined, that first reporting trip to Goris turned into the best part of three years spent living in the South Caucasus, covering the region from Armenia and Azerbaijan in the hope that more international awareness of the region would be good for all who lived there.

But the end of Nagorno-Karabakh in 2023, when it ceased to exist not in principle but in practice, came with ample warning—for more than a year beforehand, Armenians and Azerbaijanis alike had sensed that something big was about to happen, while their leaders openly stated their intentions. Those warnings were ignored or misinterpreted, and feeble diplomatic efforts to find a peaceful solution failed. Now, Armenian Nagorno-Karabakh is a relic of history, its unrecognised institutions dissolved and its people refugees, exiled from the mountains they'd tried in vain to defend. Men who took up arms to protect their homes are dead, others burned alive while trying to flee. Their widows live in rundown village houses or converted high school gymnasiums. Children who, just a few years ago, were growing up in relative peace have been made homeless or fatherless; sometimes both.

Russia, the country many Karabakh Armenians had looked to as the defender of their security, is once again in chaos: a cynical, murderous, crisis-ridden state, preoccupied with problems of its own making as a result of Putin's miscalculation in invading Ukraine. As it was in the 1990s, Moscow is utterly uninterested in looking after even its own citizens, let alone foreigners at the edge of its former empire, even if it does still expect their loyalty in what it sees as an existential battle with the democratic world. But the West has also failed in its stated goal of preventing another humanitarian crisis, albeit for very different reasons—

INTRODUCTION

economic interests, political machinations and incompetence—and has struggled even to articulate a vision for the region outside the Kremlin's sphere of influence.

One perennial problem is that it's not always clear, even to those living there, just where Armenia and Azerbaijan stand in the world. Is this strip of land on the far side of the Black Sea part of Europe? It's further east than Syria and Iraq, for example, and shares borders with places like Iran and maritime links to Kazakhstan. But, because of its history in the Russian Empire and the Soviet Union, it retains something immediately familiar to Europeans—even if it is blended with influences that are far more Central Asian or Middle Eastern, from the time when it formed an integral part of Persian and Turkic empires. The simple answer is that the South Caucasus is something entirely of its own; a uniqueness that makes it hard not to fall in love with it, but very difficult to understand for those who haven't spent time there (and even for those who have). The fate of 100,000 people in Nagorno-Karabakh, an isolated part of an unknown region, often seems like a marginal concern given problems closer to home. But, at the same time, the South Caucasus is as important now as it was in the time of the Silk Road traders, and just as hotly contested—with Russia, Turkey, Iran, Israel, the US, the UK, the EU, France, China, India and almost every other aspiring power actively protecting their interests there, in one way or another.

The events that transpired in Nagorno-Karabakh, and between Armenia and Azerbaijan, are also an early test of how our fragile international order holds up in an age when it is facing increasingly fierce assaults—a test that has exposed catastrophic shortcomings in Western foreign policy and international institutions, weaknesses that it would be a mistake to ignore. With frozen conflicts still dotted across much of Eurasia, lessons learned in Nagorno-Karabakh will likely keep leaders awake at night in other territorial disputes, like those over Kosovo, Taiwan, Georgia's Abkhazia region, and Moldova's Transnistria.

Politics is politics, but it is always ordinary people who pay the price. The great tragedy of Azerbaijanis and Armenians is not how different they are, but how much they have in common—the shared history, music, food and folk stories that come from centuries living on the same land. But they also share the experience of being failed, completely and utterly, by an international community they had believed would protect them. The two sides killing each other had the same rallying cries: to defend the graves of their ancestors and their temples. Following in the footsteps of their fathers and grandfathers, another generation of Azerbaijanis and Armenians were left to wage war, and to reap the consequences.

PART ONE

A CONFLICT UNFROZEN, 2020

1

THE BEGINNING OF THE END

It was early evening, and the sun was already going down behind the mountains, casting long shadows through the city. In the central market, traders packed up their jars of pickles and boxes of walnuts and fresh herbs for the day, while, one by one, the windows of the old Soviet apartment buildings lit up yellow.

Across town, Azat Adamyan was lighting a barbecue. His phone had rung a few hours earlier.

"We're coming to Stepanakert to celebrate our engagement," the voice on the other end said. "Can we do it at your bar?"

A single-story cinder block building, Bardak—the only pub in Nagorno-Karabakh—was where the young couple had first met, and they and their guests would need to eat and drink when they arrived.

Their journey from Yerevan took more than five hours even on a good day. A steady stream of cars and old trucks sputtered along the dusty dual carriageway as it wound its way through the foothills around the Armenian capital before tracing a course around Lake Sevan, vast and almost unnaturally blue, ice cold even in the hottest weather. It was the end of summer, but the occasional fisherman was still hawking his catch on the roadside, while stalls along the motorway sold homemade wine and cola bottles filled with bright orange sea buckthorn juice, made from berries plucked off the bushes that grow wild around the water. As the road arced away from the lake it passed through the farming village of Sotk, its dirt lanes choked with dogs, chickens and children.

Then, picking up pace as they left the houses behind, the cars carrying the bride- and groom-to-be crossed the invisible line that was the internationally-recognised border. Officially, they'd just entered the territory of the Republic of Azerbaijan; but there were no checkpoints, no document checks or cargo inspections—just the snow-capped mountains of Armenian-controlled Nagorno-Karabakh ahead. On the other side of their peaks, beyond the region's de facto capital Stepanakert, hundreds of young conscripts and volunteers settled in along the front lines for another night watching the horizon, standing guard over their tiny unrecognised country.

Bardak hadn't started out as a proper pub. It had been more of a clubhouse where Azat and his friends, most of them not yet thirty, would go to drink and listen to music, roasting potatoes and onions on top of the wood-burning stove. They'd once even barbecued a snake that had found its way onto the property. Everyone agreed that it had tasted like fish. But more and more strangers found their way into the bar as this isolated region became an unlikely destination for tourists—Italians, Germans and Brits who wanted to visit one of the world's few unrecognised states. In his mid-twenties, with a thick beard and piercing green eyes, Azat resented the idea of having to run the place as a business, plying visitors with beer, hot meals and cigarettes on the house—even letting them sleep in the bar overnight if they couldn't find a hotel. For him, hospitality wasn't an industry, but a duty, and foreigners were the least likely to be allowed to put cash in the register. When the evening dragged on too late or

THE BEGINNING OF THE END

the conversation ran out, he'd head off to bed, handing the keys to one of the regulars to lock up.

Tonight was unlikely to earn him much either. When the guests pulled into the parking lot, it turned out that they'd bought their own grilling meat along the way, so they wouldn't be buying his food. But the money didn't matter so much to Azat—charging his friends on a happy occasion felt dishonourable. And so, before long, the air was thick with the smell of barbecued pork that marks any Armenian celebration. Fatty chunks of meat, known as *khorovats*, were passed around, piled up high on boards and plates, the juices mopped up with reams of freshly made *lavash* flatbread and sprinkled with raw onion. Beer flowed from the taps—but an engagement, like any proper party, required the homemade mulberry vodka that was one of Nagorno-Karabakh's prized exports.

There were ninety-seven people in the tiny pub that night, drinking toasts to the happy couple and to the future. Guests danced and sang into the morning. It was 26 September 2020. A few hours later, the war started.

* * *

It began with artillery, a heavy bombardment along the line of contact. Up in their positions, eighteen-year-old conscripts woke to the sound of explosions. Glass shook in the window frames in Stepanakert. An apartment wall was punched in by a rocket. On television, the commander-in-chief of Nagorno-Karabakh's Defence Army told everyone not to worry—the advancing Azerbaijani forces were taking heavy losses, forced to turn back by the sheer firepower of his troops.[1] Everything was OK. Clips of tanks bursting into flames played on repeat, while newly-elected Armenian Prime Minister Nikol Pashinyan took to the airwaves to vow that his country would use all "possible and impossible means" to maintain control over the region.

"The people of Armenia are ready for this war because they have always soberly realised that the animosity against Armenia, the enmity and the hatred which the Azerbaijani dictatorship has fed its people for decades, could not lead to any other results."[2]

For three decades since the fall of the Soviet Union, a line of fortifications had divided the mountains and dusty plains of Nagorno-Karabakh. Rows of barbed wire and anti-tank spikes and landmines protected the approach to the positions. There, trenches, camouflaged sniper nests and vast concrete bunker complexes acted as the last line of defence, keeping one of the world's few "frozen conflicts" locked into an enduring stalemate. Behind this iron and dirt curtain, in an area just larger than Brunei, and just smaller than Palestine, as many as 130,000 ethnic Armenians were living out their lives, governed independently as the Nagorno-Karabakh Republic.[3] The bustling Azerbaijani-controlled cities of Barda and Ganja were only forty or fifty miles away, but they may as well have been on another planet. Nagorno-Karabakh was sealed off from the country around it, accessible only through Armenia—or through a minefield. Now, the Azerbaijanis were breaking through those defences, faster than anyone had thought possible.

It wasn't the first war Azat's generation had known. Four years earlier, in April 2016, Azerbaijan had launched a surprise offensive. Artillery shells had pounded the positions where he and his friends were doing their compulsory military service. Enemy drones had soared overhead, scouting out the lay of the land and beaming back images to generals in Baku. They were bombing heavily and Azat and his friends had come to terms with the idea that they probably wouldn't get out alive. If they did, he'd thought longingly, he would open a proper pub. By the time the dust settled after just four days of fighting, the Azerbaijani armed forces had taken several strategic peaks, giving them a clear line of sight into territory they hadn't glimpsed since the first war the

THE BEGINNING OF THE END

two sides had fought over the region three decades earlier, following the fall of the Soviet Union. The defence of Nagorno-Karabakh in 2016 had been hailed in Armenia as a victory, supposedly proving Azerbaijan was unable to conquer the region, missing the fact that this had just been the first probing attack in a long-term Azerbaijani strategy.

The violence of the 2016 skirmishes was brief, but the stories still loomed over Karabakh Armenians four years later. In the village of Talish, which had been briefly overrun before being taken back by Armenian soldiers, local media had published photographs of elderly husband and wife Valera and Razmela Khalapyan, who had reportedly been executed in their home. His body was slumped in an armchair, walking stick resting on his lap, while she lay on the ground beside him, her blood sprayed up the farmhouse door. Their ears had been cut off. More than 100 young men had been killed fighting around Nagorno-Karabakh, mostly Armenians. But Azat wasn't among them and, walking down the hill from their trench, he had vowed to name the bar whatever came out of his mouth next. There was only one word that seemed to fit the situation: *Bardak*. In Russian, the second language of almost all Karabakh Armenians, it means a total mess, a chaotic shambles, or even a brothel. And, fittingly, in Turkish, and the closely-related Azeri language, it means a drinking glass.

There were other bars in the city, but nowhere else that had the community feeling of a pub. He'd been worried that people would think the area wasn't safe anymore, that the world he'd grown up in would be emptied of its inhabitants. By opening Bardak, he wanted to give them something to stay for. But, in the end, almost nobody had left. Nobody was worried enough, even if they knew deep down that 2016 wouldn't be the last time the frozen conflict thawed.

In September 2020, it was clear things were different. If 2016 had been a scouting mission, allowing Azerbaijan to assess the weaknesses of their long-time foe, then this was the real offensive. The initial insistence of the Karabakh Armenian authorities and their counterparts in Yerevan—that things were all going to plan—soon faded. One by one, the garrisons in towns and villages stopped responding, and entire settlements went dark, to the north, south, east and west of Stepanakert. Facing a hail of missiles from Turkish-made Bayraktar TB-2 drones, squad after squad was forced to beat a hasty retreat from the front, sometimes leaving dozens of their own men behind in the chaos. Azerbaijani tanks roared through the minefields, leading the way for trucks full of soldiers. In the cities and towns of Nagorno-Karabakh, Armenian families were forced to take shelter in cellars and church basements, or to seek safety and wait out the war as refugees across the border in Armenia, racing along the roads out of the enclave before the Azerbaijanis cut them off.

This was the height of the Covid-19 pandemic: communities were crammed together, and other countries were still in various degrees of lockdown. According to research published by Armenian doctors, the daily infection rate surged past 2,000, making Armenia the second-worst country for transmission per capita at the time, increasing eight-fold since the start of the attack.[4] Many got sick, but with hospitals overwhelmed by war casualties, and themselves at risk of being hit by rockets and shells, few coronavirus patients could find medical care. And for soldiers on the front lines, fever and respiratory problems were added to the list of daily concerns, alongside the drones and artillery shells.

Then, one night in November, the sky above Stepanakert lit up. On the cliffs overlooking the city, a battle was raging for the ancient town of Shushi—the historic mountainside citadel sometimes described as the Jerusalem of the Caucasus—a holy place for both sides. Cluster munitions thumped into the cobbled lanes that great Armenian and Azerbaijani writers and composers had

THE BEGINNING OF THE END

once walked, narrowly missing the crumbling minarets of two old mosques, in parts of the city long left to fall into disrepair. Baku's special forces pushed their way up the road, fighting street to street, house to house, until there were no more streets and no more houses under Armenian control. At the centre, the historic Ghazanchetsots Cathedral lay a smoking wreck, hit by two missiles weeks before the battle began. The blue, red and green Azerbaijani flag was hoisted within view of Stepanakert and, forty-eight hours later, Armenia surrendered. After forty-four days, the war, at least for now, was over.

Under the terms of the three-way agreement signed by Russia's Vladimir Putin, Armenian Prime Minister Nikol Pashinyan and Azerbaijani President Ilham Aliyev—son and anointed successor of former President Heydar Aliyev—around 1,500 of Moscow's "peacekeepers" were to be deployed to the region, to prevent further bloodshed, until at least 2025. Armenia would agree to withdraw all of its military forces from the region, while Azerbaijan would be handed back virtually all of the "buffer zone," including a swathe of territory that sat between the Armenian border and what was left of Armenian-controlled Nagorno-Karabakh.[5] Effectively surrounded, confined to the territory of the Soviet-era Nagorno-Karabakh Autonomous Oblast, the only way in or out of Armenian-held territory would be along the "Lachin Corridor," a motorway that linked Stepanakert to the Republic of Armenia, winding its way around the now-conquered mountain town of Shusha, and ending at the city of Goris in southern Armenia. The corridor would be under the control of the Russians, who immediately began building fortified outposts along the route.

Moscow's forces rolled into Nagorno-Karabakh hours after the ceasefire was signed on 10 November, driving dozens of armoured vehicles and troop trucks in convoy through the mountain pass from Armenia to relieve the local soldiers, who were still hunkered down in their positions along the front lines. In Stepanakert, Soviet-style propaganda posters went up in shop windows, emblazoned with slogans like "forever together" and "where we are, there's peace." The Russian flag was hoisted at a disused airfield outside Stepanakert that would serve as the peacekeeper contingent's headquarters. Used in Soviet times to ferry people back and forth to Yerevan and Baku, the terminal had been renovated a decade before, but no planes had ever taken off or landed, with Azerbaijan threatening to shoot down any unauthorised aircraft flying into or out of the unrecognised republic.

The deal had sparked an outpouring of joy in Azerbaijan, where tens of thousands of people took to the streets to wave flags, chanting Ilham Aliyev's name. In Armenia, however, the ceasefire was seen by almost everyone as a total capitulation. Crowds formed outside the parliament in Yerevan on the night of 10 November, demanding to be heard by the government, insisting the surrender be revoked, that the war be won. Since coming to power in a peaceful popular revolution just three years earlier, Pashinyan's reformist administration had ordered the gates of the vast, imposing Soviet-built national assembly to be opened to the public, meaning that anyone could walk around the grounds previously reserved for the country's political elite. That night, though, they were locked—so the crowd broke them down, as the police, bewildered, outnumbered and probably equally furious, stood by.

Storming the wood-panelled parliamentary chamber, flag-waving demonstrators—several who had likely just returned from the front lines—rifled through documents and jostled for a place at the podium, impatient for their turn to denounce the sudden handover of land in Nagorno-Karabakh that their fathers had conquered three decades earlier. Outside, the crowd had spotted Ararat Mirzoyan, the young revolutionary who had been appointed speaker of the parliament, in the back of a government

THE BEGINNING OF THE END

car, trying to get away. Blocking its path, they threw open a door and pulled him out.

"Where is he? Where is Pashinyan?" they demanded, raining down blows on Armenia's most senior parliamentarian, who was later rushed to hospital for emergency surgery.[6]

Pashinyan immediately hit back—his administration hadn't sold out Nagorno-Karabakh, he insisted, blaming the regime that came before him for "selling the liberated lands for money" through incompetence and grift. "We haven't dealt properly with the corrupt, oligarchic scoundrels, those who robbed this country, stole soldiers' food, stole soldiers' weapons. I apologise for that, and I call on all the citizens who understand what is happening to prepare for revenge," he blasted.

Pashinyan's rise to power in the 2018 Velvet Revolution had been unexpected. After Levon Ter-Petrosyan was deposed in 1998, Armenia had been ruled by the oligarch-backed authoritarian elites—led first by "Karabakh Clan" leader Robert Kocharyan and, from 2008, his ally Serzh Sargsyan. Kocharyan was born in Stepanakert, and he and Sargsyan considered the defence of Nagorno-Karabakh to be the first priority of the government. As an opposition parliamentarian, Pashinyan had been more accustomed to riling up crowds through a megaphone than holding high office. Among the small, hardened activist community, he was revered as the sole MP who would tour the police stations after demonstrations, advocating for the release of those who had been arrested.

Public anger at corruption and police brutality was at an all-time high when Pashinyan and his supporters launched their #RejectSerzh campaign in 2018, in opposition to constitutional changes that they feared would hand extra powers to the presidency and keep Sargsyan in power indefinitely. With tens of thousands turning out to protests, balaclava-clad riot police detained Pashinyan and his inner circle, hunting them down across Yerevan. But, facing overwhelming popular condemnation, Sargsyan resigned and the revolutionaries were released, paving the way for Pashinyan to take control as prime minister.[7]

With his nasal voice, grey-speckled beard and pot belly, Pashinyan was a stark change from the strongmen who came before him. From the city of Ijevan, he was a Hayastantsi Armenian—from the Republic of Armenia—rather than a Karabakh Armenian, and quickly found himself at odds with the leaders in Stepanakert, who he characterised as corrupt and unwilling to send their own sons to the front line to defend their breakaway state. The response was furious, with Nagorno-Karabakh's ruling class, long indistinguishable from Armenia's, simultaneously outraged by Pashinyan's apparent lack of respect and fearful that they could soon find themselves on the wrong end of a corruption probe—for, within months of the Velvet Revolution, Pashinyan's new government had begun to clean up Armenia's act, detaining high-ranking officials accused of grift, and instituting reforms of the security services. Traffic policemen no longer asked for bribes when they pulled over motorists, and villages that had waited decades for a proper road link to the outside world suddenly had a tarmacked highway, after mayors who had pocketed the funds year after year were replaced.

And the ugliest signs of a political class with no accountability had disappeared. Back in 2001, Robert Kocharyan had entered a jazz cafe in Yerevan, surrounded by bodyguards when a former classmate, forty-three-year-old Poghos Poghosyan, had called out an informal greeting from a nearby table, "*privet* Rob!" Interpreting the remark as a sign of disrespect, Kocharyan's minders had invited him into a nearby bathroom for a quick chat. He was pronounced dead by paramedics shortly afterwards. News of the killing was suppressed, but an eventual trial saw one of the guards take the fall, handed a generous sentence of just a year on probation.[8] Pashinyan, by contrast, never gave the

THE BEGINNING OF THE END

impression that he was superior to anyone else, deriving power from the Armenian people, rather than wielding it over them.

For decades, the ruling elite had insisted that notions of democracy, liberalism and reform were weaknesses, and that Armenia had to be strong if it wanted to face down its neighbours and keep control of Nagorno-Karabakh. The brutality, they explained, was necessary. As a result, while nationalists and allies of the old regime insisted that Pashinyan was responsible for the defeat in 2020, many ordinary Armenians were prepared to overlook the military disaster because of the material improvements to their lives since he had come to power. Across the mountains in Nagorno-Karabakh, though, the mood was far more sombre. Refugees from the villages and towns that had been taken by Azerbaijan milled around the streets of Stepanakert, sifting through piles of thick winter jackets collected for those who had fled with nothing. A few thousand were from Shushi; hundreds were from villages that had once been near the line of contact but were now well behind it, their homes used as forward bases for Azerbaijani troops. Thousands were from Hadrut, a large town nestled in the crook of a mountain in the south of the region—most of the civilians had been evacuated when the bombing started, before the soldiers protecting it had been overwhelmed. It was signed over in the ceasefire. Some people had even exhumed the bodies of their loved ones and loaded the corpses into cars, hoping to rebury them when they arrived somewhere safer.

Their fears of renewed violence were only amplified by the videos that began appearing online in the weeks and months that followed. Apparently filmed on camera phones by Azerbaijani conscripts, dozens of clips surfaced on channels on the Telegram messaging app. In one, an elderly Armenian man appeared to beg two Azerbaijani soldiers for his life as his head was cut off with a serrated blade. Another showed a decapitated head perched on a disembodied pig's skull. Others showed prisoners of war being beaten and humiliated, troops emptying magazines full of bullets into blindfolded corpses. People waited nervously to see whether their houses would appear in the stream of videos showing victorious Azerbaijani troops smashing furniture and vandalising properties. In Hadrut and the surrounding villages, they had shattered gravestones, both new and ancient.

But apart from the panic was also a sense of relief. For weeks, as it became clear they were losing the war, the Karabakh Armenians had feared that Azerbaijan wouldn't stop until it had taken control of everything inside its internationally-recognised borders. That meant cities like Martuni, Martakert and, ultimately, Stepanakert. Those horrors, they worried, could soon be at their front door. But the Russians were here now—this vast superpower to the north, which had once controlled nearly a sixth of the planet, was finally back. Surely nothing could happen to them now?

* * *

At the Europe Hotel, the large guest house in Stepanakert's central square, the bar manager added a cocktail to the menu in honour of the new arrivals—the Russian Peacekeeper, a layered mix of red grenadine, blue Curaçao and white liqueur in the colours of the Russian flag. But, along a side street just a few hundred metres away, Bardak's window shutters remained firmly bolted down. A few months before the war, Azat had signed up to go to the front lines if the conflict started up again. It wasn't a decision without its critics—one night at the bar, a couple of drinkers had rounded on him, saying he was a fool to put himself in harm's way and volunteer to run around on the hillsides being shot at. For what? For someone to have to tell his mother he was coming home in a body bag?

"Are you saying you wouldn't go?" he asked one old friend, Aram.

THE BEGINNING OF THE END

"No, I wouldn't," came the reply. The disagreement was enough to end their friendship and, after pints were finished and bills were paid, the two went their separate ways.

The day after the engagement party, as the sound of explosions reverberated across the city, Azat had closed the pub and gone to fight. Like a few others who'd proven themselves in the 2016 war, he was assigned to an elite force known as the Yeghnikner, meaning deer in Armenian. The unit was led by Karen Jalavyan, a portly, greying colonel in his fifties, who ordered them to dig in around a village in the northern Martakert region, determined to beat back the Azerbaijanis or die defending the community there. Around them, the Armenian lines were collapsing as Azerbaijan's troops looked to close their pincer attack around the region. Azat was injured in a blast, shards of shrapnel cutting through his flesh and burying themselves deep in his body. He discharged himself from the hospital early so he could try and continue to help the war effort while recovering at home in Stepanakert.

Also injured in the fighting was Aram, Azat's friend who had sworn he would never serve with the army. When push came to shove he had been the first one to go to the front. His position had been hit and he was in a coma for two weeks. There were lots of stories like that, and Azat didn't feel much like opening the bar when not everyone who used to drink there would be coming back. The most haunting fate was that of dozens of young men who had been captured and vanished into the Azerbaijani prison system, with Baku frequently denying it was even holding them.

Instead of drinking, Azat would clear his head by getting out of the city, pitching a tent in the forest below Stepanakert and riding a horse he kept in a paddock there through the lush green woods around his home. But, before long, the complaints from regulars that they had nowhere to spend evenings any more became too much to ignore, and Bardak's doors reopened. Now though, the wreckage of a missile and a shrapnel-scarred bust of Lenin took pride of place on either side of the entrance, while road signs from towns and villages that had been lost went up on the walls as grim testimony to what they'd been through.

The young men who drank there knew they weren't the first to serve or suffer. Their fathers had seen terrible things in the First Karabakh War during the 1990s. Their mothers had soothed their siblings when they cried because there was no food during the long years of blockade and hardship, when unimaginable poverty hit the region at the same time as the violence. As a result, Karabakhtsis had a reputation among Armenians for being stoic, proud people who had endured much and could endure still more. When there had been almost nothing to eat during those long years of the First War, the sellers in the Stepanakert market had rolled out dough into thin parcels and stuffed them with wild greens like chickweed, dandelion leaves and chervil, topped off with a little vegetable oil, before frying them on a flat grill. The steaming pouches of *zhingyalov hats*— herb bread—were synonymous with hard times, and became the iconic staple of Karabakh Armenians. Even if all else failed, the soil of the black garden would sustain them.

But despite the reputation for being thick-skinned, they all knew people who had come back from the battlefield broken, parents who had been hollowed out by the grief of their loss. And those who'd fought knew that they too had been forever changed. Life carried on as normal after November, but in some ways it would never be normal again. Mental health wasn't something they talked about very much but Bardak became more than a drinking spot: in the words of one regular, it was a psychological centre. There was only one rule—a ban on catastrophising about things ordinary people had no control over. Nobody knew what the future held, Azat reasoned, so there was no point making others worry about it.

THE BEGINNING OF THE END

While the road from Yerevan passed a handful of gaudy, golden and tinted-glass palaces, built too close to the highway by Hayastantsi oligarchs who had plenty of money and little taste, it was almost impossible to find the same unapologetic wealth among the Karabakhtsis in Stepanakert. In Armenia proper, there was a growing trend of people taking out loans before the New Year holidays to buy piles of presents or lay on an opulent feast, while couples competed with each other over who could have the glitziest wedding. That was itself a response to the poverty after the fall of the Soviet Union, but among Karabakh Armenians, the idea was virtually unthinkable. It wasn't because of a lack of money—Stepanakert was by a long way more developed than any city in Armenia except Yerevan. And even then, locals prided themselves on having cleaner streets and safer neighbourhoods than the Armenian capital to the west. But, whether as a result of memories of scarcity in the 1990s, or because society was smaller and far closer knit, ordinary Karabakh Armenians put modesty high up the list of virtues.

Buoyed by funding from Yerevan and a major mining industry extracting gold and copper, a middle class had emerged in Nagorno-Karabakh from the general poverty that followed the Soviet collapse. The largest employer was the government, and tens of thousands were hired full-time by the security services, armed forces or civil service. Employment wasn't so much about serving a specific function as it was a social good—keeping someone in work and feeding a family—and so the massive bureaucracy created by the post-Soviet government was often inefficient and ineffective, doing the same things it had always done rather than modernising and innovating. Public sector jobs in areas like education were decently paid, and so many roles were available that some villages had more teachers than students, even where locals were subsistence farmers living in relative poverty. Many families also supplemented their income with agriculture, and those who lived in the countryside or had weekend homes grew fruit, vegetables or grapes for wine.

With its fertile soil, market tables across Nagorno-Karabakh heaved with fresh produce every summer, and were well-stocked in winter with preserves, salty cheese and homemade vodka, to accompany the ever-present *zhingyalov hats*. The breakaway region's general prosperity was underwritten by Armenia as part of a longstanding interstate loan, worth hundreds of millions per year, that had no realistic prospect of ever being paid back. While Nagorno-Karabakh had always received taxpayer funding, the scale dramatically increased after the 2020 war in order to alleviate the internal refugee crisis and avoid a massive depopulation of the region—if people couldn't find new homes and jobs, officials concluded, they would leave for better opportunities in Armenia or in Russia. And a smaller population would mean fewer boys and men to serve in the army, a national security issue in the making. For 2023, the Republic of Armenia allocated almost $360 million in funding to the Republic of Artsakh out of an overall national budget worth around $6.2 billion, while Yerevan profited from the region's natural resources, minerals and agricultural exports.[9]

Using the cash flowing in from Armenia, high-ranking officials and ministers of the unrecognised republic were able to build mansions and multi-story townhouses—more modest than those over the border—in the centre of Stepanakert, despite their paltry salaries. In many cases, public contracts would be awarded to companies controlled by their family members, or the state would swoop in to purchase bankrupt firms and rescue their well-connected owners from ruin. Even military procurement and the security apparatus weren't exempt from graft. But the kind of low-level corruption that plagued Armenia proper, and which had led directly to Pashinyan's revolution—things like paying off traffic police or bribing nurses to jump in front of

THE BEGINNING OF THE END

other waiting patients—was never an issue on the same scale here. But businessmen and officials still rubbed shoulders in the exclusive part of Stepanakert where many built their large homes. It was located just behind the iconic "We Are Our Mountains" sculpture, a statue of a Karabakh Armenian man and woman in traditional garb; known as Tatik and Papik, or Grandmother and Grandfather, they had become the symbols of Nagorno-Karabakh. Like the stone the pair were carved from, the Karabakh Armenians were made in these hills, and they would be there as long as Tatik and Papik.

Still, the Karabakh Armenians are different from those in the Republic of Armenia in other ways. Their ancient history gave rise to a unique dialect, some of which is unintelligible for speakers of standard Eastern Armenian, more melodic and with a different rhythm altogether. While the population is, on average, less religious than Armenia's, having faced tougher crackdowns on the Armenian Apostolic Church under the Azerbaijani SSR, Nagorno-Karabakh hosts some of the Church's holiest sites and most important cultural monuments. Outside Martuni, near the post-2020 line of contact, the fortified Amaras Monastery was said to have been founded by Gregory the Illuminator himself, the missionary who converted Armenia and made it the world's first Christian country. It's also believed to be the first place in which the Armenian alphabet was taught, after it was created in the fifth century by a monk named Mesrop Mashtots. Dozens of other monasteries, churches, and royal palaces have similar histories. How could Armenians not win a war over this place, this cradle of their civilization? Many, particularly those outside Nagorno-Karabakh who hadn't been confronted with the daily consequences of defeat, ultimately failed to understand that they had indeed lost. The ceasefire agreement, they came to argue, put impossible conditions on Stepanakert and Yerevan; they refused to comprehend that it was actually a statement of surrender.

During the decades when Armenia had been governed by the so-called "Karabakh Clan" of Robert Kocharyan, and then by Serzh Sargsyan, the lines between the state of Armenia and the unrecognised state of Artsakh had been deliberately blurred. Government offices had displayed maps of both Armenia and Artsakh, as though the latter were a province rather than a neighbour. On key questions like diplomacy with Azerbaijan over the future of the breakaway region, Yerevan had taken the lead—with the Armenian leadership championing Stepanakert's priorities themselves, there seemed no need for Nagorno-Karabakh to send separate representatives to talks or to form its own foreign policy. Pashinyan continued that strategy of ambiguity about where Armenia ended and Artsakh began (though more out of inertia than ideology). On paper, the Second Nagorno-Karabakh War was between Azerbaijan and what it deemed to be an illegal separatist regime occupying its sovereign territory. But in reality, Armenia itself was deeply entwined in the conflict, dispatching its own soldiers to reinforce the ranks along the line of contact, declaring martial law and a general mobilisation of reserves. The daily military briefings came not from Stepanakert but from defence officials in Yerevan, while Pashinyan positioned himself as a wartime leader, his own administration actively suppressing news of just how quickly his side was losing. The news that the symbolic stronghold of Shushi had fallen was denied for days, even as Azerbaijani troops posted pictures from the city.

When it became evident that the war was over, and capitulation the only remaining option, the lines between Artsakh and Armenia were once again hazy, with Yerevan leading the negotiations. As well as being forced to withdraw its soldiers from Nagorno-Karabakh, Pashinyan was obliged to ensure that "all economic and transport links in the region shall be unblocked."[10] This, in Azerbaijan's interpretation of the trilateral agreement,

THE BEGINNING OF THE END

included restoring road and rail connections through Armenia's own sovereign territory for Azerbaijani vehicles, allowing them to cross directly into Baku's Nakhchivan exclave and, from there, into Turkey. The move would be a major win for Azerbaijan, which was reliant on a mix of daily flights from the mainland to Nakhchivan and a road via Iran, for which its firms had to pay customs duties. It wasn't just the Karabakh Armenians on the hook as a result of the surrender, but the Republic of Armenia as well—a predicament that Azerbaijan would soon use to drive a wedge between the two.

* * *

Six months before the war, in March 2020, Karabakh Armenians had gone to the ballot box. There had been calls to pause the elections as a result of the pandemic. But Artsakh's president, Bako Sahakyan, an old-fashioned, deeply conservative former security chief in his sixties, who had held power for almost a decade and a half, pressed for the poll to go ahead, revealing that he himself would be bowing out of politics. Earmarked as his obvious successor was Arayik Harutyunyan, a portly economist who had first served as his prime minister and later, when Artsakh became a fully presidential system, as "state minister"—a title change that did little to alter the fact he was largely running the show. In 2018, Harutyunyan had resigned from the government with two other top officials, after reports emerged that state security officers had viciously beaten two men while police stood by. The incident had sparked public outrage, with protesters taking to the streets of Stepanakert calling for resignations and shouting "Nikol, Nikol"—a reference to Pashinyan, whose anti-corruption Velvet Revolution had just seen him take power in Armenia, and who had already taken aim at Nagorno-Karabakh's ruling class. Harutyunyan had taken the hit on behalf of his boss, Sahakyan, and was now rewarded for that decision—

he returned to government as president himself in the 2020 polls, with more than eighty-eight per cent of the vote.[11]

Repairing ties with Yerevan was near the top of the list of priorities for Harutyunyan, who invited Pashinyan for talks in Stepanakert. The departure of Artsakh's old guard was painted as another shake-up in the victorious Velvet Revolution, and the Armenian prime minister praised the change as the two leaders talked about security assurances for the breakaway state. But there was another pressing issue even higher up the priority list: in his inauguration speech, Harutyunyan declared that "Artsakh is Armenia, period."[12] In a symbolic move, he also mooted moving the Nagorno-Karabakh Republic's parliament up the hill to Shushi, formally overseeing construction of a colonnaded building to house the assembly—a move that sent Azerbaijani officials and commentators apoplectic with rage, given that they held up the mountainside city as a sacred home of their own people, ethnically cleansed of its Azerbaijani residents during the First War. Those plans were soon dashed, and Harutyunyan spent the forty-four days of fighting in 2020 in camouflage fatigues, visiting troops as they tried to defend positions along a rapidly moving front line that was getting closer and closer to Stepanakert.

While in many ways a democracy, political power in Artsakh more often than not wound up concentrated in the hands of the same powerful groups of lawmakers and businessmen, who had a lock on the system. As in many post-Soviet states, people generally assumed their leaders were at least dividing some of the spoils together. But there was still some room at the top for those who didn't fit the traditional mould of the macho, military-ready politician-soldier. Artak Beglaryan was one of them. At the age of six, he'd been playing outside his house in Stepanakert when he accidentally triggered a landmine laid in the 1990s. The shrapnel tore across his face, leaving him blind in one eye and taking almost all of his sight in the other. His father had been killed in

THE BEGINNING OF THE END

the First War, and his mother lived just long enough to secure him a place at a special school for blind children, in the hope that he could still get an education. A disabled orphan from a war-ravaged region, he defied the odds—gaining a place to study at university in Yerevan and then in London. But, returning to Armenia to fulfil his dream of becoming a diplomat, he found the Armenian Ministry of Foreign Affairs bemusedly unsure what to do with a blind man. And so he returned to Nagorno-Karabakh, rising steadily through the ranks from press secretary to the president's chief of staff before, a year after the 2020 war, being appointed state minister. But Harutyunyan and Beglaryan would be presiding over a shattered nation.

* * *

A year-and-a-half later, one Sunday in August, Nina Shahverdyan took her students' drawings down off the classroom walls and burned them in a dumpster behind the school where she worked. Some of the parents helped. Others were at home, weighing up what to pack into suitcases and whether to torch their houses before they left. It was 2022 and, on paper at least, the war had ended. Under the terms of the ceasefire signed in 2020, the village of Aghavno where Nina taught English was due to be handed over to Azerbaijani forces in a year's time, but an official from Stepanakert had driven into the quiet farming community a few weeks earlier and said it was already time to go—the exchange was happening sooner than anyone expected. The alternative to upholding their side of the peace agreement, local politicians knew, would be another war they'd be sure to lose.

"We spent energy, time and effort on these artworks," Nina explained to me over the phone as she tore apart her classroom. "And we don't want to see videos of soldiers stepping on them or tearing them up. Each picture carries memories—our memories. If it has to come to an end, we want to do it by ourselves."

ASHES OF OUR FATHERS

Aghavno was a tight-knit little village, perched on the hill above the Hakari river along the border with Armenia. At night, in the distance you could see the lights from the village of Kornidzor, just on the other side of the official frontier. From a well-to-do family with a picturesque town house just off Stepanakert's central square, after training as a journalist at university Nina had signed up to a program to teach children in rural communities across the unrecognised country that her ancestors had called home as far back as anyone could remember.

Nina's father was the bar manager at the Europe Hotel who had proudly unveiled the Russian flag cocktail to celebrate the peacekeepers arriving and putting an end to the conflict. But here were the Russians ushering his daughter and the few dozen children at the local school onto buses, as their parents wept and bargained over how much luggage they could take.

"If we have peacekeepers, why don't they keep the peace?" she asked in a hollow voice when I spoke to her on the phone.

Thirty years earlier, Aghavno had been known as Zabukh, and been home to a few dozen Azerbaijani families. But, as the fighting raged following the collapse of the USSR, they had been forced to flee—and in their place came ethnic Armenians looking for a better life, many moving to that part of the world for the first time: Western Armenian diasporans from Syria and Lebanon who had been promised low taxes and money to buy livestock if they'd settle in the sad, empty places left behind. Their children—and some families had five or six—knew nothing but Aghavno. And it was their drawings of mountains and trees and soldiers and bombs that were curling in the flames.

The village mattered for other reasons as well. It was among the last of the Karabakh Armenian strongholds along the stretch of land that separated Armenia from Nagorno-Karabakh, and the strategic heights around it gave whoever controlled them access to the road linking the two. Along with dozens of other towns

THE BEGINNING OF THE END

and villages in the Aghdam, Kalbajar, and Lachin regions, Armenia had pledged to withdraw its troops and hand over the territory to Azerbaijan. It had also given up the road that passed through the mountains after crossing the border at Sotk, the one the wedding party had taken the night before the 2020 war began. That left Armenian-controlled Nagorno-Karabakh entirely surrounded, and all the more dependent on that single remaining highway under Russian control.

Locals had little choice but to get used to the new arrangement. Buses, cars and trucks still flowed between Armenia and the breakaway region via the Lachin Corridor. The sign that had been along the highway for as long as most could remember, declaring that "Free Artsakh welcomes you," still greeted anyone entering the region. And, for the most part, the teenage Russians in their camouflage gear and helmets were friendly, inspecting passports and waving citizens past the checkpoints. Many of them were from small cities and towns, abroad for the first time. Some learned a few words of Armenian, greeting travellers with a cheery *barev dzez*—good day to you. Others handed out pears, plums and other fruit, smiling sheepishly at the young women making the journey to see their families in Stepanakert or to go off to university in Yerevan.

But, as the road snaked past Shushi—rebranded with a large sign reading "Shusha," the Azeri-language name for the town—there would always be Azerbaijani special forces on patrol behind the chain link fence that separated them from the Russian-controlled highway. Their faces covered, they clenched their hands around the grip of their rifles and made eye contact with any motorist who slowed down around the bend. They, and the flagpole behind them, were a constant reminder that Azerbaijan was no longer a separate country kept at bay behind a line of fortifications—only the fence, and the spotty Russian adolescents with a few weeks of basic training, now stood between it and the

Karabakh Armenians. Catastrophising over the future might have been off limits for the drinkers at Bardak, but they all knew the screw was tightening.

2

FROM ONE WAR TO ANOTHER

The village of Başlıbel lay in the crook of a mountain stream that wound its way down from the snow-capped peaks above. The low stone houses with their angled roofs fanned out in a semicircle along one side of its banks, forming interlocking lanes through which farmers drove their flocks of sheep to graze in nearby pastures.

In the mornings, gaggles of children would cross the brook and make the climb up the hill overlooking the village to the large concrete schoolhouse, for lessons on science, mathematics, and classic literature. Like all Soviet pupils, they learned Russian but, along with most of their peers in the Azerbaijani Soviet Socialist Republic, they had classes in their native Azeri language as well. In the summer, when the sun scorched the rocky ground, students would pack their books and their clothes onto the backs of horses or donkeys and set off for the highlands with their families in search of fresh pastures for the livestock—living the same semi-nomadic lifestyles their families had for centuries. Each spring, older students prepared for the final exams that could see them gain a coveted place at university in Baku, or maybe even Moscow, giving them a chance to put agricultural work behind them for good and to join the growing ranks of the educated Soviet middle classes. The graduating class would don their formal wear—dark suits for the boys and black dresses with white aprons and bows for the girls—and gather for the symbolic last ringing of the school bell.

Maharram Huseynov hadn't been to university, but he had high hopes that his two young sons would get top marks and go when their time came. He and his wife, Mehpare, lived in a one-story house in Başlıbel where the stream cut through the end of their garden. Like all the others, their home had no natural gas supply, and in winter the family would gather round the stove as temperatures plummeted to below zero. Just twenty years before, the Soviet administration had hooked the village up to the power grid, and most people still remembered what it was like to spend those long, dark nights without electric light. Now, though, a small cinema had even opened in Başlıbel, and Maharram and Mehpare would gather with their neighbours in the evenings to watch movies on the projector. Western films wouldn't often make it past the Communist censors, but Indian movies became a fast favourite, offering a glimpse into a bright and unimaginably different world, well beyond the mountains they lived in.

One night in the autumn of 1991, the lights went off. There had been blackouts before—the high-voltage cables running from Aghdam, the administrative centre of the neighbouring region, came through the Nagorno-Karabakh Autonomous Oblast. With Başlıbel a day's drive from Baku, news was hard to come by; but everybody knew there had been fighting between the Armenians and the Azerbaijanis who lived in Nagorno-Karabakh, and that the army had been sent in. The separatists were blamed for the disruptions.

This time, the power didn't come back on. Başlıbel was in darkness. Just a few weeks later, the Soviet Union was dissolved.

FROM ONE WAR TO ANOTHER

Azerbaijan suddenly became an independent country, and Moscow began withdrawing its troops from their bases, leaving its former subjects to deal with their problems on their own.

Baku was in chaos: in May 1992, the former Communist party chief clawed back power after a caretaker president who had come in to steady the ship was ousted. Four days later, he was again deposed in a bloody revolution led by a group of anti-Soviet students and other dissidents known as the Azerbaijani Popular Front. The parliamentary speaker stepped in to govern for a month, before hastily-organised elections were won by Popular Front leader Abulfaz Elchibey. Abandoned by their politicians and armed only with ageing Soviet weaponry, the disorganised bands of Azerbaijani conscripts and volunteers on the front lines in and around Nagorno-Karabakh were determined to defend their country, even if they weren't always sure who was in charge of it.

The uproar in the capital had come in the wake of news from Khojaly, a farming village in Nagorno-Karabakh not far from Başlıbel. The village stood between Stepanakert—known to Azerbaijanis as Khankendi—and the Azerbaijani-held city of Aghdam. Following the collapse of the USSR, Khojaly's population had swelled to an estimated 6,000 people, many of them Azeri refugees from villages inside Armenia who had fled at the start of the conflict. Critically, Khojaly was the closest settlement to Stepanakert airport, and taking control of it had become a major strategic goal for the advancing Armenians. Stepanakert, surrounded by Azerbaijani forces, was dependent on helicopter deliveries of food and fuel—if the Karabakh Armenians could bring in cargo planes, it would mean more vital supplies for the city. So, by February, Khojaly had itself been encircled by Armenian forces and was accessible only by helicopter from Aghdam. The garrison was on the verge of being overrun, and what remained of the local, majority-Azeri population was ordered to evacuate by 26 February—four years to the day after the anti-Armenian pogrom at Sumgait.

As the sun went down the night before the deadline, calls for helicopters to airlift civilians to safety went unanswered. Fearing the Armenians would be there any moment, locals were forced to go on foot towards Aghdam. As desperate groups of women, children and elderly residents attempted to break out of Khojaly overnight through a supposed humanitarian corridor, scrambling in darkness down the rocky hill towards the Azerbaijani lines, Armenian fighters opened fire.

Crumpled bodies lined the mountainside. Survivors and desperate relatives gathered at a makeshift morgue at the mosque in Aghdam or lined the halls of the local hospital, waiting for a glimpse of their loved ones, wailing as the corpses were brought in on the backs of trucks. Reports at the time put the death toll at around 485—but the fog of war obscured efforts to count the dead.[1] Azerbaijan hadn't even been an independent nation for a year, but it had already known one tragedy after another.

Then, in May, the better-organised Armenian troops scaled the cliffs above Stepanakert to strike at the stronghold of Shusha, the ancient mountainside town that was being used as an Azerbaijani artillery base for bombarding the Karabakh Armenian capital below. According to a Human Rights Watch report at the time, the Azerbaijani forces there had been responsible for "indiscriminate shelling and sniper shooting" which "killed or maimed hundreds of civilians, destroyed homes, hospitals and other objects that are not legitimate military targets, and generally terrorised the civilian population."[2] The routes in and out of Stepanakert had been overlooked by the Azerbaijani positions in both Shusha and Khojaly, and under blockade the capital's Karabakh Armenians had been on the edge of starvation. The Battle of Shusha and a string of other Armenian military victories ended the siege and handed

FROM ONE WAR TO ANOTHER

Armenia control over much of the region—ushering in a host of new tragedies for Karabakh Azerbaijanis.

While Human Rights Watch laid blame on both sides for violence against civilians, pointing out that "whichever side held the strategic advantage in Nagorno-Karabakh at any given moment was the one that most egregiously violated the rules of war," neither would ever acknowledge their complicity in the horrors. Each side saw their struggle as a noble battle against a brutish and genocidal enemy. Even the Armenian government of Nikol Pashinyan—the least nationalist in the country's history—has repeatedly denied wrongdoing at Khojaly, going as far as to claim that the villagers had simply killed each other.[3]

In June 1992, the Azerbaijani army launched a counter-offensive against the separatists, capturing the Armenian-majority town of Martakert the following month. The entire population fled. The American reporter Thomas Goltz, who had been among the first to break the news of the massacre at Khojaly, described the city as having been virtually destroyed, its streets lined with discarded suitcases, abandoned when their escaping Armenian owners had been forced to drop everything and run.

"It was all too clear that the Armenian civilian population had not been evacuated when the Azeri offensive began," he wrote in his memoirs. "It would be easy to call the Armenians murderously irresponsible for having left civilians as a frontline buffer in a war zone—if you didn't remember that the Azeris had done exactly the same thing at Khojaly."[4]

However, by 1993, the tide had again turned in favour of the Karabakh Armenians, buoyed by funds and volunteers from the diaspora abroad as Yerevan and the wider Armenian nation united behind a shared cause. And, once again, it would be civilians who paid the ultimate price for the fighting. Eighteen months after the power went out in Başlıbel, Azerbaijani soldiers arrived in the village, urging Maharram, his family and other locals to pack what they could and flee their homes. The Armenians were coming. Just forty or fifty miles north-east, across the mountain range, lay Martakert, which had now been retaken by Armenian forces. Twenty miles to the west was Armenia itself and the border crossing at Sotk. Başlıbel was caught in the middle. These villagers too would have to run the gauntlet.

Maharram and his family didn't have a car; they had a couple of horses, and his mother, who had trouble walking, would need to ride on one of them. Mehpare, meanwhile, was pregnant; their two sons were aged just four and one. It was April, but at this altitude still frosty. At their pace, the journey north towards the next line of Azerbaijani positions would take three days at least.

By some small miracle, a passing motorist, a rare sight on the dusty roads, stopped and had space to take the children, their grandparents and Mehpare on to safety. Maharram, his brother and cousins were forced to continue their journey on foot through the mountains, braving the cold and the constant threat of Armenian shooting. They'd only be away for a little while, they told themselves: the Azerbaijani army would soon restore order and they'd be able to return. Many would lose their possessions or even their life savings to this idea, having left them in their homes for when they came back.

Those who didn't leave suffered a worse fate, according to the survivors. Nine people who stayed behind in a shelter in Başlıbel were reportedly massacred by advancing Armenian forces and almost a dozen taken as hostages. Others hid out for weeks in mountain caves until it was finally safe to make a break for it. That same month, Kalbajar, capital of Başlıbel's region, was occupied and its Azerbaijani population was expelled. By July, Aghdam, home to tens of thousands of Azeris, had fallen too, along with everything between Nagorno-Karabakh and the Armenian border, including swathes to the north, south and east of that connecting territory. Wherever the Armenian forces moved in, a sea of desperate people surged forth—on foot, on horseback, packed into Ladas and cattle trucks, or climbing aboard helicopters. Thriving cities became ghost towns in a new Karabakh Armenian-held "buffer zone," the school bells falling silent.

Maharram and Mehpare eventually moved with their family into an outbuilding at a village hospital in Azerbaijani-held territory. The two-room house had been used by maintenance staff, and came with almost no furniture—not even glasses from which to drink the fragrant black tea that every Azeri household keeps on the boil from dawn to dusk. The government, insofar as there was a government, offered little in the way of support—the aid they received was only enough to last a few days each month for a family of five like theirs—and with hundreds of thousands of out-of-work former farmers who had lost their land, finding employment was almost impossible. Education, Maharram told his children, was the only way out. Hoping his family would never know those dark nights again, he began retraining as an electrician.

* * *

On an outcrop overlooking the port of Baku, where the sprawling tower block city meets the dark blue of the Caspian Sea, is Martyrs' Lane. Shaded from the hot sun and salt breeze by a thick canopy of trees, thousands of tombstones dot the landscape.

Once known as Nagorny Park, this was where they brought the bodies of Muslims who died for Azerbaijan's brief independence in 1917–18, fighting against both Russian Bolshevik and nationalist Armenian forces. That bloody period culminated in the so-called March Days of 1918, during which thousands of Baku's Azeri residents were killed. Months later, Baku's Armenians would in turn endure the September Days, with at least 10,000 of their community killed as Ottoman and Azerbaijani forces took the city.[5]

When the Russian Communists eventually gained control over Baku and forced this rebellious part of the former empire into the new USSR, the cemetery at Nagorny Park was destroyed and the bodies exhumed. Instead, the stretch of greenery in an otherwise dense industrial city was renamed in honour of Sergey Kirov, the ethnic Russian revolutionary and Stalin loyalist appointed to oversee the Azerbaijani SSR. A massive statue to him was erected and, at the top of the hill, a circular stone pavilion was built, housing the "Friendship of Peoples" restaurant for Soviet elites. On Moscow's orders, the memory of those who'd died for their country's freedom was swiftly erased, along with their bones. After the fall of the Soviet Union, however, the cemetery was rebuilt—like all countries, the newly created Republic of Azerbaijan needed its heroes, and this would be their temple.

In January 1990, the neighbouring Armenian SSR had announced that it would consider Nagorno-Karabakh part of its own territory and that those living there would be counted as its residents—testing Gorbachev's ability to enforce order in the South Caucasus. The resulting public fury in Azerbaijan was quickly directed at Communist officials, with the multiethnic union that spanned half of Eurasia looking increasingly unfit for the future. Old slogans about equality, friendship and brotherhood felt distinctly out of date. There would be no friendship of the peoples at this rate.

Baku's historic Armenian quarter, home to a well-to-do middle class that had historically enjoyed protection and privileges under Russian rule, was now at the centre of a pogrom. Its residents were chased through the streets, beaten, some found dead in their apartments—others thrown from balconies as neighbour turned on neighbour. Thousands of the shaken survivors were evacuated, many by ferry across the Caspian to Turkmenistan and then circuitously on to Armenia, leaving their homes and their possessions behind. What had been a thriving urban community of managers and traders and teachers would end up taking whatever jobs they could find in the impoverished country, often farming, with some of them even moving to Nagorno-Karabakh in search of opportunities.

Gorbachev sent in the troops, more to quash the growing calls for independence than out of concern for those affected by the violence. On 19 January, Soviet special forces stormed the city, cutting off its communication with the outside world, gunning down Azerbaijani National Front activists and innocent bystanders as they sought to regain control. While journalists were kept out and phone lines cut—to keep the siege of 1.7 million people a secret and avoid mass insurrection elsewhere—Mirza Khaza, an ethnic Mountain Jew and a reporter with the US's Radio Free Europe, was able to broadcast the news from the barricades, even with the sound of gunfire ringing out in the background. The Soviet Union lodged an official complaint with Washington for daring to shed light on the events. When the smoke settled, more than 130 people were dead.[6] Among them was twenty-seven-year-old Ilham Allahverdiyev, whose family had moved to Baku from the Aghdam region. When his nineteen-year-old bride Fariza heard the news, she took her own life.

The following year, after Gorbachev was deposed and the Soviet Union dissolved, the bodies of the so-called Black January crackdown were the first to be buried on Martyrs' Lane, looking down on the city they'd tried to defend. Ilham and Fariza were laid to rest side by side. But, soon, the hillside around them began to fill up with other graves, as the bodies came back from Nagorno-Karabakh. Like Armenians, Azerbaijanis engrave the faces of the dead onto their tombstones, and the shady lanes of the cemetery turned into a sea of soldiers and police officers and helicopter pilots, some smiling, others solemn. Occasionally, headstones simply read *namalum*—unknown—with the date the body was found.

Over the thirty years that followed, the city around the graveyard transformed beyond what the victims of Black January or those killed in the First Nagorno-Karabakh War would ever have recognised. The fossil fuels that lay beneath the ground, and offshore in the shimmering Caspian, made post-Soviet Azerbaijan one of the world's fastest-growing economies and bankrolled huge construction programmes that have left Baku resembling a miniature Dubai, the traces of its past torn down or, at the very least, polished up. The warrens of Russian imperial era courtyards and Soviet-era apartment blocks were razed to the ground, replaced by massive skyscrapers and tree-lined avenues. Just a stone's throw from Martyrs' Lane, the three curved glass and steel Flame Towers dominate the skyline, lit up at night by giant LEDs that alternate between showing a roaring fire and a giant Azerbaijani flag. Built on the site of the former Hotel Moscow, they alone cost an estimated third-of-a-billion dollars and were designed to look like flickering flames, paying tribute to the natural gas flares that funded the rejuvenation of the city.[7]

The political situation was no less unrecognisable. In 1993, at the height of the First War, a freewheeling army commander named Surat Huseynov staged an almost outright insurrection against President Elchibey, the Azerbaijani National Front leader. Facing charges that he had cooperated with the Russians to let the Armenians take control of Martakert and steal a march on the Kalbajar region, an accusation which could have seen him stripped of his command, Huseynov had ordered his troops to turn around—effectively abandoning the city of Kalbajar itself—and set his sights on toppling the government in Baku. With a putsch to deal with as well as war in Nagorno-Karabakh, Elchibey fled the capital. The wily former KGB chief Heydar Aliyev, who had been shut out of earlier administrations, was appointed to take over the top job. Immediately, he consolidated power in an effort to end the era of warlords commanding their own private militias. But his attempts to take back Kalbajar failed. The newly inaugurated national army was too poorly trained, underequipped and undermotivated to take the fight to the enemy, many freezing to death in the chilly mountains.

By 1994, Azerbaijani, Armenian and Karabakh Armenian officials were meeting in Kyrgyzstan to sign a ceasefire, halting the military phase of the Nagorno-Karabakh conflict indefinitely, and leaving the Armenians in control of at least a sixth of Azerbaijani territory. Later that year, Aliyev secured "the contract of the century" with Western energy firms, including British Petroleum and Norway's Statoil, which would later become Equinor. The Soviet-built oil derricks, and a floating town on stilts in the Caspian known as Oil Rocks, started pumping fuel to Europe. Buoyed with the funds brought in by the energy revenues, Azerbaijan began a slew of domestic reforms. The early days of the country's independence had been marked with chaos, street protests and a revolving door of apparatchiks taking the top jobs only to be ousted by their rivals—but the state ideology would soon become one of stability.

Having pulled the country back from the precipice, pausing the war in Nagorno-Karabakh and beginning to resuscitate the economy, Heydar (as he was universally known) positioned himself as the saviour of the nation, propagating a cult of personality that saw him installed as almost a physical embodiment of Azerbaijan. Whoever opposed him, the rationale went, opposed the national interest. Moulded by his time in the KGB and in the Politburo, having watched with horror the events of Black January and the Armenian campaign in Nagorno-Karabakh, it was clear to him that the problems arising from the fall of the Soviet Union were not how to address human rights abuses or repression, but the failure to create a unified Azerbaijan with the kind of cohesion it had enjoyed during the days of the USSR. With the spectre of renewed Armenian aggression ever-present, he and his officials maintained that strength and unity were national security priorities, giving them the freedom—even the duty—to crack down on dissent, manipulate elections and censor the media.

The topic of Nagorno-Karabakh, however, remained particularly sensitive. Revanchist groups accused Heydar of selling out the country's territory by doing a deal with the Armenians, and there were clashes between the authorities and marchers calling for action to take back Azerbaijan's sovereign territory. Quite what they'd have done differently, given that the war had long turned against Azerbaijan, was unclear. It was a question that haunted those who lost the First Nagorno-Karabakh War, much as it would haunt the losers of the Second War three decades later.

* * *

In April 2003, the eighty-year-old father of the nation was delivering a televised speech to a group of military cadets when he paused, gasped, clutched his chest and keeled over. Heydar Aliyev's bodyguards swarmed around him and the live broadcast being beamed around the country was cut. About ten minutes later, the feed came back. A defiant Heydar was standing at the podium, ready to continue his remarks, encouraged by uproarious applause.

"'I have apparently been bewitched by the evil eye—but I'm fine, as you can see," he joked.

A few moments later, he collapsed again, this time hitting his head on the lectern as he went down. The cameras were switched off and the cadets ushered out of the auditorium, only to be brought back in a few minutes later so that Heydar could finally finish his speech. He was in perfect health, the presidential press service insisted, it was just an episode of low blood pressure, and nothing would stop him fulfilling his duties. But on 12 December, Heydar Aliyev died. Unbeknownst to the public, he'd been grappling with health problems for years. His kidneys, prostate and heart were failing, and he spent his final weeks undergoing treatment at the prestigious Cleveland Clinic in the US. He was buried in a stately tomb on the Alley of Honour beside the parliament, a few minutes' walk from Martyrs' Lane; and, in death, the man who had navigated the country through its darkest days was enshrined as Azerbaijan's eternal "National Leader."

Just a few months before, Heydar had been due to stand for an unprecedented third term in office. But, days ahead of the poll, he pulled out, instead conferring his candidacy on his only son, Ilham Aliyev, who for years had been publicly groomed as his father's successor. Ilham had been educated at Moscow's prestigious foreign policy academy, MGIMO. After his father took the top job, he was appointed vice president of Azerbaijan's state oil and gas giant, SOCAR, as well as presiding over the National Olympic Committee and serving as deputy chairman of the governing New Azerbaijan Party. His marriage in 1983 to 19-year-old Mehriban, from Baku's influential Pashayev family, confirmed his place at the top of a dynasty designed to rule for generations.

As the privileged son of a powerful post-Soviet strongman, the stern, moustachioed Ilham was also haunted by whispers in the Baku bubble about his playboy lifestyle and fondness for gambling. In 1998, his father shuttered the country's casinos and outlawed the industry altogether. Those who knew him, however, said Ilham's foray into politics was more than just taking over the family business—it was rooted in the genuine belief that only he could continue his father's work. Stanley Escudero, former US ambassador to Azerbaijan and a close friend of the young leader, told the *Washington Post* at the time that "Ilham liked the ladies, liked gambling. About five years ago he had an epiphany. He was reluctant to do it [but thought] if he didn't take over, the country would be at risk of collapse."[8]

His initial public perception mattered little. Ilham swept to victory in the 2003 election against Isa Gambar, the ageing former parliamentary speaker his father had seen off in the 1990s. The night before the poll, security forces swooped in to arrest dozens of Gambar's supporters outside his party's headquarters. The next day, the opposition took to the streets, with thousands demonstrating against a result they claimed had been engineered in the Aliyev family's favour, smashing shopfronts and clashing with the police. Hundreds more were detained. While Western nations called for Baku to ensure free and fair democratic elections, Turkey, Russia and Iran were quick to congratulate the country's new forty-two-year-old president, who had gained more than seventy-five per cent of the vote.[9] Two years later, in 2005, parliamentary elections that gave Aliyev's party the most seats were again marred by a crackdown on opposition politicians, the arrest of activists and consistent reports of vote rigging. Thousands of people took to the streets calling for a new election, while the government blamed irregularities on a small number of local officials, sacking them and holding a limited number of rerun votes.

With his hold on power cemented, Ilham Aliyev quickly moved to fill his father's footsteps, marrying his own political agenda with a potent strain of Azerbaijani nationalism and authoritarianism. On the international stage, he played up his country's increasing strategic importance—here was a secular Muslim country at the intersection between Russia, Iran and Central Asia that was only too happy to work with the West. At home, his government continued to turn the bloody history of the 1990s into a national religion, complete with high holidays like Martyrs' Day—dedicated to the victims of the First Nagorno-Karabakh War—and the International Solidarity Day of Azerbaijanis, designed to unite the Azeri diaspora. In international rankings, Azerbaijan lingered close to the bottom of the table for political rights, civil liberties, democracy and freedom of the press.

Quietly and incrementally, the state doctrine became more and more virulently anti-Armenian, as righting the historical wrongs suffered by Azerbaijan's people became the heart of Aliyev's governing mission. In one school textbook, distributed to Azerbaijani children, Armenians were blamed for the Soviet purges initiated by Stalin's regime, held up as an example of the neighbouring country's desire to wipe out the Turkic population of the South Caucasus. The violence of 1918 was also put down to the region's Armenians who, educators wrote, "went berserk and burned men, women and old people. Children were impaled on bayonets. These maddened Armenian executioners then collected copies of our sacred book, the Qu'ran, made bonfires of them and threw Muslims, bound hand and foot, into them."[10]

A growing market for pseudo-scholarship quickly appeared, patronised by national institutions, with anthropologists and historians prepared to argue that Armenians were actually not indigenous to the region, but had been relocated there by the Russian Empire and later the Soviets, in order to form a barrier between Azerbaijan and Turkey, dividing the Turkic world. The "true" origins of these people was up for debate, but consensus in Baku generally settled on them being from India or Syria and having appropriated the culture and land of the now long-extinct Armenian kingdoms. The Hays, as Armenians refer to themselves, were not the same people as the ancient Armenians; Hayastan, as Armenians call Armenia, was not a legitimate country. The ancient monasteries throughout their nation and across Nagorno-Karabakh had in fact been built by Caucasian Albanians, an ancient Christian people eventually subsumed into modern-day Azerbaijan. Amaras Monastery, the birthplace of Armenian Christianity and the Armenian language? Caucasian Albanian. *Khachkars*, the engraved crucifix stones that Armenians have been erecting for millennia as a monument to their faith, were supposedly fabricated, newly carved and made to look weathered in an effort to manufacture a historic claim on Azerbaijani land.

ASHES OF OUR FATHERS

In 2016, Sabir Akhundov, a Baku schoolteacher and historian, summed up how the tragic events of the past were being memorialised: "Azerbaijan's post-Soviet memory politics are great at uniting society. Too bad it's against external enemies."[11] By and large, when it came to the official version of that history of oppression and brutality, the Russians were let off the hook, and all the world's evils were laid at the door of the Armenians. And, while Aliyev built closer ties with the West, securing military aid including equipment and other assistance from countries like the US and UK, he also carefully balanced relations with Moscow, bolstering trade and paying frequent friendly visits to Putin.

* * *

Heydar Aliyev had treated the Nagorno-Karabakh issue with caution, reluctant to reawaken the memory of defeat or face criticism for signing the ceasefire with the Armenians, but his son was single-minded in his mission to restore Azerbaijan's territorial integrity and undo his father's humiliation. At international meetings, he repeatedly brought up the continued Armenian occupation and Yerevan's disregard of UN resolutions, while diverting oil and gas money to pay for a massive PR campaign designed to show the world the consequences of the conflict. As diplomatic outreach to Yerevan, designed to resolve the standoff, waxed and waned with no results, it became increasingly clear that—as Heydar in Azerbaijan and LTP in Armenia had both found—the two sides were unable to agree a compromise. They each remained confident that events would swing in their favour. An unverified audio recording, purportedly leaked and dating to 2016, appeared to reveal that Belarusian President Alexander Lukashenko had told Armenian President Serzh Sargsyan that the government of Azerbaijan was prepared to pay $6 billion for the return of the occupied territories around the former Nagorno-Karabakh Autonomous Oblast.[12] Sargsyan reportedly replied that he could not hand over the land where "the blood of 5,000 Armenian soldiers was shed" in the First War. Lukashenko himself later backed up the claims.[13]

This tense state of affairs worsened with Pashinyan's appointment as Armenian prime minister in 2018; his anti-corruption, pro-democracy revolution flew in the face of Baku's commitment to stability above all else. Talks between the two countries soon broke down, and a war of words followed. In an effort to smooth his own troubled relations with the Karabakhtsis, Pashinyan embarked on a tour of Nagorno-Karabakh months after being elected and taking office, often appearing in military fatigues and, as Harutyunyan did, said in a Stepanakert speech that "Artsakh is Armenia—full stop," backing full integration of the region into his country.[14] A few weeks later at Russia's Valdai conference—an annual gathering of regime officials and favoured elites—ahead of a joint appearance with Putin, Aliyev retorted that "Karabakh is Azerbaijan—exclamation point!"[15]

What mattered more than punctuation, though, was Pashinyan's visit to Shushi that year, where he walked smiling through the streets of "the Jerusalem of the Caucasus," this symbolic cultural heartland for both Armenians and Azerbaijanis. On the cliff that Armenian fighters had scaled to capture the city in 1992, the new prime minister locked arms with locals and soldiers, dancing with joy. With the Karabakh Armenian leader Arayik Harutyunyan's announcement of plans to move the breakaway republic's parliament to Shushi as a symbol of its dominance, this was enough to eliminate any remaining doubt the Azerbaijanis may have had: Yerevan and Stepanakert were unwilling to negotiate a solution. Over the course of three days in July 2020, just months before the Second War broke out, crowds marched in Baku and other major Azerbaijani cities, incensed by the deaths of two senior officers during border clashes that month. The demonstrators accused military chiefs of incompetence, and demanded all-out war with Armenia. Something would have to be done—and plans had likely been in motion for a long time.

On the morning of 27 September, hours after the engagement party at Bardak in Stepanakert, President Aliyev appeared on television screens across Azerbaijan. The Armenians, he claimed, had broken the ceasefire and begun pounding the line of contact with artillery, after months of provocations that had left Azerbaijani servicemen injured and dead. This, he blasted, was a manifestation of "Armenian fascism" and demanded an immediate military response.

"What are Armenian soldiers doing in our lands?! What is the Armenian army doing in our lands?! It is no secret that 90 percent of the personnel in the 'Nagorno-Karabakh army' are Armenian citizens," Aliyev declared, rubbishing the idea the soldiers were just a local Karabakh Armenian defence force. "Armenia is an occupying state—this occupation must, and will, end." He raised his clenched fist. "We are on the right path! Ours is the cause of justice! We will win! Karabakh is ours! Karabakh is Azerbaijan!"[16]

With tens of thousands of Azerbaijani troops immediately pouring across no-man's-land and forcing the Armenians into retreat, Aliyev transformed into the country's camouflage-clad commander in chief. Operation Iron Fist had begun, and the nation was at war. An emergency UN Security Council meeting convened two days later called for an end to hostilities, but to no avail—as officials in Baku saw it, Armenia had ignored four UN resolutions calling for its military withdrawal from Nagorno-Karabakh over the last thirty years, so why should Azerbaijan be bound by the supposed international order when its enemies weren't?[17]

The conflict wouldn't last long, though: with their more advanced military hardware—much of it flown in from Israel in exchange for huge cash payments and the regular flow of oil and gas—and having benefitted from regular drills and exchanges with NATO-trained Turkish troops, the forty-four days of the Second War would see an almost uninterrupted series of Azerbaijani victories.

A string of villages along the line of contact was first to be secured, while elite troops took control of the strategic heights. In this mountainous theatre of war, having oversight of the surrounding area and controlling the high ground is half the battle. But ordinary Azerbaijanis also found the front lines coming to them—rockets fell on civilian settlements on the Azerbaijani side of the line of contact, as they had before on the Armenian side. The nearby city of Ganja saw dozens injured. Harutyunyan, the Karabakh Armenian president, confirmed he had given the orders but insisted they were targeting military installations.[18] Then, on 17 October, a Soviet-designed Scud missile slammed into a residential square in Ganja, obliterating several homes, killing seven and leaving thirty-three injured.[19] The following week, Smerch missiles began exploding on the streets of Barda, also on the Azerbaijani side of the line of contact, killing twenty-six in the space of two days.[20]

The attacks did little to change Baku's resolve, and soon the Armenians were pulling out of strategic towns far past the demarcation line, as the Azerbaijani offensive picked up pace, having already made its way through the fields of landmines and fortifications. Talish to the north was captured, then the destroyed city of Jabrayil in the "buffer zone," which had long since been picked to its bones by looters and scrap collectors. Then, in the most significant victory since the start of the fighting, Hadrut fell, marking the first time a major Karabakh Armenian town had been conquered. But none of that remotely compared in significance to the battle for Shushi, the holy city on the hill that offered a direct view of Stepanakert. Just months after Pashinyan had danced on Shushi's cliffs, elderly men danced in the streets of Baku among the traffic, celebrating the reclaiming of the city—now renamed Shusha—for Azerbaijan. Thirty years of occupation, of humiliation, of feeling like a third-rate country that couldn't control its borders, had just ended.

* * *

On 10 November, Aliyev signed the ceasefire deal with Pashinyan and Putin. The Azerbaijani president again appeared on television, this time in an ecstatic mood. "An end is being put to the Armenia-Azerbaijan Nagorno-Karabakh conflict today," he said.[21] A total cessation of hostilities would begin that evening at midnight Moscow time, with both sides holding in their current positions. Along the new line of contact, the Russians would station its peacekeeping forces. They'd be deployed in parallel with the withdrawal of Armenian troops back to the Republic of Armenia and would guard the new Lachin Corridor. What had once been one of two roads linking Nagorno-Karabakh to Armenia would now become a humanitarian highway that cut through Azerbaijani-controlled territory.

Aghdam and Kalbajar districts would have to be handed over to Azerbaijan within weeks, and Lachin district by the end of the year. Armenia would have to restore transport links along its borders with Azerbaijan after three decades of the two sides keeping them closed. Prisoners of war would be exchanged, the bodies of the dead handed over. "We brought them to their knees, and they are on their knees now," Aliyev grinned in his jubilant speech, taunting his rival on national television, "*na oldu* Pashinyan? What happened?" The two men couldn't have been more different personally or politically, and this was Aliyev's chance to goad the Armenian prime minister and everything he stood for.

Days later, Aliyev and his wife Mehriban, both dressed in fatigues, visited Shusha so the president could raise the flag himself, walking past apartment blocks where the Armenian population had lived—now empty. Also on the itinerary was Aghdam, a once-thriving city now branded by Azerbaijan as the Hiroshima of the Caucasus: the place had been looted beyond recognition following its capture by the Armenians in the First War. Everything from building bricks to roof tiles had been removed and sold during the thirty-year occupation. The once-bountiful vineyards had been levelled and no single building stood undamaged. Construction materials had been removed and used to build homes elsewhere, while wood had been used to heat homes during the years of grinding poverty and isolation endured by the Karabakh Armenians during their time in control of the territory.

The few Armenians who had moved into Aghdam, usually to graze cattle or to support nearby military installations, had lived in squalor, without electricity or, often, even running water; they had shared the shattered buildings with both their livestock and regular rotations of soldiers. One woman who had taken up residence in a former Azerbaijani home while supporting the military detachment had decided to relocate there permanently, despite the tough conditions, refusing to leave her youngest son's grave after he died in a car crash and was buried in the dusty soil. Now, with her neighbours, she'd had to pack up her scant possessions and leave the destroyed city behind. Aghdam's mosque, where the bodies of Khojaly massacre victims had been taken in 1992, survived the worst of the damage—it had been left standing deliberately, to serve as a distance marker for zeroing artillery and mortars in the event of an Azerbaijani attack. Its historic interior had been used during the three decades of occupation as a cattle shed, the floor covered with animal waste.

In Baku, on a strip of land between the grand park where Heydar Aliyev is buried and the city's bustling car market, a field of graves was quietly dug for Azerbaijan's latest generation of fallen soldiers. Satellite imagery dating back to 2015 appeared to show the site being cleared, with empty plots popping up as early as 2018. This, officials would later announce, was to be Martyrs' Lane Two, and it would be the final resting place for more than 100 young men who had died during the Second Nagorno-Karabakh War. The total Azerbaijani death toll was over 2,900, with many of the fighters' bodies sent back to their villages for burial by their parents.[22]

Later, Aliyev would concede that Azerbaijan had in fact started the 2020 war—but maintain that it was Armenia who had begun the whole conflict, back in the 1990s.[23] And, as time dragged on, he would blame Armenia for risking a third war, too. Baku came to argue that the armed formations in Karabakh holding the line behind the Russians weren't local self defence units, but the same old army of occupation, commanded and supplied from Yerevan through the Lachin Corridor. They would have to disband too, or face being destroyed. The victory in 2020, Baku was convinced, was the start of a clear and irreversible path to Nagorno-Karabakh giving up first its weaponry and then its autonomy.

Pashinyan, meanwhile, was refusing to open up the transport links, ignoring his obligations under the terms of the ceasefire deal. Baku wanted a corridor through "Zangezur," the alternative name for Armenia's southernmost Syunik province, creating a Russian-controlled highway that would separate Armenia and Iran while linking mainland Azerbaijan both to its Nakhchivan exclave and to Turkey. While the Armenians saw the trilateral agreement as a list of territorial concessions required to end the 2020 war, Aliyev saw it as a roadmap for him to take control of the entirety of Nagorno-Karabakh—either voluntarily or, if need be, by force. It would be up to the Russians to decide whose version of the agreement they upheld.

The ceasefire clearly wasn't the last word the Armenians had hoped it would be, but for many it was the end of an era. Fifteen days after it was signed, the Kalbajar district was handed back to Azerbaijan. Among the territory that changed hands was the

FROM ONE WAR TO ANOTHER

village of Başlıbel. After several months of demining, Maharram Huseynov would be able to return home for the first time in thirty years—to find a village levelled to its foundations, and to find the graves of his forefathers.

PART TWO

THE FALL OF NAGORNO-KARABAKH, 2022–3

3

"IT'S STARTED"

"It's not safe to go ahead," the soldier at the checkpoint told the driver of the rickety white minibus. "They were shelling the highway just a few minutes ago." Squeezed into the back seat between two cameramen sweating in the summer heat, I breathed a sigh of relief as we pulled into the layby and the door slid open. At the side of the road, a handful of troops and dozens of Kalashnikov-wielding police officers were milling around, some smoking, some watching black smoke rise from the hillside.

Two nights before, on 12 September 2022, an Azerbaijani friend had sent me a message—"the operation will probably begin tonight." I read it twice. An acquaintance of his with close ties to the military had posted something on Facebook about how the hours ahead would be difficult, but God was with the army. Twenty minutes later, an Armenian contact wrote: "it's started."

An artillery barrage pounded targets inside the Republic of Armenia, with explosions heard across much of the east of the country. Goris was being hit, the mountain town located at the Armenian end of the Lachin Corridor. So too was Jermuk, a quiet mountain spa town, where dozens of tourists suddenly woke to fires raging along the hillside, the sound of automatic gunfire in the distance. I had hitched a lift with the Armenian public television network, and our minibus was making a beeline for the border village of Sotk, the farming community that used to be the last stop on the old road to Stepanakert, before that route came under Azerbaijani control. Now, it was one of the tensest parts of the front line. If Sotk fell, the Azerbaijanis would be able to reach the shores of Lake Sevan, cutting off one side from the other. It seemed an all-out assault was underway: just two years on from the Second Nagorno-Karabakh War, the two countries were at war once again, this time inside Armenia itself.

Unable to carry on for the time being, we parked at a little shop by the highway for cigarettes and water. As he counted change out of the register, the man behind the counter, Artush, told me it was the best day for his business since he'd opened fifteen years ago. It wasn't often that the local gendarmerie sent all its available men, most of them carrying impressive bellies and wearing their thick Soviet-style uniforms, to stand guard on the road outside. In this thirty-degree weather, the fridge full of cold drinks was virtually empty. But Artush was more worried than he'd been in 2020, when the fighting was raging on the other side of the hills.

"Even during the war it wasn't this bad. I don't know what we did to deserve this."

This wasn't the conflict anyone had expected. For thirty years, the focus of the conflict had been Nagorno-Karabakh. After the scale of the defeat there, few could say whether Armenia would be able to bear the brunt of this new offensive; the 2020 ceasefire ending the Second War had given Baku's forces control of the entire shared border, and they were now using it to stage incursions into Armenian territory. In the early hours of the morning, I'd texted Leyla Abdullayeva, the smooth-talking spokeswoman for the Azerbaijani Foreign Ministry.

"IT'S STARTED"

"All responsibility for the current provocations lies with the political-military leadership of Armenia," she replied in a long voice message, maintaining that the shelling was only targeting military installations. Meanwhile though, reports were coming in of massive Azerbaijani troop movements, pushing into Armenia under the cover of the barrage. The invasion was underway.

A shout went out from the bus. We were cleared to go. I strapped on my flak jacket and my helmet and we were waved through, driving towards Sotk in the distance. The sky was bright blue, speckled with white clouds—and long black plumes of smoke rising up over the houses. Every thirty seconds or so you could still hear the blast of the artillery in the distance, but the shells now seemed to be landing somewhere else, far away. The driver hit the accelerator and we sped past farm after farm, some with fields aflame, while the camera crew filmed out of the window.

Soon we screeched into the village. Just off the main square was a family home with a porch running the length of the building. A round had just missed the house, hitting a tree in the front yard. There was a crater next to the shattered trunk, and dozens of tiny, not-yet-ripe apples had been sprayed around it like shrapnel. The blast had also ripped apart the side of the corrugated iron roof, metal peppering the plaster walls with holes. The door was open—whoever lived there had left in a hurry. Inside, in the carpeted living room, there was still food on the table, while upturned potted plants and broken glass covered the floor. Children's soft toys had been placed on the bars across one window in a colourful nursery room. Somewhere in the distance, the calming tones of a wake-up alarm played endlessly on a forgotten phone. I wondered how this met anyone's definition of a military installation.

At another house, just past the shuttered school, I peered over the high fence into the garden. Looking back at me were maybe

100 sheep, staring up in silence, shut in when the owners fled. In a village like Sotk, a flock would be someone's entire livelihood, their life savings. When they needed money for home repairs, they'd sell a few lambs; and when their son was getting married, they'd kill one and barbecue the meat for their guests. Just down the dust track, a shell had ripped into a fence post, sending mud and metal flying. A giant Armenian sheepdog, known as a *gampr*, barked at the new arrivals, straining against its chain outside the house where it had been tied up and left behind. Outside, shrapnel had shattered the windscreen of an SUV and macerated the cab of an old tractor. Another house nearby had burned completely to the ground.

It was scorching hot and I was overheating in my heavy body armour. I unclipped the clasp on my helmet and placed it on a rickety wooden bench at the side of a lane leading down from Sotk back to the main road. The breeze felt fresh and cooling, and I leaned against the wall of a farmhouse for a few moments to catch my breath. Through the gap in the gate, a small dog appeared, tied to his kennel. I bent down to stroke him. Suddenly, screams filled the air. I didn't understand the words but I instinctively knew what the tone meant. In the sky, there was a whistling noise. The two cameramen threw themselves into a ditch along the side of the road. I rounded the gate and lay down against the wall, almost jumping on top of the dog. Clasping my hands over my head, I immediately regretted leaving the helmet on the bench. There was a distant bang, then another. We jumped up and made a run for the bus. A car carrying the two or three soldiers who'd stayed behind in Sotk roared past, getting out as quickly as they could.

Late the night before, the Russian government had announced that it had brokered a ceasefire, sweeping in to restore order in its former colonial hinterland. It was broken minutes later, assuming it had ever actually come into effect. The Russian FSB border

"IT'S STARTED"

guards, who drive convoys up and down the border roads when things are quiet, plastering billboards on the side of their barracks that say things like "security and peace," were now nowhere to be seen. The Armenian army reported that it was facing down Azerbaijani ground advances just a few miles from Sotk, as well as in the Syunik region around Goris in the south, and it was becoming increasingly clear to them that nobody else was going to help. Outgunned and outmanoeuvred, they dug in for the inevitable battle to the death. It was a former Azerbaijani diplomat who had given me the frankest assessment of events, in a phone interview that morning: "for thirty years, this conflict played out on our soil. From now on, it will play out on Armenia's." The Armenians would have to decide what mattered more to them, Nagorno-Karabakh or their own country—because failure to acquiesce to Baku's terms would mean losing everything.

Still catching my breath from the run back to the bus, I sent a message to an Azerbaijani official who knew me well and was always happy to give me the unvarnished truth about what was going on.

"You say you're only hitting military targets," I wrote, "but that can't be true—I was just in a border village and you weren't far off hitting me."

A reply came seconds later.

"Thanks for your opinion," smiley face, "hope you're OK."

Someone in the front seat shouted a question: "English boy! Are you scared?"

Sitting there was an Armenian cameraman I'd met a couple of times in Yerevan. He'd not been there on the drive down and had somehow managed to talk his way on board the packed bus to get through the military checkpoint. Whoever had originally been sitting in the seat was nowhere to be seen. This cameraman had made a name for himself as a fixer in Nagorno-Karabakh two years earlier, getting reporters into and out of some of the toughest spots, even during the fall of Shushi when the city was almost totally surrounded. For journalists willing to take the risk, he could work wonders, but for the army officers and ministry officials trying to keep tabs on foreign reporters, he was a constant headache—leaning on passing acquaintances and charm to get places those in charge didn't think anyone should be.

"Do you have a lighter?"

I passed one forward, the smell of cannabis soon filling the bus.

After that things were quiet on the two-and-a-half-hour ride back to Yerevan, except for the constant ping of Telegram notifications as news broke of the political response to the invasion. Prime Minister Pashinyan gave a televised address to a terrified public convinced that an all-out war was underway, and that this time it would be much closer to home.

"We want to sign a document, as a result of which we will be criticised, cursed, called traitors," a tired-looking Pashinyan said.[1] "The people may even decide to remove us from power. But we will be grateful if as a result of this Armenia receives lasting peace and security on an area of 29,800 square kilometres," he explained, referencing the size of Armenia inside its internationally-recognised borders—excluding Nagorno-Karabakh. A ceasefire had now finally been agreed, and was seemingly holding, ending this Two Day War, and now was the time for diplomacy.

The reaction was instantaneous: Pashinyan was preparing to sell out the nation, to sell out Artsakh. The opposition called for every patriot left in the country to turn out to protest that evening in Yerevan, while demonstrations were also being organised in Stepanakert. A few hours later, the prime minister again took to the airwaves—this time in a hastily arranged Facebook Live stream.

"I have just been informed that people are spreading news claiming that I have signed a document. There is no document," Pashinyan insisted. "No document has been signed, no document

"IT'S STARTED"

is going to be signed. There is no discussion of a document. This is being done to weaken the resistance of our soldiers standing at the border."[2]

Quite how propaganda was to blame for the supposed misunderstanding, given Pashinyan himself had brought up the idea of a document that same afternoon, was unclear. As a revolutionary, he'd been able to shout whatever he liked through a megaphone. Now he was finding out that in office his words had consequences. And it was his government facing massive street protests of the kind he used to organise.

Thousands of people were already gathering on Northern Avenue, the long shopping street in the centre of the capital. Chants of "Nikol! Traitor!" and "Resign" were going up and down the column of marchers on repeat. Spotting an obvious foreigner, one woman started shouting something at me that I couldn't make out. I carried on in the long line that snaked around the central opera house and up towards parliament. The police had parked their cars along the road, their blue lights illuminating the city, but stood back as the angry crowd moved in. As they had been in 2020, the gates of the national assembly were locked. The wave of people thronged around them. While a hardcore contingent at the front shook the barriers and shouted at the colonnaded building that used to house the Soviet of the Armenian SSR, most just milled around, trying to find their friends or scrolling the news on their phones to see what Pashinyan would say next. Just like their prime minister, none seemed to have a clear idea of what the government should actually do when faced with the prospect of another war with Azerbaijan, except go back in time and win the last one.

I snapped a few pictures of the scene. Almost instantly, hands were placed on each of my shoulders, holding me back. I was surrounded by four or five guys, and the woman who had been shouting at me earlier was with them, yelling at those around her that I was a spy.

"Who are you?" the middle-aged guy holding my right arm asked.

"I'm a journalist. I'm a foreigner," I tried to explain, as calmly as I could. I'd dropped my backpack off at the apartment before coming out to cover the protest. My press card was inside it.

"It's OK, everything will be OK—unless you're a *gondon*," he said, using a Russian slur that literally means condom. "What documents do you have?"

It was a question I dreaded. With its longstanding hunger for Azerbaijani oil and gas, and close political ties to Baku, my country, Britain, was a long way off being popular in Armenia. Unlike the United States or France, the UK had never formally recognised the Armenian Genocide, and was widely seen as an ally of Azerbaijan. I pulled out my passport and my recently-expired Turkish residency permit came with it. The men all looked down at it and then up at me—Turkey, as much as Azerbaijan, maybe even more so, was the enemy. I wasn't just a Brit but evidently a Turk too. The shouting woman went quiet and smiled, vindicated in her suspicion that I was a saboteur of some kind.

"I'm in Armenia to report on the conflict," I blurted out, "I think it's important that the world knows what is happening here." It was an explanation that had won over plenty of people before, and I was hoping it would work this time. I tried to pull up proof on my phone, an article or something, but with thousands of people in one place the network was sluggish to the point of being unusable. Very convenient, they must have thought.

"Show us your phone," one of the guys chipped in. "Yeah, show us your messages. WhatsApp. WhatsApp!"

Here I had to draw the line. From the early warning I'd had the night before to my comment requests to the foreign ministry and my exchange with an official as I left Sotk, my messages were filled with Azerbaijani names. Armenian names too, but it would be the Azerbaijani ones that got me beaten to a pulp before the cops even bothered to get out their cars.

"IT'S STARTED"

"Look," I said, pulling up a video a friend had sent me, shot by the Armenian public TV crew a few hours earlier in Sotk. It was grainy but you could still make me out, in the same outfit, running hell for leather towards the bus in a press vest and helmet as the subtitles explained how a group of reporters had come under fire earlier on the border.

"You can tell it's me because I can't run very fast," I said, pointing down to my out-of-shape body and my clothes covered in dust. One laughed, then the rest. The mood lifted.

"I'm sorry," my interrogator said, releasing my arm, "but I hope you understand why we have to check."

I mumbled something to the would-be vigilantes about how I'd be the same if it was my country, turned on my heels and darted off, catching a glimpse of the still-suspicious woman, now visibly disappointed that I'd escaped a well-deserved beating.

It was little wonder people were petrified and furious: by the end of what was being called the Two Day War, more than 200 Armenian servicemen were reported dead or missing, and 140 square kilometres of Armenian territory had been captured.[3] The army had only a small stock of outdated equipment—the Russians, who were usually the sole supplier, hadn't delivered on any orders since 2020 and, after the ceasefire that ended the 44 Day War, the Armenians had left much of their best hardware in Nagorno-Karabakh, knowing they'd be unable to take it back across the Lachin Corridor if hostilities resumed there. It was a miscalculation that had left the country's ground forces facing down a vastly superior enemy on its own territory.

In Yerevan, students set up collection points on street corners for the public to donate tinned food, socks and packs of cigarettes for the boys at the front, even as central government publicly played down the risk of further fighting. One group of boys camped outside in a tent on a boulevard among the grey stone buildings, asking passersby to spare whatever they could for the army. However, in an unusual turn of events, the Azerbaijani Ministry of Defense quickly released its own casualty figures, admitting that eighty of its troops had died in the clashes;[4] and, despite Azerbaijan's material gains, there seemed to be a sense of surprise among those I spoke to that the Armenians had been able to slow or, in many areas, stop the offensive altogether. The Second War in 2020 had created a sense on both sides of the border that Armenia was a spent force, defenceless against its foe, but in the heat of the battle Armenian troops had held the line as often as they'd lost it. They might have been outnumbered and outclassed, but they were fighting on home soil.

In Jermuk, the mountain spa town synonymous with sparkling water and childhood holidays, the armed forces had been taken by total surprise. It took me days to get permission to drive up there, including an abortive afternoon sitting at the block post at the start of the road, chatting with the soldiers for hours as various officials back in Yerevan rang each other to work out whose job it was to decide if I could proceed. Unlike in Ukraine, which was far better used to dealing with international journalists, the paper press accreditation cards handed out by the Armenian Ministry of Foreign Affairs meant virtually nothing and offered no special access. Worse still, they were written entirely in English, a language that most of the sentries and police officers couldn't read.

A few days after the end of the Two Day War, I was finally allowed to enter Jermuk, along with a few other reporters, a military attaché and an official from the Ministry of Foreign Affairs. The small group I was with felt conspicuous in what had become a ghost town. A missile stuck out of the ground on the road along the hillside, while a funfair at the bottom of the ski slope, which had borne the brunt of the shelling, was littered with broken glass, shattered gazebos and an upended test-your-strength machine. The fire station where lookouts were billeted

"IT'S STARTED"

had been shelled and only a small group of local men who wanted to defend their houses had stayed behind after their families fled.

In the makeshift command centre, young soldiers stood with their backs against the walls to form an intimidating human corridor to the commandant's office for the journalists who had been given permission to enter the now-closed city, under escort with the Ministry of Foreign Affairs. Batting away questions about military capabilities, hardware and strategy, the overweight, chain-smoking officer in charge of defending the area—who had sent several of his troops home in caskets that week—leaned in and let out a stream of consciousness:

"The problem with Azerbaijanis," he said, "is that they are Muslims. They're circumcised. This makes them more aggressive. And they move to the West, they become consumerists, they want to buy new fridges and televisions, and they become gay."

The Foreign Ministry minder clapped his hand on the table—"this is all off record."

* * *

The fighting in September 2022 sparked an unprecedented international reaction. Clashes in Nagorno-Karabakh were a frequent affair, and even the full-scale Second War in 2020 had been met with a muted response from the West. The issue, officials and diplomats had concluded, was complicated. By the letter of international law, the land was the sovereign territory of Azerbaijan, and wading into this bitter ethnic standoff offered little to no benefit for any outside power. And, as of 2020, Russia controlled access to the breakaway region, making it almost impossible for outside observers to get in anyway. But this new, two-day conflict was a separate issue altogether—this was a war that was formally between two nation states, at the juncture between Europe and Asia. This was a situation where something could be done.

ASHES OF OUR FATHERS

Western governments were quick to decry the violence, initially calling on both sides to return to the negotiating table and avoid a direct military confrontation. US Secretary of State Antony Blinken immediately became a regular on the call sheets of both Aliyev and Pashinyan, while his spokesman, Ned Price, indicated that, in Washington's assessment, the shelling had hit Armenian civilian infrastructure—contradicting Baku's claims and corroborating what I was seeing on the ground.[5] Near-daily contact underscored that this was an issue the White House and the State Department were taking very seriously. The EU went further, in rhetoric at least: its top diplomat, Josep Borrell, initially called on both sides to show restraint, before laying the responsibility for the escalation squarely on Baku.[6] Turkey, by contrast, broke with its NATO allies to back its friends in Azerbaijan, accusing Armenia of being responsible for "provocations" that had triggered the attack.[7] But the overriding sense was that Azerbaijan had overplayed its hand, and would have to stop the offensive or face repercussions.

Azerbaijani officials were incensed at the West's attitude: for thirty years, officials blasted, the Armenians had occupied Karabakh, and not a word from Brussels or Washington—but one little foray onto Armenia's turf and they ride in, desperate to help. Besides, the government line went, Azerbaijan and Armenia had never actually signed a treaty officially agreeing where the border was, so who could say what constituted an incursion? If Yerevan wanted its territory respected, it would have to sign a deal and agree to respect Baku's as well, including Nagorno-Karabakh.

The critical verdict, though, fell to Russia to give. After all, it was the only outside power with boots on the ground, through its peacekeepers in Nagorno-Karabakh and its border guards in Armenia. Along with Belarus, Kazakhstan, Kyrgyzstan and Tajikistan, Yerevan was a founding member of the Collective Security Treaty Organization (CSTO), a Moscow-led defence

"IT'S STARTED"

alliance intended as the Kremlin's own version of NATO. Azerbaijan had opted out in 1999, meaning the choice of which side to support should have been straightforward for the alliance. With the security situation worsening, Pashinyan invoked Article 4 of the bloc's constitution, which states that an attack on one member is an attack on them all. The CSTO was obliged to respond: to weigh in on Armenia's side and either bring the Azerbaijanis to heel or roll them back to the border. Or so Yerevan believed. Whatever hopes Pashinyan had for intervention, however, were quickly dashed by the pact's Russian secretary-general, Stanislav Zas, who refused to issue a statement blaming Baku, and said that a fact-finding mission would be sent to work out what had really happened.[8]

Alexander Lukashenko, the bombastic dictator of Kremlin satellite state Belarus, minced his words even less. In one of his typically rambling press conferences, he said the conflict was "very sensitive" for countries like Russia, because of its own large Muslim population, making it unwilling to rile Azerbaijan.[9] Armenians had often believed that Russia, as a fellow Orthodox Christian nation, would protect them but, with a rapidly-growing Muslim population of somewhere between fourteen to twenty million people—many of them in Russia's historically rebellious North Caucasus—turning the conflict into a religious one would have been dangerous for the Kremlin.[10] Lukashenko also praised Azerbaijan's strongman Aliyev as "our man" in the region. With the brutal suppression of Belarus's own liberal, reform-minded opposition two years earlier, during presidential elections widely understood to have been rigged in Lukashenko's favour, he and the Velvet Revolutionary Pashinyan had little in common.[11] Aliyev himself was well aware of this, happily pointing out that "we have more friends in the CSTO than Armenia."[12] Pashinyan may have been a democrat and a liberal, but he hadn't started out as a critic of Russia's role in the region, accepting it as a fact of life. Now, with Moscow's image as Armenia's security guarantor shattered, that would soon change.

A couple of days after the Russian rejection, a group of well-built men with crew cuts and wraparound sunglasses strolled into the lobby of the Marriott Hotel on Yerevan's Republic Square, one of them wearing a stars-and-stripes patch on his combat jacket. Someone notable was evidently planning a visit, and the rumour mill quickly went into overdrive. It was US Vice President Kamala Harris. No, it was President Joe Biden himself, moved by the plight of the Armenian people to intervene personally in the conflict. When Nancy Pelosi, Speaker of the House of Representatives, published a statement revealing that she was the high-ranking politician packing her bags for Armenia, half the country was Googling to find out who she was. But Pelosi was the obvious choice for the Biden administration—she had a record of hotspot diplomacy, having been to war-torn Ukraine months earlier and, as recently as August, having paid a nail-biting visit to Taiwan that saw China stage dramatic wargames in the waters around the island. She was also far enough removed from the executive branch that she could act independently. This would give the White House plausible deniability in case Ankara went ballistic over this apparent intrusion into Turkey's zone of interest—Washington's NATO ally had become an increasingly important, but unreliable, partner since the invasion of Ukraine in February.

On 19 September, Pelosi's convoy of black sedans sped through the streets of Yerevan. Wherever she went, a crowd of US-flag-toting Armenians was there to greet her, waving and smiling and pleading for photos. At a roundabout behind the opera house where her cortege was expected, a crowd of young people, elderly men and women, families with children, gathered to catch a glimpse. Some held up the star-spangled banner or the Armenian tricolour, others brandished signs reading "fuck the

"IT'S STARTED"

CSTO" or "Putin is a murderer." But the mood was still tense. The crowd spotted that one photographer's press card had his nationality down as Russian.

"Why don't you go back to Russia and report what's happening there," one middle-aged woman spat, "you're an occupier!"

Calmly, he explained that he worked for an opposition media outlet that the Kremlin had long since banned from operating inside Russia, that he couldn't go home or he would be arrested, and that he'd been working in Ukraine when Putin unleashed his savage war on the country. He got an apologetic hug.

"All my life we have been a Russian colony," said one protester, Anna, who had brought her seven-year-old daughter to the rally. "It's time for us to try something else."

At a press conference in the parliament, the oleaginous speaker Alen Simonyan greeted Pelosi like a long-prophesised saviour, along with the stalwart pro-Armenian Democrats Frank Pallone, Jackie Speier and Anna Eshoo, herself an Assyrian-Armenian American. Pelosi was excoriating in her criticism of Azerbaijan, painting the conflict as a battle between Yerevan's democracy in the wake of the Velvet Revolution and Baku's authoritarianism. Pallone, Chairman of the House Committee on Energy and Commerce, said that "the US is very concerned about Armenia's security, we want to do whatever we can to be more supportive of Armenia's security and we're going to work to see what can be done to help." Asked whether Yerevan's security relationship with Russia was a barrier for more support, he demurred, saying only that that was the business of Armenian leaders.

In a typical display of government media management, the audio for the translator failed during the Q&A, for which three local outlets had been pre-selected to ask the only questions, pushing the US delegation for lukewarm platitudes about how Armenia was right and Azerbaijan was wrong. Nobody questioned what the support meant in practice or whether the US was really prepared to risk the ire of Ankara in order to support Armenia. I shouted out a question during the awkward silence while the technicians fiddled with the wires, asking whether the US delegation was able to offer anything more than supportive words, and what that would mean for ties with Turkey. Simonyan shut down the query, interjecting before his guests had a chance to answer.

Two months later, a white Ilyushin passenger plane touched down at Zvartnots Airport just outside Yerevan, bringing an altogether different group of visitors. On board was Russian President Vladimir Putin, en route to a November 2022 summit of the CSTO that had been scheduled long before the Two Day War kicked off. The capital was in security overdrive for the visit—an extremely rare overseas trip for Putin, who had been bunkered down in Russia since the start of the war in Ukraine nine months earlier—and police cruisers lined the route to the conference venue, a grand hotel. Workers in the surrounding buildings had been ordered to leave as authorities swept the floors to ensure a sharpshooter couldn't pick off the world's most notorious strongman from afar as he walked into the meeting. Along the route, Putin will have seen two sides of Armenia out the window—first, a small group of supporters brandishing Russian flags and a banner declaring that the two countries would be "together forever." But, as he got closer to the venue, more and more protesters will have come into view, dwarfing the pro-Russian gaggle. The "fuck the CSTO" signs were back, this time accompanied by not just American but Ukrainian flags.

If it had taken place in Russia or Belarus, this display would have been enough to see everyone involved beaten by the police, paraded before a judge and then summarily thrown into jail. But this wasn't Russia or Belarus, as was becoming evident with each passing day. This level of political opposition to Russia from all walks of society was unprecedented in Armenia, which had his-

"IT'S STARTED"

torically enjoyed some of the closest ties with Moscow of any nation. And, crucially, the anti-Russian sentiment hadn't existed on anything like the same scale before Putin abandoned his ally. Had the Kremlin deployed troops in response to the Two Day War and issued a stern warning to Baku, the crowds would have been a fraction of the size. As much as Armenians might have preferred to live under Pashinyan than Putin, they'd have continued to hold their nose for the latter, if he was seen as being on their side in the conflict with Azerbaijan.

It wasn't just the public in outright rebellion against Moscow. Chairing the meeting of autocrats, Pashinyan sharpened his criticisms of the bloc; he'd inherited Armenia's membership from previous governments. He accused the alliance of ignoring his calls for help and thereby doing "grave harm to the image of the CSTO both inside our country and outside its borders." Finally, when the moment came for the leaders to sign a joint declaration on their continued cooperation, Pashinyan leaned in towards the microphone, explaining that it did not include a clear assessment of who was to blame in the most recent round of fighting with Azerbaijan. "I will not sign this document in this form, thank you very much," he said. Putin dropped his pen. Lukashenko threw his hands up in exasperation. The room looked on in stunned silence. "Thank you very much," Pashinyan repeated.[13]

The gulf between Armenia and its former colonial overseer was, for the first time in recent history, cracking open. Azerbaijan—which arguably had the greater grievances with Moscow, given the Russians' role in the March Days massacre of Azeris in 1918, Black January in 1990, and the First Nagorno-Karabakh War—had championed a two-track policy, balancing the interests of Putin and the West. Unlike Aliyev, Pashinyan was seemingly preparing to tear up that post-Soviet status quo.

Weeks before the procession of strongmen landed for the CSTO meeting, one of Russia's leading propagandists, Russia

ASHES OF OUR FATHERS

Today chief Margarita Simonyan, claimed she had been banned from entering Armenia—a move that, if confirmed, would be certain to anger the Kremlin's political machinery.[14] Herself a descendent of Armenian Genocide survivors who had fled Turkey for southern Russia before being exiled to the east during Stalin's purges, Simonyan—no relation to the Armenian speaker of parliament—had become one of the most fanatical cheerleaders of Putin's increasingly paranoid and murderous trajectory. Her loyalties to the Russian regime had led her into uncomfortable contortions, from denying its obvious role in the downing of the MH17 passenger jet that killed 298 people in 2014 to cooking up conspiracies about biolabs in Ukraine.[15] Now, serving the country that brutalised her own family meant turning fire on Armenia, the land of her forebears.

The hawkish commentator condemned the Pashinyan government's failed prosecution of pro-Russian former President Robert Kocharyan for alleged abuse of office and authorising violence against protesters, despite him being ultimately acquitted by a court in 2021.[16] Simonyan also hit out at Yerevan for not recognising Ukraine's Crimean Peninsula as Russian, despite Pashinyan not having come to power until four years after the illegal invasion of 2014. Responding to the attacks, Pashinyan said only that "Armenia has not recognised the independence of Nagorno-Karabakh too, but does it mean that we are not defending Nagorno-Karabakh? No."[17]

Besides, the decision to recognise Crimea would have put Armenia among just a handful of obedient Kremlin partners, including North Korea and Syria—a prospect that even the old Sargsyan regime had seemed to balk at. The Crimea dispute also had dangerous echoes of the Nagorno-Karabakh conflict, with Putin's pro-annexation case boiling down to disagreeing with the Soviet decision to transfer the territory to the Ukrainian SSR, and brandishing an illegal, one-sided referendum engineered by

"IT'S STARTED"

Moscow in favour of the peninsula returning to Russian control. Ukraine's pro-democracy, anti-corruption Maidan Revolution, which had ousted the Moscow-backed old guard in 2014, also had clear parallels with Pashinyan's Velvet Revolution four years later.

When Russia's "little green men" seized government buildings across Crimea in March that year, Armenia in fact initially backed Russia's claim. The country even voted against United Nations' resolutions condemning the occupation and human rights breaches on the peninsula every year for six years, from 2016 to 2021, irrespective of the change of leadership in Yerevan.[18] However, the question of recognition had been kicked down the road, winding up on Pashinyan's plate as he took office. Early on, and eyed closely by Moscow, he had refused to fall into line, telling the Parliamentary Assembly of the Council of Europe that "it is very difficult to make a choice between one friend and another friend."[19] This answer, which endeared Armenia to neither side, also raised eyebrows in Stepanakert, which had issued its own statement during the annexation, painting Crimea's patently fabricated referendum as "yet another manifestation of realisation of the right of people to self-determination."[20] Pashinyan's equivocation wasn't a change in policy for Yerevan, but it meant that relations got off to a rocky start.

Following the 2020 war, Simonyan had become even more incensed by, and unpopular with, the government in Yerevan. "Any Armenian that dares criticise Russia now, should go cut out his dirty tongue," she had said, painting Pashinyan's push for democracy as the reason it had lost so much territory.[21] Armenians only had themselves to blame, she'd claimed, "for giving power to a national traitor who had a falling out with the only supporter of the Armenian people [Russia] and created conditions for this war." If she really was banned from the country in 2022 as she insisted, then this was a major sign that Pashinyan and his officials were reaching a conclusion of their own: that

Russia wasn't the friend it made itself out to be. Either way, Simonyan's claims opened the floodgates for more public criticism of Armenia's longstanding alliances: "Ban the CSTO like you banned Margarita Simonyan," read one placard outside the summit Putin was attending.

However, extricating Armenia from Moscow's self-declared sphere of influence would be no easy task. The borders with Turkey, Iran and Azerbaijan were all under the control of Russia's border guards per the terms of a post-Soviet agreement with Moscow. The Kremlin also had a cast iron hold on the economy and security sector. Russia was both the main destination for Armenian exports, namely ores and precious metals mined from the rocky hills, and also the main source of imports—things like consumer goods and fuel. Russia's state energy firm Gazprom had a monopoly on natural gas imports via a pipeline that runs through Georgia, and owns much of Armenia's energy infrastructure; previously, it had offered supplies at a substantial markdown to its ally, but there was increasing nervousness that Moscow could jack up the price whenever it wanted, given that there was no alternative provider. Russia also had a virtual monopoly on grain and petroleum, and owns Armenia's now largely defunct train network, the sum total of which is a rail link between Yerevan and the Georgian capital, Tbilisi. And, with relations deteriorating, Moscow even temporarily banned the import of Armenian dairy products, threatening to sink the agricultural sector.

For decades, the Armenian general public had seen Russia as a brother nation. Homemade signs on village streets bore the flags of both countries and farmers would paint the tops of their silos in both Armenian red, blue and orange, and in Russian white, blue and red, side by side. That was changing fast, with a growing sense that Armenia's vast northern neighbour was no longer on its side. One poll published in the summer of 2022

"IT'S STARTED"

found that, even before the September offensive, only around one in three Armenians surveyed believed that Russia was Yerevan's "main friend," down from almost half in 2013, with France now taking the top spot.[22] After those two, the most popular answer was that Armenia had no real friends—a cynical position, but one that had felt increasingly true in recent years.

Eyeing the growing power vacuum left by Moscow's disinterest and Armenia's divided loyalties, Western powers saw an opportunity to tackle Russian influence while, at least in theory, helping to bring stability to a fragile region on the Eurasian fringe. Just weeks after the September 2022 clashes, the European External Action Service (EEAS), the EU's diplomatic service, said—at Yerevan's request—that it would deploy a civilian monitoring mission to Armenia's tense borders. Initially, the idea had been for a cross-border peacekeeping commission, but Azerbaijan had flatly rejected the idea of yet more foreigners along the frontier, in addition to the Russians. Baku's approval wasn't needed to operate inside Armenia, however, and forty observers were quickly despatched to the town of Goris as an advance party, taking up residence in an office within the grounds of Hotel Mirhav, a leafy hillside complex boasting, in my view, one of the country's best restaurants. It kept the Europeans supplied with *tolma*—the hand-rolled, meat-stuffed vine leaves served throughout the South Caucasus—and homemade wine.

Equipped with a small but growing fleet of blue-and-white SUVs bearing diplomatic plates and the gold-starred EU flag, the monitors began establishing routes along the most dangerous parts of the Armenia-Azerbaijan border, peering through binoculars at the sets of military positions facing off against each other. Then, in January 2023, an official at the EEAS confirmed to me that the European presence was to be ramped up rapidly.

"There was a mutual understanding with authorities in Yerevan that there is a need for a renewed presence, but the previous one was too small. Up to 100 monitors will now be deployed to the region as part of a fully-fledged Common Security and Defense Policy mission," the diplomat said, confirming they would have a two-year mandate in the country.

Azerbaijan, which had opposed the move from the start, was incensed. Aliyev had described the EU deployment as "very unpleasant" and argued it would actually undermine negotiations[23]—presumably, in his view, negotiations would be undermined by anything that made Armenia feel that its current position was secure, and that it wouldn't have to capitulate to his demands in order to survive. On a long call in which we discussed Baku's deteriorating relations with the EU, Vaqif Sadiqov, the head of Azerbaijan's diplomatic representation in Brussels, insisted his country had "legitimate security questions" over the venture, not least because many of the observers were, by nature of the job, retired police officers or gendarmes. "It's easy to see how a civilian mission becomes a paramilitary force," he claimed. But in a battle between Azerbaijan's advanced armed forces and a group of unarmed Italian, German and Romanian fifty-somethings, it is hard to see how Baku would struggle to hold its own.

The broader issue was that, despite the fanfare launching the EU monitoring mission, it was powerless to stop further escalations, and was regularly silent when they took place. In order to avoid misunderstandings or putting their observers in harm's way, the mission shared its weekly patrol itinerary with the Azerbaijani side in advance. Clashes frequently happened when the mission wasn't in the area. Markus Ritter, a greying former German policeman who looked as though he'd stepped straight out of a Nordic noir whodunnit, was always careful to point out that his job was not to report publicly what was going on, but to report back to Brussels what was going on. Brussels would then seemingly do nothing with the information. Even in country, though, the mission made staggering displays of incompetence.

"IT'S STARTED"

On 15 August 2023 after a spate of sometimes fatal clashes, Armenia's Defence Ministry spokesperson Aram Torosyan announced that Azerbaijan had shot at positions just south of Sotk, and that EU observers had been in the line of fire.[24] In a rare and unprecedentedly speedy public statement, the official Twitter account of the EU monitoring mission posted a screenshot of Torosyan's Tweet with a giant red "false" stamp over it, insisting that none of its observers had been involved and effectively saying the Armenian side was lying.[25]

The Defence Ministry, however, moments later released a video in which an EU monitor in a blue high-vis was taking shelter in a frontline bunker, pointing across the hill to Azerbaijan, from where he said they had come under fire.[26] The mission was forced to issue a correction.[27] Within a few months they were looking for a new local press officer. And, as if the incident needed a final touch of confusion and unprofessionalism, the head of the mission, Markus Ritter, would later claim the video had been faked and filmed by a staff member "for his home, to be more interesting," and that it had been leaked by one of the Armenian escorts.[28] Whether it was communications chaos or a case of conflict cosplay gone wrong, it had a catastrophic impact on the reputation of the mission. While its investigative powers evidently weren't up to much, from an Armenian perspective the monitors were more useful as human shields to deter further all-out offensives. If some retired Belgian police officer were blown to smithereens by an incoming shell, the brutal rationale went, that would be an escalation that the EU would struggle to ignore.

Unsurprisingly, the Russians were about as pleased with the EU's presence as the Azerbaijanis were. A CSTO mission had actually been ready and waiting for deployment all along, Foreign Minister Sergey Lavrov claimed, despite the bloc having publicly reneged on its commitments to Armenia.

On the ground, the Russians proved actively obstructive: the EU mission was entering into territory that had, since the fall of the Soviet Union, effectively been under the control of the Russian border guard. Despite the monitors being accompanied by local Armenian officials, the Russian conscripts and their bosses would frequently try to block their convoys, even when gently reminded that this was the territory of the Republic of Armenia, and the Defence Ministry could take its guests anywhere it liked. The worst affected locations were the eastern side of the southern border, past the town of Meghri, where the territory around the village of Nrnadzor was tightly controlled and all foreigners were turned away by the Russians. Just north was the village of Nerkin Hand, a regular hotspot for tensions, where Azerbaijani troops well inside Armenian territory virtually surrounded the settlement on four sides, with a lone, Russian-controlled road cutting through the mountains—a microcosm of Nagorno-Karabakh inside the Republic of Armenia. Access for the monitors to Nerkin Hand was largely impossible, meaning that provocations would happen out of sight and out of mind—with Moscow an even less competent and reliable observer than the EU mission. Like in Nagorno-Karabakh, if gunshots rang out in the woods and only the Russians were around to hear it, it may as well not have happened. And that suited Azerbaijan just fine.

Baku's message had been heard loud and clear in Yerevan—if Armenia continued to maintain its designs on Azerbaijan's internationally-recognised territory, Aliyev would have no qualms about not respecting Armenia's internationally-recognised territory either. And while Pashinyan had his sights set on a rapprochement with the West, the Armenians knew they would ultimately be alone. A battery of talks between the two sides had been immediately put on the table after the Two Day War, some mediated by the EU, others by the US and a small number hosted by Moscow. Recognising the severity of the threat, the

"IT'S STARTED"

Armenian prime minister began the long process of weakening the country's stance on the status of Artsakh. While carefully avoiding sparking outrage at home, Yerevan officials now routinely referenced their commitment to honouring the Alma-Ata Protocols, the 1991 agreement among former Soviet Republics to respect each other's territorial integrity. Successive Armenian leaders had ignored the declaration—Pashinyan no longer could.

* * *

A few days after the ceasefire had come into force, ending the Two Day War, I went back to Sotk. This time, other outlets had also sent reporters to cover this dramatic escalation in the decades-long conflict. The Ministry of Foreign Affairs had even arranged a bus, air-conditioned and far more comfortable than the one I'd squeezed into while the fighting was still raging. All was quiet in the village now, and what had seemed like a hellish vision from the front lines now felt surprisingly underwhelming. Apart from a few shrapnel marks here and some shattered roof tiles there, the village looked largely like any other. The inhabitants had returned—some just to lock up and clear out their homes while they moved their families somewhere safer. In front of the village administration building, one foreign news crew was recording a piece to camera. The presenter had strapped on his body armour to show that he was somewhere incredibly dangerous, while his producer kicked back out of shot, wearing shorts and a t-shirt in the September heat. A colonel in the armed forces was marching around trying to show others where shells had landed, pointing at indentations in the mud, or broken windows that could have been broken for years. The whole thing felt faintly ridiculous now that the smoke had lifted.

An old blue Lada pulled into the square. "Where are you from?" shouted the man at the wheel, getting out and coming over to shake hands with me.

ASHES OF OUR FATHERS

"I'm Andranik," the driver said. He was maybe only just forty, but his dark beard was flecked with white. "This is Aram."

He pointed to his young son, playing on a phone in the back of the car. Sotk isn't a village that usually attracts a lot of foreign visitors and, as if from nowhere, a welcome committee was appearing, with neighbours dropping whatever they were doing to come and meet the strange interlopers who were photographing their broken fences. From the trunk, Andranik pulled out a large plastic jug.

"Have you tried Armenian vodka? I made this myself."

At a picnic bench nearby, he and a few other locals laid out a spread of lavash flatbread, pickles, sweet sugar biscuits, and a sour cream dip, to take away the burn of the alcohol. Someone produced a stack of small metal shot glasses of the kind that almost every man in the country seems to keep to hand at all times. Packs of slim white cigarettes, named Ararat after the mountain, were handed out. Someone raised a glass. "To peace!"

The vodka tasted like gasoline. You could feel it sliding down your throat, corroding a hole in your stomach lining. The sour cream was quickly passed around and the glasses were refilled. On the hillside above the village, an Azerbaijani flag fluttered in the breeze. The forward position gave Baku's forces a commanding view of the entire area.

"To friendship between peoples!" another man shouted, raising his glass in the direction of the outpost.

My eyes watered from the vodka, as Andranik explained how he made it from local apples, how the apples were better here than anywhere else, how almost all of the people living in Sotk had been refugees who'd fled villages inside Azerbaijan during the First War, how the apples there were even better than the apples here. Behind me an Australian journalist, the only other member of the press group to have broken off and joined the locals for a drink, was throwing up on his shoes.

"IT'S STARTED"

"Someone go and get some meat," Andranik shouted. "We will cook up some *khorovats*!"

With the sun going down and the vodka already taking its toll, staying for dinner was out of the question.

"We'd love to," I said apologetically, "but we're worried the barbecue will smell so good the Azerbaijanis will want to come down from that position up there." I pointed up to the sandbags on the hillside.

"Don't be," he answered without missing a beat, "they're Muslims—they don't eat pork anyway."

* * *

Rumours continued to swirl that Azerbaijan would resume its offensive at the first available opportunity, which many believed would be the moment Pelosi left the country. The only way to remain safe, a common joke went, would be to kidnap her and have her driven around the borders in a jeep as another human shield. But, just a day after she'd arrived, Pelosi was wheels up from Zvartnots and the Armenians were once again alone.

The most dangerous place in the country, conventional wisdom held, was the southern province of Syunik—a wild, sparsely inhabited mountain region that formed a narrow divider between mainland Azerbaijan and its exclave of Nakhchivan. This was where Baku's long-vaunted Zangezur Corridor was supposed to be. It also hosted an airport that served as a base for the Russian peacekeepers operating in Nagorno-Karabakh, with a row of helicopters lined up along the landing strip, occasionally flying patrols around the area. But the atmosphere in the region was one of fear, despite the foreign military presence and the arrival of the EU monitoring mission.

Syunik is the most remote part of Armenia. A three-hour drive from Yerevan, you drive south-east through the fertile fields of the Ararat plains and begin the climb up into the mountains. At the top, where a highland plateau opens up that is covered in snow for eight months of the year, you find the Gates of Syunik, two pillars on each side of the road that mark the start of this southernmost region. From there, it's another hour and a half to the stony-grey streets of Goris, the first of the province's major cities, once the last stop before Azerbaijan's border on the road east to Nagorno-Karabakh. If you stay on the winding high-altitude highway instead, you pass south through the historic monastery town of Tatev, with its breathtaking cliffside chapel, rebuilt after being sacked by invading Seljuk Turks in 1170. Another hour and the road reaches Kapan, a forlorn mining town on the border, where you can see Azerbaijani positions from the main road, and then Lernadzor, with a massive Russian-run uranium mine. Another ninety minutes' drive and you reach Meghri, which means "honey town" in Armenian, a popular stop-off for Iranian truckers to have a final cold beer before crossing the nearby border to make their deliveries. Winding through Syunik takes longer than travelling across the entire rest of Armenia.

Despite its vast open space, green forests and natural resources, the entire population of Syunik is less than 150,000, with a lack of economic opportunities and tough living conditions forcing a generation of young people to seek work elsewhere.[29] Many villages are now no more than lanes of houses built out of concrete and corrugated metal with their little vegetable gardens out front, surrounded by the older, crumbling stone ruins of buildings that had once been inhabited when the region was still thriving. Vast decaying Soviet industrial complexes sit empty, their iron gates padlocked and their statues of distinctly Russian-looking workers eroding in the rain and the wind.

Syunik's depopulation is more than just a missed opportunity for Armenia: many analysts see it as a security threat, given Azerbaijan has consistently set its sights on the region. As well

"IT'S STARTED"

as the proposed Zangezur Corridor—named after Syunik's historic title—President Aliyev has repeatedly described the region as a rightfully Azerbaijani homeland. In 2018, he said that a return to Syunik, as well as Yerevan and elsewhere, "is our political and strategic goal, and we need to work step-by-step to get closer to it," leaving open what that would mean in practice.[30]

By 2022, the Azerbaijanis were already looking very close. Following the 2020 war, the entire eastern border of the region had come under Azerbaijani control. In Kapan, the newly built civilian airport was now effectively the front line: a camouflaged Russian position sat on the edge of the tarmac, while an Azerbaijani outpost looked down on it from the hillside opposite.

The ceasefire that ended the Two Day War was certain to collapse, everyone in Armenia seemed to insist, and what would inevitably come next was a pincer attack from both mainland Azerbaijan and Nakhchivan that would cut Armenia in two and cut off Syunik, with Baku's forces meeting in the centre at Sisian, a small, quiet town on the way to Goris. On the afternoon of 19 September 2022, in the central administration building in Sisian, the mayor of the local region, Armen Hagopjanyan, was meeting with security officials. Intelligence—or at least rampant speculation—indicated that the Azerbaijanis would attack at any moment, likely when the sun went down, because they knew the Armenians didn't have night vision equipment. Men in tatty camouflage gear were carrying heavy holdall bags and talking into radios. This was the new front line.

"Journalists are less than useless to me right now," Hagopjanyan said. "But I can offer you some exotic local juice."

An assistant returned from the room next door with a bottle of Fanta, while his boss, smiling at the naivety of a foreigner, explained that things were tense.

"We pray nothing will happen, but of course we will defend our land if it does. There's no other option."

With the Russians, he went on, "we see the flags, not the help. And I won't answer any more questions about them."

Sisian, Hagopjanyan went on, had already taken in 650 displaced people who hadn't thought it was safe to return to surrounded Nagorno-Karabakh after the 2020 war. Locals were becoming resentful of the fact that these refugees had received priority access to schools, and that what little welfare support the region could offer was going to people from outside the community.

"We have elections coming up and I'm not so popular right now," he said, "I might be wearing a white shirt but I can take it off and someone else can have my job if they think they can do it better."

In a ground floor apartment not far from Hagopjanyan's office, Armen Hagopyan and his wife Anna were deciding whether to pack up their things and flee their home yet again. They were Syunik natives, but in the 1990s they had moved to Aghavno, as part of the settlement policy incentivising outsiders to relocate to Nagorno-Karabakh. They'd built a house there and they'd raised their three young sons. But, with a vague inkling that the conflict could start up again, they'd kept an apartment in Sisian, and had uprooted the family after the 2020 war. Now, with Aghavno handed to Azerbaijan following the Two Day War—and given back its Azeri name of Zabukh—they didn't think it was safe to go back, and were considering whether they even wanted to stay in Armenia. Between the pandemic and the Second War, the children had missed more than a year of school. As they played in the kitchen, their parents wondered aloud whether they should move abroad.

"I don't want my son to see war," Hagopyan said, pointing towards twelve-year-old Tigran and his younger brothers. "But military service is compulsory in this country—you have to do it to become a man."

4

JERUSALEM OF THE CAUCASUS

Broken glass crunched underfoot in the abandoned apartment. Furniture lay strewn across the living room, while in the kitchen a stack of pickling jars and empty cognac bottles gathered dust. Glass cabinets had been pulled over, a wooden television console smashed into pieces. It had been a year and a half since Azerbaijani forces stormed the town during the Second War, but it still looked and felt like a battlefield.

Alvina Nersesyan had fallen in love with a man from Shushi. She was from Yerevan, and had had plans to become a university lecturer, with opportunities for travel or even a job abroad. Instead though, the young couple had decided to move in with Alvina's in-laws in this relative backwater of Nagorno-Karabakh. She'd found a teaching job at Stepanakert University, making the drive down the hill from Shushi to work every morning, past lines of centuries-old buildings that had long since fallen into disuse and disrepair. She and her husband had bought an apartment of their own in Shushi, where they had their two sons.

"From one balcony you could see the Green Chapel, and from the other you could see Ghazanchetsots Cathedral. Everybody needs a place where they can feel peace, and there you felt closer to God," she'd explained to me.

It wasn't an easy place to live—there were no movie theatres or bars or upscale shops like you had in Stepanakert, and in winter the wind would whistle through the hills, making Shushi far colder than the big city below. It had a population of just a few thousand, many living in the dilapidated Soviet apartment blocks around the historic centre. From the outside, they might seem run down, but most families had spent huge sums on renovating the interiors—putting up wallpaper, laying new floors and tiling bathrooms. But by 2022, the place was abandoned. In one now-empty stairwell, a former resident had painted a trail of bright red love hearts along the crumbling walls leading up to their apartment. From the shattered window you could make out the caved-in roof of a school, and dark green military trucks lining up outside the building. Since the 2020 war, it was serving as the operational headquarters for an elite Azerbaijani army unit.

When the war started in September 2020, Alvina's husband told her to take the kids and go somewhere safe—she had family in Yerevan, they could stay there. They'd packed a few changes of clothes and she'd grabbed her laptop. Nobody thought to pack documents or family photos. They'd be back in a week or two, she told her boys, even as their dad and uncle enlisted to fight on the front lines.

Now though, the muddy streets of the city were empty of residents and rumbling with heavy machinery—diggers to clear out the rubble for new buildings, trucks hauling building supplies from Baku. At floodlit construction sites, crews of workers, many employed by Turkish firms, toiled around the clock. The masterplan for the city's rejuvenation called for conference centres, restaurants, and homes for 25,000 people by 2040.[1] The building that Arayik Harutyunyan had hoped would house the Artsakh parliament building and reinject life into Armenian-controlled Shushi had been bulldozed and would now be the site of a five-star hotel, a symbolic show of opulence and wealth triumphing over the Karabakh Armenians' democratic republic. On one billboard, a camouflage-wearing President Aliyev brandished his fist in the air—"dear Shusha, we will revive you!"

Along the walls of the old fortress, the Armenian lettering had been removed and replaced with the Azerbaijani version of the name. The Shushi where Alvina's children grew up was gone: this was Shusha now. Young conscripts and construction workers would pose beneath the gate for Facebook posts; their relatives and school friends—who had little chance of obtaining the government permit needed to enter the military-controlled Karabakh region—could only look on in envy.

For both Armenians and Azerbaijanis, the city is hallowed ground, its history a microcosm of the conflict around Nagorno-Karabakh. The question of who first built on the site of this mountainside fortress is fiercely contested, as with every part of the region's history. The official Azerbaijani position is that it was founded in 1725 under the rule of the Karabakh Khanate—Armenians trace its history back to at least the 1400s. But, by the 1800s, it had become a home for both peoples, and the undisputed jewel in the crown of the entire South Caucasus—its most prosperous trading town, made famous for rearing the hardy Karabakh horses prized by Russian and Persian armies alike. While the majority of Shusha's inhabitants were ethnic Azeris, there was a prominent Armenian quarter with a rich civic and cultural life. But in the early 1900s, against the backdrop of collapsing Russian Imperial rule, ethnic and religious violence broke out between the two groups, and local Armenians rebelled against Azerbaijani rule over Karabakh.

In February 1920, having declared independence as Russia descended into civil war, the leaders of the new Azerbaijan Democratic Republic announced the end of Karabakh's effective autonomy: its ethnic Armenians would be subject to rule from Baku. That sparked an outright rebellion. According to historian Richard Hovannisian, on the night of 22 March 1920, a band of around 100 Armenian fighters slipped into Shusha to launch a stealth attack on Azerbaijani troops garrisoned in the city, many of whom had taken over Armenian homes. However, poor coordination and ill-discipline among the ranks of the Armenian militia saw fighting break out before they managed to enter the fort, alerting the Azerbaijanis and scuppering the plan. Fearing reprisals, several thousand local Armenians fled through the dark fog, and those who remained faced furious retribution.

"The enraged Azerbaijani troops, joined by the city's Azerbaijani inhabitants, turned Armenian Shushi into an inferno," Hovannisian writes, with homes, churches, schools and libraries set ablaze.[2] The community's bishop, Vahan Ter-Grigorian, had his tongue ripped out, and was decapitated, his dismembered head marched through the cobblestone streets on a spike. Hundreds of ordinary Armenians are said to have died in the resulting pogrom, many killed after gathering and begging for protection in the courtyard of one grand Armenian-owned mansion. The merchant and intellectual classes of the city were gutted. The violence only ended when the Soviet Red Army arrived to subjugate the region; the concept of competing Armenian and Azerbaijani nation states was smashed by the Bolsheviks, left to lay dormant for eighty years. Shusha, meanwhile, remained virtually entirely Azerbaijani-inhabited through the Soviet period, and the Communist government in Baku cleared much of the destroyed Armenian quarter's unsightly ruins to make way for six- or seven-story apartment blocks.

When the First War began, Shusha's Azerbaijanis were suddenly on the front line, the city turned into an artillery base guarding the approaches to and from Stepanakert. As Armenian forces scaled the cliffs and captured it, the entire remaining

JERUSALEM OF THE CAUCASUS

population was forced to flee, their apartments quickly given to Armenian refugees from elsewhere in Soviet Azerbaijan—foreshadowing by thirty years the bulldozing of the 2020s, to make way for Azeri returnees.

At a carefully choreographed June 2021 summit, held among the sun-bleached shells of old buildings, Aliyev welcomed Turkish President Recep Tayyip Erdoğan to the heart of newly liberated Karabakh. The sorry state of this hallowed city was chalked up to Karabakh Armenian negligence when, in fact, much of the widespread destruction was a consequence of over a century of ethnic conflict, in which Armenian Shushi and Azerbaijani Shusha could not both exist at the same time. Aliyev and Erdoğan signed a declaration expanding relations between their two countries, pledging to bolster economic and military ties, and to lay the foundation for Baku's natural gas exports to flow through Turkey to Europe. The most pointed part of the text, however, was for Armenia—envisaging the creation of the Zangezur Corridor that would link mainland Azerbaijan to its exclave of Nakhchivan and Turkey, connecting the two Turkic nations, and overcoming what Baku saw as the irritating Armenian presence that separated them.

On the hillside, Azerbaijani troops stood constant watch as a procession of VIPs and foreign dignitaries were shown around Shusha on guided tours pointing out both the depth of destruction and disrepair following thirty years of Armenian control, and the sheer scale and ambition of Aliyev's plans. Little camouflage firing posts had been erected outside the city's limits, along the cliffside where Pashinyan had once danced. They gave Azerbaijani forces a clear line of sight into Stepanakert. Shusha was famous for its fog, but on clear days you could make out the dome of the Karabakh Armenian government building down there, and the central market, not far from the newly reopened Bardak pub. A line of Russian peacekeeper positions stood between them.

ASHES OF OUR FATHERS

On my first visit to Shusha in 2022, I woke up early and took a walk through the battle-scarred streets to those cliffs, to watch the sun rise over Nagorno-Karabakh. Sitting on a boulder, I messaged a Karabakh Armenian journalist I knew. She commuted to work in the city below, and I wondered whether she was on one of the buses I could just about make out in the distance. The Lachin Corridor was off limits to foreigners, with the Russian peacekeepers turning away anyone without an Armenian or Russian passport, so I was finding it impossible to get access to the parts of Nagorno-Karabakh still under Armenian control. From Azerbaijani-controlled Nagorno-Karabakh, it felt like a world away, even if it was just down the hill.

Two or three miles below, Alvina Nersesyan and her children had returned from Yerevan and tried to restart their lives in Nagorno-Karabakh, this time down in the capital. Her home and possessions had been lost, but her husband had survived the war. Stepanakert University had reopened, even if not all of its students were still alive. And while normal life carried on, every time the family drove past the mountainside town above, she could feel her children tense up, knowing they were unlikely to ever go back to their old life. It was OK, she told them, just because somebody else is in control of it doesn't mean it isn't still your homeland.

Among the ruins and the restoration work in Shusha, house museums sprang up to commemorate the great Azerbaijani writers, poets and composers who once called it home, while the city was anointed the Turkic world's capital of culture for 2023. Specialists were brought in from Europe to work on Karabakh's historic sites, and international firms won lucrative tenders to build new, high-tech towns and public buildings. Baku was determined to show the world just how much it was investing into the newly-recaptured region. This was why I'd been given rare access to Shusha, as one of the first foreign reporters to visit since the Second War. Even many of the lower-level officials I'd met in Baku hadn't yet had the honour of permission for a pilgrimage to the city. My only condition for accepting was that I'd pay my own way—Baku is notorious for its strategy of inviting journalists, analysts and other miscellaneous foreigners to the country, putting them up in luxury hotels and plying them with the best hospitality it has to offer. Others are invited to opulent receptions at Azerbaijani embassies across the world, designed to charm officials and civil society figures.

One Azerbaijani policymaker put it more bluntly in comments to researchers from the European Stability Initiative:

"'There are a lot of deputies in the Council of Europe Parliamentary Assembly whose first greeting, after 'hello', is 'where is the caviar?'"[3]

Over the best part of three decades, caviar diplomacy has made Azerbaijan a large number of friends—albeit usually relatively junior politicians or slightly obscure experts—prepared to go out to bat for the country at any opportunity. The Council of Europe Parliamentary Assembly, known as PACE, has been a key target—it offers all the legitimacy of the continent's chief international political exchange as a forum for meeting politicians, but without the scrutiny facing actual decision-making institutions. But members of the European Parliament are also frequent honoured guests, with Azerbaijan's ambassador to the EU, Vaqif Sadiqov, hosting friendly receptions in the garden of Baku's beautifully-designed embassy in a leafy suburb of Brussels. A number of parliamentarians have been flown into Baku for high-profile events since 2020, meeting their Azerbaijani counterparts before touring the liberated territories. In some cases, they failed to disclose their trips even to the committees they purported to be representing, while opposing motions critical of Azerbaijan and even booking rooms in the European Parliament building for Baku's visiting diplomats to host outreach sessions.

However corrosive this strategy has been for European democracy, the impact on media coverage of the Nagorno-Karabakh conflict and of Azerbaijan's domestic political situation has been worse—a string of otherwise reputable outlets have, almost from nowhere, run glowing stories about Azerbaijan, by reporters who had never previously covered the South Caucasus. Most did no original research beyond writing up what their Foreign Ministry tour guide told them as they shuttled between lavish lunches and lavish dinners, and few bothered to publicly disclose that they'd been wined, dined and party-lined. Almost all of the articles that resulted from these junkets were one-sided, and some were patently ludicrous. Because the region was so under-covered, so largely unknown by editors and readers, many flew under the radar where similarly negligent reporting on, say, Israel and Palestine, or Serbia and Kosovo, never would have. Even if Armenia wanted to replicate the same media strategy, it has neither the resources of its petro-state neighbour nor the administrative effectiveness to pull it off—the idea would've been discussed in meetings for weeks, until some civil servant earning a few hundred dollars a month realised that it would require them to do some work, and then it would have been shelved indefinitely.

Azerbaijan, with its vast fossil fuel revenues and its retinue of foreign PR firms—including several based in London—maintained a slick operation. In 2022, more than 200 "journalists" visited the country, the vast majority of them likely on trips organised and funded by the government, and by 2023 that had more than doubled to over 480.[4] The criteria for being invited on one of these press tours were usually fairly loose—while reporters with a clear track record of covering the region were mostly excluded, freelancers who were setting foot in the South Caucasus for the first time were the most highly prized. Others given tours of Baku's skyscrapers and the ruins of Aghdam were often a random assortment of tabloid columnists or even interior design bloggers. But aside from the puff pieces, the strategy had an unintended consequence—it undermined more serious coverage of the country and meant any efforts to tell the Azerbaijani side of the story were treated with deep suspicion by those following events in the South Caucasus.

For, beneath the talking points of the lobbying effort, there were of course genuine Azerbaijani grievances. With Nagorno-Karabakh still under military jurisdiction following the 2020 war, and with regular clashes along the front lines, I'd been forced to accept a surly Foreign-Ministry-approved driver who spoke neither English nor Russian, but who had apparently undergone landmine training to ensure that our black sedan wasn't suddenly shredded by one of the hundreds of thousands of devices still stuck in the ground. On the way to Shusha, we pulled into a popular stop for press junkets and politicians' visits: the Ağalı smart village. Surrounded by dusty hills, this collection of 100 or so houses was the first major project designed to rehouse Azerbaijani refugees from the region who had fled during the First War. The administration buildings, a post office and a public services hub surrounded the ghostly central square, and I was ushered into an upstairs office for tea with the mayor—who, as it turned out, wasn't originally from Nagorno-Karabakh. I interrupted the long list of planned developments and improvements to ask if anyone actually was.

"Well, if you want to speak to a former refugee, we can find one," came the reply. The mayor called out to the elderly man who had served us the little glass cups of black tea, who now appeared again with a shallow dish full of boiled sweets.

Mohubbet Samadov was sixty-nine years old and he'd been born in the original Ağalı village, along the road to Shusha. When the fighting started during the Soviet collapse, he'd been well into his thirties, farming the dusty soil to feed his children and his parents. The surrounding region, Zangilan, was bordered by Armenia in the west, but largely cut off from it by the mountains. To the south, Iran lay just across the river Aras, behind a long fence. Ağalı, tucked in Azerbaijan's southwestern corner, was a long way from the Soviet Nagorno-Karabakh oblast, and the only Armenians he'd ever met by 1993 were roving traders who came to buy agricultural produce or sell their wares to the locals. But, in October that year, in one of the last great offensives of the First War, Armenian forces had gained a foothold in the hills and begun to push south into the province. Mohubbet and his family fled, fearing for their lives.

He put down his cup and picked up a tissue from a wooden box on the table, wiping tears from his eyes as he explained how he and his family had lived in squalid conditions for the best part of the three decades that followed, despite Azerbaijan's increasing wealth. While the glass and steel Flame Towers were erected, while Martyr's Lane was refurbished, surviving First War refugees had effectively been left languishing without safe accommodation in shantytowns and barracks, a permanent spectacle for foreign visitors to show how much Azerbaijan had suffered at the hands of the Armenians.

Now, following the Second War, Mohubbet and his family had been given a home of their own, becoming an altogether different exhibit—one that showed resilience, and the desire to reverse the wrongs committed against them.

Suddenly very composed, Mohubbet concluded, "I want to thank victorious President Ilham Aliyev for giving us our home back."

Just a few hundred metres up the hillside from the identikit houses lay the original Ağalı, the village he remembered so clearly that he could find exactly where his house had been, among the few remaining stones that hadn't been plundered during the thirty-year Armenian occupation.

* * *

JERUSALEM OF THE CAUCASUS

It was getting dark in Shusha on the evening of 4 August 2022. I'd pulled into the city a few hours earlier after the long drive from Baku, checked into an eerily quiet hotel and headed downstairs for a bowl of soup and a plate of Soviet-style *stolichniy* salad—a mix of chicken, eggs, peas, potatoes and pickles bound with mayonnaise. My arteries hardening with the cholesterol, I stepped out through the manicured garden for a walk around the abandoned city.

The empty apartment buildings stood with their doors open and their windows dark, except for the occasional ground floor flat where a construction team had set up camp. Along one of the main streets leading towards the centre, what had once been Armenian-owned businesses were now hollow shells, daubed with graffiti written by the soldiers and with no glass left in the windows. The little white signs on almost every doorway reading "*minalar yoxdur*" (cleared of landmines) were another constant reminder that this was a city that had only recently changed hands. I walked around the newly-restored statue of legendary Azerbaijani singer Bulbul, and past the empty pedestals that had once held up busts of venerated Armenians. Along one side street, close to the ruins of centuries-old homes that had long fallen into disuse, there was the largest mound of rubble I'd ever seen. Concrete and bricks and bathtubs and chequered blankets and wooden floors and shards of furniture had all been bulldozed into a vast heap on the outskirts of town.

Further towards the centre were the hollow archways of the building that had once served as a bazaar for local Armenians. But just beyond it, in a clearing, a massive white marquee had now been set up by the Azerbaijanis. A cheer rang out from the crowd inside. Maybe forty or fifty young people were there, watching the football on a projector screen. Qarabağ FC were playing—the premier Azerbaijani team founded in the city of Aghdam, where what was once their stadium is now a dusty disused field. After the First War, the team had been relocated to the outskirts of Baku, and had come top in the country's premier league every year since 2014, hounding out rivals like Sumgait and Neftçi, the former oil workers' club. They were winning again tonight and the spectators, who turned out to be a group of foreign-born Azeris on a special cultural exchange, were delighted. As the final whistle went, I accosted a few to ask what they thought so far. "We might live far away, but this is our land, this is where we belong," one, a Polish-Azerbaijani university student explained. Another, one of the group's chaperones, was an Azerbaijan-born French citizen living in Paris. One of her grandfathers was from Aghdam, and she'd brought with her a board game she'd designed that allowed players to chart a course around the entirety of Azerbaijan, discovering its cultural landmarks as they went.

The walk back to the hotel was dark, without street lamps or the light from buildings. In the distance though, I could have sworn I'd seen the occasional flash, and what sounded like bangs sounded out somewhere in the distance. Was it thunder? Fireworks celebrating Qarabağ FC's victory? I wasn't sure. As I rounded the corner, I came face to face with a sentry in full uniform, holding his assault rifle out in front of him. "Can I see your papers?" I pulled out my passport and my press card, which this time I'd remembered to bring with me. "There's a curfew at 10pm, you know?" I didn't. I checked my watch: it was 10.20. Obviously not an enemy spy or saboteur, I was waved on.

The next morning, opening my laptop in the hopes of getting some work done on my article before breakfast, I spotted a new statement from the Azerbaijani armed forces. A firefight the previous morning, Baku claimed, had killed one of its servicemen, Anar Kazimov, not far from where I was sitting. Now, "Operation Revenge," it said, had begun. Special forces had carried out a major offensive to take control of strategic heights along the line of contact, and work had begun on reinforcing their new positions with supply roads. Where were the Russians, supposedly here to hold the line? A statement on the extremely outdated website of Moscow's peacekeeping contingent confirmed that two Karabakh Armenian troops had died and fourteen more were injured, but boasted that "the command of the Russian peacekeepers, in cooperation with the Azerbaijani and Armenian sides, resolved these incidents. There were no violations of the line of contact between the parties." And yet, reality seemed to be on the side of the Azerbaijanis and Armenians, who both acknowledged that territory had changed hands.

Operation Revenge, the largest threat to the post-war status quo since 2020, seemed to have gone unnoticed by Moscow. Even less useful for understanding what was going on was the joint Russian-Turkish monitoring centre, which had been established following the 2020 war to observe and document any ceasefire violations using drones and surveillance cameras. The following year, a portacabin village had sprung up near Aghdam to accommodate it, but that was more or less the last anyone had heard of the venture. It stayed quiet on key questions of responsibility for clashes, rarely if ever issuing statements and not even bothering to create a proper website for its findings.

Back in Baku, at a meeting with a senior Azerbaijani military officer, I asked how it was possible that, within twelve hours of a clash on the contact line, they had managed to launch a multi-pronged, well-coordinated campaign on mountainous territory, with its own branded codename. "Ah," he said, "we just wait for the right moment and then we strike." Meanwhile, Gegham Stepanyan, the Karabakh Armenian human rights ombudsman, told me in a message that Stepanakert was increasingly coming to terms with what was going on. Russia wasn't punishing aggression along the line of contact, and now Azerbaijan was "taking advantage of the situation."

* * *

ASHES OF OUR FATHERS

The 2020 ceasefire came with uncertainty for many Armenians, but few more than the priests living in the vast Dadivank monastery complex, an ancient stone compound fabled to have been built in the first century CE. The towns and villages of Kalbajar district around it were passing to Azerbaijani control under the trilateral agreement of November, and the black-robe-wearing clergy were preparing to take down their most valuable religious artefacts and leave with the steady stream of local residents. Among them was the abbot, Father Hovhannes Hovhannisyan, a greying, bearded priest who, when the war started, became a social media sensation after posing with his AK-74 in one hand and a golden cross in the other. He launched a public appeal for trucks to help the priests haul out the monastery's bells and inscribed cross-stones.

As the handover deadline loomed, dozens of Armenians made the journey from Stepanakert, or along the Lachin Corridor from Armenia itself, to see the hallowed monastery for the last time, and come to terms with losing one of their nation's cultural homes. Some wept, others took photos with Father Hovhannes, who wore a thick padded camouflage army jacket over his robe and dog collar. His phone rang—it was the president in Stepanakert.

"Do not touch Dadivank, do not touch the crosses, we will not give up Dadivank," Arayik Harutyunyan reportedly said.[5] A deal had been done; the priests could stay at the monastery, guarded by the Russian peacekeepers—a little bubble of Armenian life surrounded by Baku-controlled territory.

According to Sarhat Petrosyan, former head of Armenia's property planning committee, the reprieve was the result of a mapping detail. While Azerbaijan had been expecting the ancient church to be given up as part of the deal, once charts published by the Russian general staff were superimposed over Google Maps, this showed Dadivank outside the new Azerbaijani area of control. A day later, a spokesperson for the Armenian Church confirmed that the Russians had moved in and a number of priests would stay behind to worship. Inside the wrought metal gates, the green-clad peacekeepers parked an armoured personnel carrier, patrolling the perimeter of the vast monastery grounds. Each week, the local priests would pass the Russians the names of up to ten Karabakh Armenians living nearby who wanted to worship at Dadivank. By 2021, the lists were coming back with each and every name struck off in rejection, as Moscow tightened its procedures. The three monks and three deacons who'd stayed behind under Russian guard were virtually cut off from the world, with no congregation left to preach to.

Azerbaijan was furious with the monastery's special status, declaring that its real name was Khudavang and that it had actually been built by the wife of Caucasian Albanian Prince Vakhtang, not by Armenians. Its rightful inheritors, therefore, were the descendants of the Caucasian Albanian people, namely Azerbaijan's minority Udi people. "Armenians have nothing to do with this place," concluded Mubariz Gurbanli, the chairman of the State Committee for Work with Religious Organisations.[6]

Despite frequently being cast as a conflict between Christians and Muslims, the standoff between Armenians and Azerbaijanis lacks a clear religious dynamic, and this has been the case since well before the 1990s. As in many former Soviet states, the role of any kind of faith had been largely minimised in society for decades. As a result, Azerbaijan is one of the most secular Muslim nations in the world. Like their counterparts in cosmopolitan parts of Turkey, many Azerbaijanis drink alcohol, and only a small minority regularly pray at mosque. The country's Christian minorities—its ethnic Russians and the Udis—have built churches, while the Jewish community is held up as an integral part of society, showcased by the government as an example of its tolerance. While Muslim nations across the Middle East and further afield have faced the radicalising influences of Sunni

Wahhabism and Iran's Twelver brand of Shia Islam, Azerbaijan has remained a largely irreligious state, where religion, as in many countries, is more about culture than commandment.

Armenia, meanwhile, is often ranked as among the most religious Christian nations in the world. But beyond professing a belief in God, Armenians' faith is often more personal and spiritual than organised. Unlike in neighbouring Georgia, where the leadership of the Georgian Orthodox Church has significant authority in society, Armenians rarely say the clergy has a monopoly on truth, and their iconic hillside places of worship are used more as backdrops for occasions like weddings and christenings than for regular services. Among Karabakh Armenians in particular, irreligiousness is even more pronounced, having faced tougher scrutiny in the Soviet era than those in the Armenian SSR. And, when it came to geopolitics, one of Armenia's closest partners was the theocratic Islamic Republic of Iran, while one of Azerbaijan's most important partners was the State of Israel.

The problem with Nagorno-Karabakh's churches wasn't that they were Christian, it was that they were Armenian—and acted as monuments to the existence of a people on land the Azerbaijanis said they had no historical claim to. Likewise, Yerevan's Blue Mosque, a domed architectural jewel from the 1700s in a city where most buildings of that period have long since disappeared, has survived because it was considered to be Persian, not Azeri—despite having been built by the Turkic-Iranian Khanate, which controlled the city at a time when it was home to hundreds of thousands of people who would now be considered Azeri. This is ethnic hatred, pure and simple, looking for a version of history in which to substantiate a basic premise that the two nations are like oil and water—have never mixed and would never be able to. Coexistence had been possible under the yoke of the Russian Empire and the Soviet Union, but it was a coerced form of coexistence, based on the idea that the things separating Armenians and Azerbaijanis, like religion and nationality, were worthless. It also divided them into two separate states within Moscow's union, laying the foundations for the conflict that would come.

While many of the apartments of Shusha's former Armenian inhabitants still stood—empty and ignored, their doors beaten down by soldiers—Azerbaijan had been quicker to act on more obvious reminders of the city's dual heritage. The iconic Ghazanchetsots Cathedral, which was hit by two missiles during the 2020 war, was fenced off and covered with green construction netting. A bored-looking armed guard patrolled the entrance, but couldn't explain why it was off limits given there seemed to be no work taking place. The building was put up in the late 1800s, damaged in the Armenian pogrom of the 1920s, and reportedly used as an ammunition store for the Azerbaijani garrison that held the city during the First War. It was repaired by the Karabakh Armenians later in the 1990s while other buildings were left to crumble, and became a major symbol of the breakaway republic. In October 2020, the cathedral, still damaged from the rocket attack a few weeks earlier, had been filled with well-wishers. Even as the war raged, a young couple from Martuni were married there by a priest, the bride in a flowing white dress and traditional metal headdress, the groom in military fatigues, having been given just a few days off from the front line. It was the last wedding to be held in Ghazanchetsots—now renamed Gazanchi Church by the Azerbaijanis.

According to Azerbaijani sources, despite inscriptions on the walls confirming it was built with the support of the Armenian Apostolic patriarchate, the great cathedral was actually a Russian Orthodox church, established to serve the tsar's armies in the region.[7] It would therefore have to be "reconstructed" to undo the supposed Armenian vandalism, officials said. As concern grew about the fate of the historic site, one Baku historian, Adalat Mustafayev, explained the government's position:

"Throughout history, there have been no Armenians on the territory of Karabakh. Therefore, the presence of an Armenian church in Shusha is impossible."

While Azerbaijan never published plans to show what Ghazanchetsots Cathedral was supposed to look like, the most immediate changes were made to its pointed roof, damaged by missile strikes. This was removed and the tower left as a sort of impotent rotunda, uncharacteristic of Armenian churches in the region. However, while the spire didn't exist in the Soviet period, early photos from the Russian Imperial era show a similarly pointed roof, likely damaged during the destruction of Shusha's Armenian quarter in the 1920s. The Karabakh Armenian restoration in the 1990s appeared to have been broadly consistent with the historical form, but it was clear that Azerbaijan wasn't interested in that version of the past. And, on top of that, Armenians were quick to point out that they had also actually paid to restore the city's upper mosque, arguing that the wider state of disrepair and dereliction was the result of poverty rather than malevolence.

The Green Chapel, the other place of worship Alvina Nersesyan had been able to see from her balcony, faced similar treatment. The first time I saw it in person in 2022, its dome had been removed and photos had surfaced online of its interior having been trashed, candlesticks broken and altar destroyed, obscured from view by a heap of rubble. Again, the official objective, Azerbaijani media confirmed, was to return it to its "historic" condition—which presumably meant the days immediately after the anti-Armenian pogrom a century earlier. But clips uploaded by Azerbaijani conscripts of them triumphantly tearing down metal crosses or smashing gravestones were just the tip of the iceberg.

JERUSALEM OF THE CAUCASUS

Baku's Nakhchivan exclave was once home to a historic Armenian population, which had almost completely emigrated to the Armenian SSR by the end of the Soviet period. Since the 1990s, Azerbaijani authorities have pursued a seemingly deliberate policy of erasing that cultural history. Caucasus Heritage Watch, a satellite mapping initiative based out of Cornell University in the US, found in 2022 that of 110 "mediaeval and early modern" Armenian monasteries, chapels and graveyards in Nakhchivan, virtually all have now been destroyed, scarcely a headstone surviving to testify to the community that once lived there.[8] Mostly the old Armenian sites have been left empty, the dust reclaiming them, but in some cases a monument or a mosque was built on top of the bulldozed ruins. Now, experts fear that Nagorno-Karabakh's rich cultural fabric will face the same systematic policy of destruction and relabelling. Those concerns have only been compounded by the post-2020 destruction of swathes of the historic Armenian village of Mets Taghlar, its almost 200-year-old bridge and cemetery; and the constant claims since the Second War that Armenian heritage is "really" Caucasian Albanian.

Azerbaijani commentators wrote off the Caucasus Heritage Watch report, largely because one of its authors was an Armenian, but in fact the group also published a seminal analysis of the destruction of Azerbaijani cultural sites in Nagorno-Karabakh during the thirty-year period between the two wars. Almost sixty per cent of the mosques and burial sites studied have been damaged to a greater or lesser degree, with only around a third broadly unchanged since the First War. While most have been allowed to slip into disrepair or dismantled for building materials, many were seemingly deliberately targeted by the Karabakh Armenian administration. But the report's conclusion riled the two sides, dismissing both the Azerbaijani claim that sixty-five out of sixty-seven mosques were destroyed and the Armenian insistence that the damage was done by Soviet authorities.

The Karabakh Armenians may not have liked to talk about it, or may even have rushed to justify it as a wartime necessity, but they knew that the land they lived on or used as their "buffer zone" had once been home to hundreds of thousands of ordinary Azeris. By contrast, the newly victorious Azerbaijani state now regularly maintains that no native Armenian population has ever lived there. Shusha, like the real Jerusalem to which it is so often compared, had become the site of a battle over its shared past that one side intended to win.

In the centre of Shusha, a construction fence shielded one of the city's two historic mosques. It had been used as a cattle shed, its historic floors coated with a thick layer of manure, its walls daubed with Armenian graffiti. As late as 1988, it had played host to weddings between a small number of young mixed Armenian and Azerbaijani couples, with guests from both communities dancing together the dances they knew by heart, lighting candles and breaking bread. Like Ghazanchetsots, the mosque too was now off limits, as a stocky man in shorts and trainers rushed out of a portacabin to tell me. He introduced himself as Ali, and just a year-and-a-half ago he had been one of the first soldiers to storm the city. He had been wounded in battle, awarded a presidential pension and offered a cushy job helping with the restoration.

"I want to sincerely thank the supreme commander, President Ilham Aliyev, for making all this possible," he said the moment he found out I was a journalist, and then disappeared into the bushes to pick a handful of walnuts and berries he wanted me to try.

"The fruit here is so sweet," he said, "because it's given by God."

5

A TALE OF TWO ARMENIAS

The table in front of us heaved with dozens of dishes. There were smoked cheeses, fried pastries, fresh-cut cucumber, tomatoes and herbs, honeycomb and pots of preserves, as well as large bowls of green beans cooked in tomato sauce and, of course, *menemen*—eggs scrambled with tomato and green pepper, a staple of every Turkish breakfast. Outside the cafe window, the water of Lake Van disappeared into the distance.

It was the summer of 2023, and it had been a three-day journey from Yerevan to get to one of the easternmost cities in Turkey. Van may be only a little more than 100 miles from the Armenian capital, but there is no direct route between the two—the border between the two countries has been sealed for thirty years in retaliation for the First Nagorno-Karabakh War. Instead, a rattling sleeper train packed with holidaymakers took me to the Georgian coastal city of Batumi, a dizzying resort filled with glass skyscraper hotels, popular with Russians and Armenians alike. From there, at a depot where traders sold loose tobacco and fresh pastries, a bus was waiting to take me across the border.

Along the highway that follows the curve of the Black Sea coast, huge well-lit tunnels have been blasted through the hills.

ASHES OF OUR FATHERS

The road inland was newly-paved and dotted with giant posters of recently re-elected President Recep Tayyip Erdoğan. A few hours after leaving the coastline behind, more and more military checkpoints begin flanking the highway. This is Kurdish country—home to most of the estimated twenty-million-strong minority group that has for decades clashed with the Turkish state. Just six months before, in November 2022, a bomb had exploded on Istanbul's unimaginably busy İstiklal Avenue, killing six people and injuring another eighty-one. The terror attack had been blamed on the outlawed Kurdistan Workers' Party and, ahead of the national elections in May 2023, police had launched operations to arrest tens of Kurdish politicians, activists and journalists. While outright fighting between Turkish troops and Kurdish militants has largely calmed down in recent years, in Van the atmosphere remained tense.

In February, weeks before the election, a magnitude 7.8 earthquake had hit south-eastern Turkey and Syria, levelling millions of buildings and taking the lives of more than 50,000 people, largely in Kurdish-majority areas.[1] With footage of entire floors of apartment blocks stacked pancake-style on top of each other, anger had quickly turned against corporate construction companies and the system that had allowed them to skirt around earthquake safety rules, meaning that many of those who were in bed at 4.00am on 6 February had no chance of escaping before the ceiling above them came down. I'd been in Istanbul that morning. When I turned up at my regular cafe with copy to file on what the catastrophe meant for Turkey and for Erdoğan's political future, the shutter was still down. Sam, the normally cheerful owner, himself a Kurd from Diyarbakır, had turned up ten minutes late with tears in his eyes.

"My best friend is under the rubble. He's a civil engineer. Imagine, an engineer crushed by a building that wasn't built properly. How can they get away with this?"

A TALE OF TWO ARMENIAS

In the end, though, Erdoğan comfortably won May's elections. But Van province heavily backed his challenger, Kemal Kılıçdaroğlu, in hope of securing a more Kurdish-friendly administration. They failed, and while no officials have been held to account for the devastation of the earthquake, Erdoğan has since reshuffled his top team to bring in more officials of Kurdish descent, including the foreign minister. But it wasn't a Kurd I was in Van to have breakfast with.

Özcan had been born and raised in Van, the leafy city around the lake. He and his eight brothers and sisters had grown up and gone to school there, prayed at their hometown's domed mosques and had children of their own. But ever since he was a child, he'd understood that the family was different to their predominantly Kurdish neighbours. In 1986, the police had turned up at their front door to take away their father. He'd come back nearly two weeks later, having been tortured. Within a year, he was dead, living his final days furious with the humiliation he'd suffered at the hands of the authorities.

Özcan took a sip of hot black tea from the glass and explained how, from a young age, he knew his parents were Armenian. It wasn't something they talked about outside the house, but his mother had made sure her children knew where they came from—and why her husband had been targeted. From 1914, Anatolia and eastern Turkey descended into brutal violence as the forces of the Ottoman Empire launched a campaign against the population of more than a million Western Armenians living under its rule. Formally, they were already second-class citizens, having faced a flurry of arbitrary prohibitions at the hands of sultans through the ages—including being banned from owning weapons or riding horses. These harsh conditions had made rural life almost unbearably hard, and increasing interference from the state had bolstered the ranks of self-defence units and anti-government movements, which were subject to a blanket ban from

1915. So too had recent violence against the Armenians, not least the Hamidian massacres of 1894–7, when tens of thousands had been killed and many more forced to convert to Islam as the Ottoman authorities grew suspicious of any group that it saw as a threat to the foundations of its increasingly shaky state. Among those committed to defending themselves against a future onslaught was the Armenian Revolutionary Federation, or Dashnaktsutyun party, a pan-Armenian nationalist faction that fought for independence.

As news came in that entire Armenian communities in cities further west—Erzincan, Erzurum, Diyarbakır—had been forced to pack whatever possessions they could carry and join their neighbours on long forced marches into the unknown, or else face being massacred, Özcan's grandfather, Hovhannes Pashonyan, decided to flee. For a Van Armenian, or Vanetsi, there were only two obvious routes out: east to the Persian Empire or north to the Russian Empire. Moscow had long been seen as a steadfast ally of the Ottoman Armenians, bound by their shared Christian faith. The First World War had just begun, putting the Ottomans and the Russians on opposing sides, and this had been given as a reason why not just the Armenian farmers of the east but also the Armenian merchants and intelligentsia of the bigger cities, including Istanbul, were suspect and treacherous. In January 1915, Russian troops defeated a larger Ottoman force at the Battle of Sarikamish near the border city of Kars, and top commander Enver Pasha quickly blamed the Ottoman Armenians. Hovhannes decided to go north to Russia.

In April 1915, many of the Armenians remaining in the city of Van rose up, led by the Dashnaktsutyun (or Dashnaks). They had been promised that if the self-defence militias clashing with Ottoman forces laid down their arms, the violence would stop. It didn't. Fearing that the state was now intent on killing or dis-

A TALE OF TWO ARMENIAS

placing them no matter what, armed bands known as Fedayi launched an attack on the Ottoman patrols encircling the city. In retribution, the Armenian quarter was shelled, even as Armenian refugees from other parts of the country continued to flood in. As the siege went on, Russian forces—often under the command of Armenians from inside their empire—launched a push into eastern Turkey, aiming to reach Van. So too did ethnic-Armenian militias from Persia, the crisis drawing in fighters from across the two empires that had partitioned the once great Armenian kingdom in 387 CE.

In Russia, Armenian exiles were sending weapons to the resistance in the Ottoman Empire, trying to defend their hometowns and take the fight to the Ottoman troops. Their efforts failed: by August the Russians were in retreat back to the South Caucasus, with Armenian refugees often fleeing alongside them to escape brutal retribution. The Ottomans, facing catastrophe on other fronts in the First World War, were pulled back, and the Russians moved in again, capturing swathes of territory in the Armenian-inhabited east. But, once again, the chaos of the war kicked in—the February Revolution of 1917 saw Russian troops mutiny and the tsar deposed. The Ottomans regained the upper hand, taking back the territory they had lost. The remaining Armenians fled, many forced south to a refugee camp outside of Baghdad.

Those Ottoman Armenians who didn't or couldn't flee now faced death, either directly at the hands of the Ottoman Empire's ethnic-Turkish forces, or on death marches into the deserts of Syria. Often poor farmers from isolated villages, they were rounded up by gendarmes and put into temporary settlements in places like Malatya, Sivas and Muş before being forced to traipse through the wilderness towards Aleppo. The route was strewn with the bodies of those who died of thirst, hunger, illness or bandit attacks. Once in Syria, the ordeal didn't end for the tens of thousands of dishevelled, brutalised Armenians who survived the journey: in open-air concentration camps at Deir ez-Zor, without access to food and clean water, they were stripped of their belongings—although some were fed or helped to escape by local Arabs. Women and girls were often captured by or sold off to Bedouins along the road, forcefully tattooed as marks of their new ownership, while children were placed in non-Armenian families, never told about their true heritage. Men were simply told they were being conscripted into the army, then executed on the outskirts of town. In cities along the Black Sea coast, particularly Trabzon, there were reports that the Armenians had been told they were being rehomed and had been loaded onto ships, which were then sunk once out to sea. Further inland, they were said to have been executed by firing squads on the sides of ravines, their bodies flowing down the river, or set on fire. In Istanbul, where Armenians had been a sizable presence since before the 1400s, the educated elite was targeted first, destroying the cultural and intellectual life of the Ottoman Armenians and undercutting their ability to organise or advocate for themselves.

For those who had always seen themselves as part of this land, the loss was incomprehensible. Among them was Komitas, the Armenian priest credited with cataloguing and resurrecting thousands of pieces of Armenian and Kurdish folk music that would otherwise have been lost to time and neglect. He was spared being subjected to the horrors himself as a result of diplomatic pressure from the US, but was broken watching the destruction of the communities he loved. He would die in an asylum in France.

Meanwhile, the other major Christian minority of the Ottoman Empire, the Greeks of the Mediterranean and Black Sea coasts, were similarly killed or hounded from their homes, many escaping by ship as their chief population centre, the seaside city of Smyrna (now İzmir) was set aflame. So too were

A TALE OF TWO ARMENIAS

hundreds of thousands of Assyrians, native to the interior of the Ottoman Empire.

The legacy of that bloody period shaped the entire region, creating a massive Armenian diaspora wherever desperate people could find safety—from Aleppo to Baghdad and Beirut. From there, some descendants of the virtually annihilated Western Armenian population moved abroad, forming new communities across the world, notably in the French cities of Paris and Marseilles; in Russia's Moscow, Rostov-on-Don and Krasnodar regions; and in the US, particularly in and around the Los Angeles suburb of Glendale. Scratch a diasporan Armenian, a *spyurkahay*, and you'll uncover a tiny piece of that history: a member of Buenos Aires' estimated tens of thousands-strong community, for example, could have one grandparent born in Diyarbakır, one in Aleppo, one in Istanbul and one raised in an orphanage in Calcutta. Eastern Turkey itself, the ancestral homeland of the Western Armenians, was now empty of Armenians—their homes torched or given to Turks and Kurds, their fields ploughed by those who'd driven them out.

Except, it seemed, Hovhannes. He may have fled in 1915, but he was one of a small number of Armenians who decided to return from what was now the fledgling Soviet Union, in 1923. Maybe he hoped that the end of the First World War would mean the end of the purges; maybe the pressure of Stalin's repression drove him to cross the tense frontier—or maybe he simply missed home enough to risk his life. Either way, he returned across the River Aras, a journey that most fleeing Armenians only made once. In a village outside Van, he was taken in by a Kurdish family he knew from his previous life, assuming a new Kurdish name himself to disguise his identity. He was lucky—as ethnic minorities in the Ottoman Empire, the two groups had been pitted against each other. Armenian property had often ended up in the hands of Kurds, and it was

Kurdish bandits who had looted the columns of desperate refugees as they fled the cities the two communities had once shared. It might be us now, went the bitter Armenian warning, but it will be you next.

Within three generations, Hovhannes' grandchildren would all be born Turkish citizens, raised Muslims in a majority Kurdish community, never to learn his Armenian mother tongue. But they lived on the land they belonged to and, through the stories they passed down, they knew who they were. By Özcan's count, there are as many as 140 families of Armenian descent in Van alone, although most would rather not remember that fact. The local authorities and their Kurdish neighbours also have a good idea of who is Armenian and who isn't—with xenophobia and persistent rumours about buried gold flaring into occasional violence. In 2007, Özcan was shot in one such row. He proudly pointed to the wound as we talked and ate. But with eight siblings and nearly ninety cousins and extended family members, they can look after themselves, he insisted.

* * *

We finished our thick Turkish coffees and climbed into an off-road SUV to go and see the village where Özcan's family once lived. The road out of town passed through a gendarme checkpoint, where soldiers took down the names and addresses of those coming in or out—security measures imposed in the name of tackling Kurdish separatist terrorism. Convoys of armoured cars rolled past along the highway. Another hour's drive away, the village was a small maze of mud-brick huts, animal enclosures and new concrete buildings, their compound gates facing out into the street. Women in thick headscarves carried their children in the scorching sun, while a shopkeeper arranged stacks of soft drinks and canned goods on stalls. Just past the houses, on a hill above the road, a vast temple suddenly came into view.

A TALE OF TWO ARMENIAS

Built on what was believed to be the site of the tomb of Saint Bartholomew—one of Jesus' apostles, said to have been among the first to bring Christianity to the Kingdom of Armenia—the colossal church had remained the focal point of the surrounding region's diocese long after the Ottoman conquest. Fortified with a curtain wall and watchtowers on the commanding heights, its impenetrable defences had likely saved it through centuries of turmoil. Until, that is, the modern era. Empty since it was looted at the height of the purges in 1915, St. Bartholomew Monastery now lies in ruin, its dome and roof caved in. Some Armenian sources allege it was blown up by the Ottoman army, while others argue it was damaged in an earthquake, as it had been so many times in earlier history. But, by the 1990s, its cavernous structure had been taken over by the Turkish gendarmes, who'd installed a pill-box at the turn-off from the road and draped rolls of razor wire around the perimeter, turning St. Bartholomew into a makeshift fort from which to fight against the Kurdish separatists, who were at that time waging an all-out war against the government, as the government waged an all-out war against them. Now it had been abandoned even by the police, although the razor wire remained. Along the facade and across the church's now-crumbling archways, where crucifixes and Armenian script had been lovingly etched into the stone, there were bullet holes and the carved names of bored officers once stationed there. There was no sign of the restoration work that had been promised for more than a decade by local Turkish officials.

The death and destruction unleashed on the Armenians was well-documented in the foreign press. A *New York Times* front page declared in 1915 that at least 800,000 had already been killed,[2] while an editorial in Britain's *Independent* published explosive photos of lined-up bodies, asking "shall Armenia perish?"[3] But despite the public outcry, little of any substance was done to end the catastrophe or hold the Ottoman authorities to account. A cover illustration for American satirical magazine *Puck* highlighted the dilemma: a racialised caricature of a Turk holding a sword above the head of an inaccurately European-looking Armenian woman, while John Bull, in a Union Jack waistcoat, watches on from across the water, sitting beside a lockbox of profits from British trade with Turkey. "It's 'ard to 'ave to disturb 'im—'e's such a good customer," read the caption.[4] The magazine wasn't alone in noting the lack of consequences for the slaughter. Decades later, in 1939, Adolf Hitler backed up his genocidal rhetoric using a speech in Obersalzberg to rhetorically ask "who, after all, speaks today of the annihilation of the Armenians?"[5] A week later, he ordered the invasion of Poland and the start of the systematic, industrialised murder of Europe's Jewish population.

The genocide of 1915 is recognised by more than thirty national governments and parliaments, including France, Germany, Russia and, as of a 2021 statement by President Joe Biden, the United States.[6] However, Turkey's official position is that the Armenian genocide is a myth, although it acknowledges many of the individual events, simply arguing that they were justified within the circumstances. According to the Turkish Ministry of Foreign Affairs, which has spent significant time and effort cultivating an academic framework for its version of history, the estimates of between 600,000 and 1.2 million Armenians dead and countless more displaced are inaccurate, and must be understood in the context of "an imperilled empire waging and losing battles on remote and disparate fronts."

"Armenians have attempted to extricate and isolate their history from the complex circumstances in which their ancestors were embroiled. In so doing, they describe a world populated only by white-hatted heroes and black-hatted villains. The heroes are always Christian and the villains are always Muslim," Turkish diplomats argue, in an English-language position paper that

A TALE OF TWO ARMENIAS

appears high up the list of search engine results for anyone looking for information on the subject. At the same time, Ankara blames the Armenians for their fate, insisting "the Armenians took arms against their own government. Their violent political aims, not their race, ethnicity or religion, rendered them subject to relocation."[7]

Mevlüt Çavuşoğlu, the pugnacious former foreign minister fired in Erdoğan's 2023 post-election reshuffle, went further during his time in office. In April 2022, Turkish Armenians protested his state visit to Uruguay to sign a free trade agreement, exactly coinciding with the 107th anniversary of the genocide; he sneered with laughter at them out of the window of his SUV, pushing his middle finger and thumb together, raising his index and little finger to form the sign of the Grey Wolves.[8] The gesture was a show of support for the pan-Turkist paramilitary movement that violently targets non-Turkic ethnic minorities, denies the events of 1915, and has been known to harass Armenian communities.[9] Çavuşoğlu's gesture sparked a diplomatic incident, with the president of his host country describing the taunt as "regrettable."[10]

Turkish people, Azerbaijanis and scholars have a right to question the historical facts. But much like Holocaust denial or, say, the refusal to accept the crimes of British colonialism, the overwhelming body of evidence, of scholarship, of oral history, points solely in one direction. And those whose starting point, for political or personal reasons, is that these events never took place, or didn't take place as mainstream historians say they did, rarely refute individual pieces of evidence—instead seeking to muddy the waters and write off the entire field as biased against them and paint the Armenians and Turks of the time as being as bad as each other.

That denialism is best encapsulated in the city of Iğdır, Turkey's closest to the Armenian border, less than 100 miles from Van, around the colossal snow-capped Mount Ararat. Once the defining geographical feature of the Armenian homeland, mythical and almost sacred, the mountain now sits inside Turkey's borders, but towers over the modern Republic of Armenia—for many Armenians, it is forever out of reach, a reminder of the very real closed border now between them and it. A farming community, Iğdır is home to the Memorial and Museum of Martyred Turks Massacred by Armenians, an extensive exhibition topped by three giant swords that jut into the sky, making it the tallest monument in the country. It is dedicated to the tens of thousands of Turkish civilians the government says were killed at the hands of Armenians between 1915 and 1920, reversing the allegations against itself and directing them back at those making them.

Iğdır itself was originally included in the Armenian First Republic, proclaimed in 1918 when both the Ottoman Empire and the Russian Empire were collapsing. The Ottomans' defeat in the First World War saw the empire's territories carved up, with Palestine and Syria handed out as mandates to the victorious British and French. At talks held in France in 1920, the Allied Powers also initially proposed that the Armenian First Republic be awarded a huge expanse of land that had made up historical Armenia, including Van, Erzurum and Trabzon, and named Wilsonian Armenia after its proponent, President Woodrow Wilson. However, when the Ottoman Empire descended into all-out civil war that year, the new Turkish government declared war on the Republic, taking back Armenian-controlled territory that the Ottomans had lost during the war with the Russians. While Armenian fighters were able to prevent a total Turkish invasion from the west, the Bolshevik Red Army was advancing from the northeast, and the Republic was summarily quashed before the end of the year. There would be no independent Armenian state again until almost the end of the century.

A TALE OF TWO ARMENIAS

But the imperial collapse also meant that the officials responsible for the genocide had been deposed. The Young Turk movement in power since 1908 had been ousted, and the new post-Ottoman government put its leaders on trial in Istanbul in 1919, both for their crimes against the Armenians and Greeks, and their role in the empire's defeat. The chief defendants were Enver Pasha, who had served as defence minister, navy minister Djemal Pasha, and grand vizier Talaat Pasha—but all three had fled abroad following the fall of their government. They were found guilty by the court-martial and sentenced to death in absentia. In practice, they continued their lives abroad in comfort and relative safety, benefitting from the lack of international extradition systems.

On the morning of 15 March 1921, Talaat Pasha stepped out of his Berlin apartment for a stroll. He'd been living there under the name Ali Salih Bey and had shaved his distinctive moustache to ensure he wasn't recognised; he was being looked after in semi-secrecy by a large exile community of former Young Turk security officials and diplomats. As he walked down the street, a man came jogging towards him and shot him dead with a pistol. The assassination was the culmination of months of work to track him down by the Dashnaktsutyun, which had been surveilling his apartment and the businesses of former Ottoman officials across Berlin as part of what they named Operation Nemesis: an Armenian campaign to kill those the international justice system had failed to hold to account—in some cases, carrying out the death sentences handed down by the Istanbul tribunals.

The gunman was Soghomon Tehlirian, an Armenian from the town of Erzincan. He'd lost almost his entire family in 1915—including his mother, brothers and sister, and had been determined to avenge them.[11] It wasn't Tehlirian's first killing either; he was credited with the murder of Harutian Mgrditichian, an Istanbul Armenian who had worked with the Ottoman security services to draw up lists of intellectuals for deportation and slaughter. Standing over Talaat's body, he was arrested and put on trial by the Germans. Hauled before the court, he was a pitiable character, suffering night terrors, sudden collapses and even seizures that physicians told the judge were the result of having lost his loved ones so brutally. He was ultimately acquitted by the jury and released. Just over a year later, Djemal Pasha was killed by Dashnaktsutyun assassins in Tbilisi, while travelling from Kabul to Berlin. All in all, by 1922, seven leading Young Turks blamed for organising the deportations and killings lay dead.

Decades later, Operation Nemesis would inspire more violence in the name of avenging the genocide. In the 1970s, the Armenian Secret Army for the Liberation of Armenia emerged, its stated intent to create Wilsonian Armenia and unify both the Armenian people and their former lands, whether they be under Turkish or Soviet rule. This secret army was known for the killings of Turkish diplomats, for storming the Turkish embassy in Paris in 1981 and taking fifty-six hostages, actively targeting civilians with a gun attack at Ankara airport in 1982 and the bombing of a Turkish Airlines check-in desk at Paris Orly airport in 1983.[12]

Not all responses to the genocide have been violent. In eastern Turkey, being open about being an Armenian is still nearly impossible. But in Istanbul there is a more sizeable community, caring for still-intact churches and running businesses that are conspicuously Armenian if you know what to look for—which most of their neighbours don't. In nationalist Turkish parlance, they are the *kılıç artığı*, or "leftovers of the sword": those who survived the purges. President Erdoğan himself has used this term to describe "terrorists who are still in our country, although their numbers have decreased," prompting outrage.[13] Istanbul's Osmanbey district is home to many of the great city's dwindling Armenian population; there is an Armenian private school and a

A TALE OF TWO ARMENIAS

handful of *meyhane*-style cafeterias that lay out plates of mezze and grill up lamb or chicken skewers to order. In one such bar-restaurant, after I talked in broken Turkish to the elderly owner about his dreams to visit Yerevan before he dies, a waiter appeared at my table with a serving plate. "It's sausage from Armenia," he said, lowering his voice to a gleeful whisper, "it's pork!"

But, just up the hill, across the dual carriageway, is the parallel neighbourhood of Talaatpasha, officially named in honour of the man once sentenced to death in this city for his crimes against the very community still clinging on to its existence here.

That complex divide was one that Hrant Dink, one of the best-known Turkish Armenians in recent history, personified until his death in 2007. Born in the east of the country, he served as editor of Istanbul's influential Armenian- and Turkish-language newspaper *Agos*, and chronicled the stories of those who'd died, those who'd fled, those whose lives had been forever changed. However, he still described himself as a patriotic Turkish citizen who wanted to see the country acknowledge its past and then move on; who wanted a democracy where ideas could be discussed freely and without the millstone of guilt around Turkey's neck. Denialism, he felt, came not from the fact that Turks were bad people—but "because they think that genocide is a bad thing which they would never want to commit, and because they can't believe their ancestors would do such a thing either."[14] As he often pointed out, there were even Turks and Kurds who had saved and sheltered Armenians, like those who took in Özcan's grandfather—but their heroism and sacrifice was now a taboo subject in the country they loved. One such Turk was Ali Kemal Bey, a liberal politician and great grandfather of former British Prime Minister Boris Johnson, who served as interior minister for three months in 1919, and who accused the Young Turk regime of sanctioning massacres and looting Armenian property. He was lynched for his dissent.

Dink was a patriot insofar as he was passionately striving for what he saw as a better Turkey, more secure in its past. His version of patriotism, however, demanded challenging the idea that Turkishness is an ethnic identity, rather than a civic one, and that minorities are by their very nature a dangerous separatist and secessionist threat. The creation of a monolithic Turkish ethnostate has been championed by every government since the fall of the Ottoman Empire as a way to rally together a huge and deeply varied country where many—if not the majority—of people have at least some heritage from decades of intermarriage with those they shared their land with, namely Armenians, Kurds, Greeks, Bulgarians, Arabs, Assyrians. In the narrative of the state, they were all now Turks, with one flag, one government, one sense of self.

Dink's unequivocal insistence that "I am not a Turk, I am an Armenian citizen of Turkey" contradicted the very foundations of the state and saw him prosecuted, unsuccessfully, on charges of denigrating the Turkish national character.[15] But at the same time, he also vigorously opposed French proposals for a law banning Armenian genocide denial, fearing they would ultimately lead to free speech restrictions and were part of a cynical Western effort to rile Ankara. If the law was passed, he vowed, he himself would fly there, dance up the Champs-Élysées while denying the genocide, and be the first tried for breaking it.[16] His legal entanglements didn't end there: he received a six-month suspended sentence in 2005 for an article in which he suggested that Western Armenian diasporans would have to move past the history of 1915 and "replace the poisoned blood associated with the Turk, with fresh blood associated with Armenia."[17] What he meant was that clinging on to bitterness over their lost homeland would hold his people back, and they should look to their state to invigorate their future—but that was of course not how the remarks were interpreted. An interview with Reuters in which

A TALE OF TWO ARMENIAS

Dink used the word "genocide" saw another case opened. Friends urged him to leave Turkey, but he replied simply that "whenever I go abroad, I miss my country so terribly."[18]

On 19 January 2007, a man approached Hrant Dink on the street outside the *Agos* offices in Osmanbey and shot him three times in the head, killing him instantly. Two young men were handed hefty prison sentences for the murder, but it sparked a fierce debate about what the police and security services had done in the lead up and aftermath. A decade later, the former head of Turkey's police intelligence, Ali Fuat Yılmazer, told a hearing that the attack was "deliberately not prevented" and "this murder was made possible on purpose" because officials had simply ignored the threats to Dink's life. British journalist Robert Fisk described him as the 1,500,001st victim of the Armenian genocide.[19]

Instead of being silenced, though, Turkey's small Armenian community and their allies were incensed, with more than 100,000 people from across the city marching at his funeral and many Armenians taking an increasingly active role in political life.[20] By 2015, there were three openly Armenian candidates for parliament and, in 2021, one of the few who'd been elected, Garo Paylan, introduced a bill to recognise the genocide once and for all, and see the names of those responsible for it stripped from public place names. The bill failed, but Dink's dream of open discussion of history had been realised. Now, a memorial tile marks the spot where he fell in Osmanbey, although it's occasionally accompanied by a large banner hung across the street by the Grey Wolves.

That debate was a long way away from Van, however, where there is no living trace of Armenian public life. Driving back from Özcan's village, we pulled in at a second old church partly hidden behind a handful of farmhouses. A beautiful circular chapel with a huge domed roof, it was obviously Armenian, with curled script and crosses carved onto the walls by long-dead worshippers. But it was in a catastrophic state of disrepair—one of the window arches had caved in, while large bricks that had withstood centuries had been prised off the facade. A gallery above the entryway had been entirely dismantled. As we looked around the forlorn and cavernous hall, a group of giggling children watched on.

"Are you here for the treasure?" one boy politely enquired in Kurdish. Just two days before, a couple of men searching for gold and other precious relics had smashed one of the arches, he explained, and broken through the interior wall to find a space where the bones of a priest had been interred. They'd found nothing of value and thrown the bones away, but would probably be back again soon. I thought back to stories I'd heard of Holocaust survivors returning to their family homes to find that whichever German had moved into their home had wound up smashing it to pieces looking for the pot of gold that all Jewish people surely had and must have stashed somewhere.

"What do you think about Armenians?" Özcan asked the group.

"They're bad people," came the answer, accompanied by a gap-toothed grin.

"No they aren't," he replied with infinite patience. "Who's telling you that? Your parents? At school?"

They all nodded.

* * *

In 2014, Ruben Vardanyan climbed Mount Ararat. He was on top of the world. Two years before, he'd sold the company he'd helped found—Russia's first post-communist investment bank, Troika Dialog—to financial giant Sberbank, for more than a billion dollars. The heavy-set, full-bearded Russian-Armenian businessman was now a multimillionaire and a favourite of the Kremlin, appointed to prestigious roles with national institutions and settling into life as a philanthropist.

A TALE OF TWO ARMENIAS

By summiting Turkey's highest peak, Vardanyan was fulfilling a promise. His father was an Armenian from Van, the same place as Özcan, and had escaped with his sister while his family perished in 1915. He'd grown up in an orphanage outside Yerevan and had made his son swear that, no matter what else he did with his life, he'd make it up the mountain they had always looked at from afar, a reminder of where they'd come from. It was easier said than done: ice and snow make the climb impossible eight months of the year, and even in the summer the four-day ascent would be no easy feat for a well-fed oligarch who spent most of his time living in comfort, between boardrooms and chauffeured cars. But he'd made it. And, as he stood at the top, looking out over the two Armenias—the land they'd lost and the land they still had—he knew there was more to do.

In September 2022, Vardanyan announced that he was moving to Nagorno-Karabakh. "After the 2020 war, we Armenians around the world have a duty to join together with the people of Artsakh. We should be providing not just moral support, but concrete help," he said in a surprise message posted to his Facebook page. "Today the people of Artsakh are in a very difficult psychological state; they have no confidence in the future. Residents who survived two wars and lost their relatives and friends in the struggle for independence, feel abandoned."[21]

For years, Vardanyan had been building a brand in Armenia. He was the patron of a United World Colleges school for gifted students that he'd helped build in the leafy resort town of Dilijan, bringing a huge injection of cash to the area. He'd built the Wings of Tatev, the world's longest non-stop double-track cable car, which linked the historic Tatev Monastery with the busy road that leads to Goris, cutting out half an hour of switchbacks for tourists and locals. And he'd funded the Aurora Prize for Awakening Humanity, awarded on behalf of the victims of the Armenian genocide for humanitarian work, with the winner receiving $1 million. The move to Nagorno-Karabakh, he insisted, was about putting his mouth where his money was.

Seven months before Vardanyan's Facebook pledge, Moscow had launched its catastrophic full-scale invasion of Ukraine, turning Russia into a pariah state and with no sign of the conflict ending any time soon. Vardanyan had been included in a blacklist published by Kyiv, because of his commercial role in strategic industries "that undermine or threaten the territorial integrity, sovereignty and independence of Ukraine." Troika Dialog had famously funnelled money to Putin's allies and helped them invest it in America and Europe, making Vardanyan a prominent target.[22] He'd also been named alongside a dozen other prominent Kremlin oligarchs in a draft of the US Congress's proposed Putin Accountability Act, developed weeks before Moscow declared war as a shot across the bow.[23]

As part of his move to Nagorno-Karabakh, Vardanyan renounced his Russian citizenship altogether—despite there being no clear legal need to do so as he was already an Armenian dual national. His billion-dollar empire would be looked after by his partners and transferred to a family foundation, he confirmed, raising speculation that he was simply bowing out of Moscow high society to avoid being sanctioned and having his foreign assets frozen. Others wondered why he had gone to the crisis-hit region. Was it linked to his praise of Moscow's role in the 2020 ceasefire?

"I am grateful that Russia is present in Artsakh today and peacekeeping troops are protecting the security of Artsakh people," he said in his Facebook address. "I believe that the mandate should be secured for the period until we are ready to fully ensure the security of the people of Artsakh ourselves."

Vardanyan denied he had political ambitions, while at the same time hinting he could seek office in the breakaway state to "serve" rather than "exercise power as a ruler." There had long been rumours he could consider making a play for the top job in

A TALE OF TWO ARMENIAS

Yerevan, now possible after giving up his dual citizenship, and he'd formed close ties with A Country to Live In, a political party in Armenia. Moving to Stepanakert was a curveball, keeping him out of the fray of mainstream politics but at the same time cementing his perception among Armenians as a potential leader in times of crisis. And, within three months of arriving in Nagorno-Karabakh, he had secured for himself one of the most influential political roles in its unrecognised administration. He would become state minister—the equivalent of prime minister—while the incumbent, Artak Beglaryan, would quietly step down to become his advisor.

But Vardanyan had plans to shake up Stepanakert's sclerotic corridors of power, sidelining the traditional Soviet-style bureaucrats who made up much of the Artsakh government, bringing in his own people to take up key roles in media relations and strategy. Often professionals he had cultivated during his career in the corporate world, they were a stark change to the low-paid officials who toed the line, and who did what they did because that was how things had always been done.

"Every nation has its roots," he said in an interview with Russian newspaper *Kommersant*, sitting in the garden of the iconic Gandzasar monastery near Kalbajar.[24] "Those roots are not just heritage or history, they are the foundation and the future. If the roots are destroyed the tree will not survive and will not produce fruit. Artsakh is unique not just in terms of nature and history, but as the cradle of Armenian and Christian civilization." The message was clear: Ruben Vardanyan was going to save Nagorno-Karabakh to save both Armenia and Armenians everywhere.

In Stepanakert, his arrival was greeted with joy by many ordinary people—here was a man with huge personal wealth and contacts abroad who could surely do something positive for their imperilled homeland. Even if the rumours were true and he had been sent by the Kremlin, which few believed, then at least that showed Moscow cared about their situation and wasn't about to abandon them. In Yerevan, however, the arrival of this charismatic outsider who had spent most of his adult life in Russia was a cause for concern. One senior official in the Armenian government went as far as to ask me, given I had been in contact with Vardanyan, why I thought he was here and what he really wanted. That question consumed Nikol Pashinyan's inner circle for weeks, with the embattled prime minister's advisors fearing he could be a potential domestic political rival, a Putin-backed stooge, or both.

My personal assessment was less dramatic. Russia already had far-reaching influence in Nagorno-Karabakh, holding sway with its leaders and security apparatus, as well as its literal army on the ground to secure its foothold. It was hard to see why Moscow would parachute in an unpredictable oligarch to represent its interests when it already had the stern-faced General Andrey Volkov, who had been appointed to head the peacekeeping contingent at the start of 2022. The most straightforward answer seemed the most likely: Vardanyan was a hero in his own mind. Like many men who have made all the money they could spend in a lifetime, he'd come to the realisation that there are no pockets in a funeral shroud. He wanted a legacy, he wanted to be a saviour to his people, and do something more meaningful than mixing with the rich and powerful. Nagorno-Karabakh was the crisis calling out for a leader, and from everything he'd ever said, he clearly had no doubt he could be that leader. Besides, if his success was so great, his talents so appreciated by the Armenian people, who knew where it would lead.

The Azerbaijanis were less impressed. The cadre of diplomats and officials who had spent years dealing with the Karabakh Armenians knew their opposite numbers well, in many cases having kept back channels open with them on a semi-informal basis. They knew how Stepanakert's bureaucrats would act and react, and an unpredictable outsider was the last thing they wanted to have to handle. President Aliyev had long insisted that Yerevan had no right to use its separate negotiating track to talk about the rights of the Karabakh Armenians, given that he saw this as a purely internal matter for Azerbaijan, and maintained that his government would consult with local leaders in Stepanakert on the subject. While talks had never shown any signs of delivering on his one and only non-negotiable term—complete capitulation and acceptance of rule from Baku—his subordinates at least had been able to build working relationships with their counterparts. Now, one of Vardanyan's first moves was to sideline Stepanakert's seasoned team of negotiators, resolving to lead the tense talks himself, while proudly announcing that he wanted to use the Russian peacekeepers to bolster Artsakh's defence forces and ensure the Azerbaijanis could never again beat them by force. Aliyev immediately announced that his government would have no dealings with Vardanyan. Baku was ready to talk, he said, "with Armenians living in Karabakh, with people who live in Karabakh and want to live there, but not with people like Vardanyan, who has been sent from Moscow with a clear agenda."[25]

Azerbaijan had big plans for the future of Nagorno-Karabakh, and Vardanyan's arrival meant they would have to be implemented without delay—to reinforce just how precarious the Karabakh Armenians' situation was, and to dispel any notion that they could continue to operate as an autonomous state. There had long been allegations that Armenia was using the Lachin Corridor to bring in weaponry and rotate army volunteers. The Russian peacekeepers didn't search vehicles as they travelled into Nagorno-Karabakh along the mountain highway, so this was an obvious way for those fearing a new Azerbaijani offensive to ensure they could defend themselves. Suspicions were bolstered when a group of fourteen unidentified Iranian nationals also entered the territory, according to Baku's claims—which was unusual, given that anyone other than Armenian or Russian passport holders were generally turned away by Moscow's peacekeepers.

"The Corridor is not being used for its intended purpose and this must be stopped," Azerbaijan Foreign Minister Jeyhun Bayramov said in late November 2022, claiming that, along the line of contact, Baku had uncovered landmines manufactured after the 2020 war, suggesting they had been brought in by road.[26] Armenian officials, however, argued that the devices in the photograph had actually been captured by the Azerbaijanis from around places like Sotk and Jermuk when they'd invaded Armenia itself that September, in the Two Day War. The allegations, Yerevan said, had been concocted as a pretext to restrict movement along the corridor.[27]

The row was largely ignored, dismissed as the usual unverifiable claims and counterclaims constantly traded by the two sides. But against the backdrop of Azerbaijani anger at Vardanyan's arrival and the breakdown of talks, they struck me as significant. I messaged a senior official in Baku—was this just a protest lodged with the Russians or was this something Azerbaijan would actually act on? "Diplomatic options have almost been exhausted," the official replied. "What if we were to install a [border] post at the entrance of Lachin and finish the whole process? How can you breathe with no air?"

I sent a frantic email to my editor—it was a Sunday, but we should get a story up as soon as possible, before whatever was about to happen happened. We did. And then we waited. Monday came and went as normal, then Tuesday. Had I simply bought into Azerbaijani hubris? How could they really challenge Russian control over the Lachin Corridor, effectively tearing up the 2020 ceasefire? Then, on Wednesday, on the morning of 3 December, a small group of civilian Azerbaijani officials pushed past the chain link fence that separated the territory they controlled from the Lachin Corridor, insisting they be allowed to inspect vehicles travelling along the highway. As young Russian peacekeepers tried to contain the situation, the flow of traffic ground to a halt, leaving people stuck in their cars for hours.

This time, the complaints were ostensibly over the Karabakh Armenians mining gold—the region's huge industrialised mines were a major employer for the local population and contributed the largest share of any sector to the breakaway state's revenue.[28] According to the Azerbaijani officials, however, the deposits on Baku's sovereign soil were being illegally plundered, with the precious metal exported under the protection of the Russians. On top of that, they alleged, the mining operations were poisoning the environment and threatening the local ecosystem. "The Lachin Corridor is serving as an entryway for military criminals and marauders," wrote the popular nationalist news outlet Caliber, which has close links to the Azerbaijani Ministry of Defence.[29]

Russian commanders were quickly on the scene and invited the angry officials to join them for talks on establishing a monitoring mission. The road reopened. As a proof of concept, though, the incident had shown that this vital artery for the Karabakh Armenians could be blocked by Baku without serious consequences.

Just over a week later, on 12 December, a crowd of people in warm winter gear appeared and walked past the line of Azerbaijani soldiers where the Lachin Corridor passes around Shusha, taking up positions on the tarmac. As the Russians watched on, the Azerbaijani civilians unfolded pop-up marquees and made it clear they were in for the long haul. From the hill above, they brought down barrels to light fires in and unfurled homemade placards calling for an end to "ecocide." Once again, the traffic ground to a halt. This time, it wouldn't ever restart.

For Azerbaijanis, the impasse was them finally standing up after three decades of displacement and destruction in Nagorno-Karabakh; for the Armenians, though, it was hard not to see it as the latest in a full century of efforts to wipe them out altogether.

6

BLOCKADE

A steady procession of families made their way up the hill to Yerablur military cemetery. It was 2 January 2022—Armenian Christmas Day—and they'd come to see their boys, on a rocky outcrop that overlooked the exhaust-choked road to Yerevan's airport. Past the chapel and through a parting in the trees, the rows of graves were split into two sections. On one side were those who died in the First War of the 1990s, their portraits looking out proudly on the flower-strewn tombs of their victorious commanders. Further down were the soldiers from the Second War in 2020, and there were more of them—lines of white marble headstones, topped with colour photographs of smiling teenagers, most just eighteen or nineteen. Beyond that, marked out with string in the red dirt, were the plots left empty for the seemingly inevitable next war.

Parents, grandparents and younger siblings gathered around to light incense, some joking and telling stories, others wailing uncontrollably as thick black smoke rose up from the incense burners. One grave had been decorated with balloons for what would have been its occupant's twentieth birthday, and someone had left a box of foil-wrapped liqueur chocolates on his headstone as a gift. At the edge of the cemetery, a group of four or five men in winter coats stood in a circle at the resting place of their fallen comrade, passing around a small bottle of cognac and making toasts. With almost 4,000 soldiers having been killed or gone missing during the fighting in a country of under three million people, almost every young person has classmates who never came back.[1] At Yerevan's prestigious American University of Armenia, one staff member told me, faculty would send round emails whenever one of their students was killed, confirming their name and hailing them as a fallen hero. By the end of the forty-four-day Second War, they'd sent seven emails.

After the ceasefire was signed, the professors would have to deal with a wave of boys coming back to study after having witnessed horrors their peers could never comprehend. One group of enrolees, after being cut off from their unit by the advancing Azerbaijanis, had survived for days in the attic of a building, wedging the trapdoor shut and laying silently as their enemies combed the surroundings for stragglers. They were eventually reunited with their families, with only frostbite and trauma to show for their service. Others had nightmares of watching banned white phosphorus munitions—which Azerbaijan denies using—exploding over the lines in front of them, burning their friends alive or leaving them with deep, disfiguring burns.[2]

Yerevan is a small city of just over a million people, and those tragedies touched almost everyone living there. It is hard to see Armenia as a country scarred by war from the well-heeled centre, with the iconic Mount Ararat looming over its volcanic pink stone buildings and its large boulevards lined with shops and restaurants. But the suburbs tell a different story. On the walls of their shabby Soviet-built apartment blocks, murals are painted of the boys who lived there and didn't return. It is often those from the poorest families who have suffered the most.

BLOCKADE

For those who'd lost their sons in the Second War, the defeat hit hard—the war of the 1990s had been hard-fought, claiming in excess of 9,000 lives, but it had entered the national consciousness as a triumph. What had this younger generation fought and died for, when the government had been forced to give away the land they'd spilled their blood for? As 2022 began, the sense of defeat in Armenia was palpable. While there was broad support for the Karabakh Armenians, there was also a sense of complete helplessness, an inability to even contemplate what could be done in the face of overwhelming force from Azerbaijan. The opposition—the loosely-allied ranks of pro-Russian politicians and nationalist demagogues who had been in power for two decades before the war—had no ideas either. They insisted Pashinyan was a traitor, or worse a "Turk," an ethnic slur used by nationalistic Armenians against Turkic peoples from both Turkey and Azerbaijan. But they stopped short of revealing what they would have done differently. The debate boiled down to whether the war had been lost because Pashinyan's Civil Contract party had failed to manage the armed forces in the first two years after taking office; or whether the blame lay with the decades of corruption and complacency under their predecessors—now the core of the opposition.

In February 2021, months after the ceasefire was signed, a cadre of forty military officers led by the army chief of staff—a Moscow-trained career officer named Onik Gasparyan—issued a statement claiming Pashinyan and the civilian government were "unable to make the right decisions in this critical moment of crisis for the Armenian people."[3] Accusing officials of seeking to pin the blame on the armed forces (Gasparyan's deputy had been sacked), the top brass warned that "inefficient governance and very serious foreign policy mistakes have put the country on the brink of destruction." Pashinyan was furious, decrying the statement as a coup attempt and calling on his supporters to rally in

Republic Square, as anti-government protesters set up barricades around the parliament and called for his resignation.

Gasparyan was sacked, and Pashinyan announced a snap election for June—if it was the will of the people that he be turfed out of office, the people would be able to give their orders through the ballot box. His opponent was a familiar face, the former strongman President Robert Kocharyan, whose jubilant campaign pledged to bring back a sense of security to Armenia, expecting a coronation while condensing his policy pledges to a simple "trust us." Voters didn't, and Pashinyan secured almost fifty-three per cent of the vote to Kocharyan's twenty-one per cent.[4] Because of the distribution of the vote across constituencies, and a parliamentary system that gives the winner a boost to ensure a stable majority, this handed Civil Contract a massive seventy-one out of 101 seats in parliament.

Armenia's political crisis had been solved, but there had been no substantive public discussion of what to do about Nagorno-Karabakh or how to deal with Azerbaijan. The result also emboldened a small but well-represented group in the pro-Pashinyan camp that saw the Nagorno-Karabakh conflict as a perpetual burden for Armenia—harming its international standing and its economic ties with neighbours like Turkey, and condemning another generation to fight a war that wasn't really in the interests of their own Republic. It was the Russians who had created this border issue, it was the Russians who had stepped in to play peacekeeper, and so, they concluded, from here on it should be a problem for Moscow and not for Yerevan.

However, by 2022, the situation in Nagorno-Karabakh was fast deteriorating, and ignoring it was becoming impossible. The group of Azeri activists stormed the Lachin Corridor in December and stayed there, their numbers growing. Describing themselves as eco-protesters, it was clear to everyone that they had been organised by the Azerbaijani government, which has a long history of violently cracking down on demonstrations it doesn't approve of. Few if any of those occupying the road had a track record of green activism, despite living in a petro-state that offered up plenty of opportunities for dissent, and they would all have needed the state's permission to enter Karabakh, which is usually off-limits. While many I spoke to undoubtedly cared about the environment—pushing for low-waste packaging and building a Christmas tree from recycled plastic bottles—taking action was far easier when Armenians were the target for criticism, rather than their own leaders. Their signs were printed for them professionally in English and Russian, and they had been gifted jackets by the Azerbaijan Youth Foundation, founded by the ruling family's multibillion-dollar private fund.[5] President Aliyev himself was soon lavishing praise on the demonstrators, describing them as "our pride" and declaring that 2023 would be "the last chance" for the Armenians to reach a peaceful agreement over the future of Nagorno-Karabakh.[6]

Many were students, reportedly given dispensation to miss class so that they could take part in what was being presented as a civic duty. Hotels were booked for them so they could get some sleep and warm up during breaks from the twenty-four-hour vigil on the road, although one incident saw a number of the protesters booted out, after exuberant teenagers away from home allegedly trashed their rooms with a wild party. At the same time, their encampment on the tarmac next to Shusha had become a media circus, with Baku's state television companies sending crews to produce daily packages extolling the activists' principled stand against Armenian exploitation of their country's natural resources. Several protesters threw up the ultranationalist Grey Wolves salute.[7] In one clip, a supposedly environmentally-conscious protester, a middle-aged woman in a fur coat, shouted slogans through a megaphone while brandishing a white dove. Presumably intending to launch it skywards as a symbol of peace, she seemed not to notice that the bird hung in her fist limp and lifeless as she shook it. When she threw it up in the air at the end of her speech, it fell back to the ground with a grim thud.[8]

While the protesters were careful to point out that they were making way for Red Cross vehicles and the olive-green convoys of Russian peacekeepers, civilian Armenian traffic had been blocked—held back by Moscow's contingent to avoid a direct confrontation. The impact in Nagorno-Karabakh was immediate. Supplies usually brought in from Armenia were suddenly not arriving; shelves for eggs, fresh produce and medicines were bare within just a few days. "There is no access for any cars, including those carrying food and healthcare supplies," Artak Beglaryan, now serving as advisor to State Minister Vardanyan, told me over the phone. "We don't have any helicopters and the Azerbaijani side threatens to shoot down any flying object, so resupplying by air is not an option either. Every day, the humanitarian catastrophe is growing deeper."

The sense that the Karabakh Armenians were under blockade had been underlined when, a day after the start of the self-described eco-protest, natural gas supplies to the region were cut off, leaving homes unheated in the freezing weather. Azerbaijan's state gas company claimed the outage was because of the cold temperatures, and the flow was restored three days later.[9] It was a reminder for those living in Nagorno-Karabakh that not just their food but also their warmth was at the mercy of Baku. Meanwhile, in Stepanakert's central market, traders sold jars of pickles and blocks of long-lasting salty cheese, as the women on the hotplates fried up batches of *zhingyalov hats*, the reliable staple in times of scarcity.

Before the end of January 2023, winter stockpiles of food dwindled. Local authorities began to issue ration coupons, printed on coloured paper. A shopkeeper's assistant would break off the squares of paper while someone else bagged up portions of the most in-demand essentials. After queuing, sometimes for hours, a family of four would come away with two kilograms of sugar, two kilograms of buckwheat, two kilograms of rice and two kilograms of pasta for the month, those on the ground told me ruefully. Perishables like eggs were sold on a first-come, first-served basis, as nobody knew how many would arrive from the farmers out in the villages. Crowds jostled to see whether they could get hold of the few items of fresh produce that arrived each morning. At the same time, neighbours swapped products they didn't need and lent each other what they had, and online exchanges sprang up to facilitate trades, like a bag of potatoes for a few jars of preserves. As the blockade dragged on, these choices became tougher and tougher. With baby formula having disappeared from shops, nursing mothers began breastfeeding the children of other women who weren't able to. Parents cut up old clothes to use as diapers, ensured their kids had eaten enough before eating themselves, and wondered what to say to the older ones when they asked for candy or ice cream. After a few weeks, the only widely available products in shops were cigarettes and alcohol, and eventually even the cigarettes ran out.

With the noose tightening around them, the biggest question for many Karabakh Armenians wasn't how to leave the region, but how to get back in. Thousands of people had been cut off from their families and their homes since the activists began their sit-in just weeks before the holidays, when many had been travelling to see friends and relatives; the Armenian government had been forced to book out hotels in the border city of Goris so that they had somewhere to stay. Now, by February, groups of displaced people were milling around the Armenian mountain town, waiting for news from their loved ones and discussing rumours that there were ways to get through the blockade. There were teachers cut off from their students, leading remote classes from their hotel rooms. In the cafeteria of one boarding house, I met thirty-eight-year-old Oksana, who had travelled to

Yerevan for an operation to remove a cancerous tumour from her thyroid. Her young son had come with her, and now both were stranded, with a worried husband and two other children back in Stepanakert, presents for the New Year holidays waiting for them under the tree. "We're not refugees," she insisted, "because we have homes to go to—we just can't get there." On New Year's Eve they'd gathered in the hotel cafeteria, where the staff had made lunch for them and brought a few toys for the children. Oksana had tried not to let her son see her crying.

On the other side of Goris, the comfortable Hotel Mirhav was hosting around twenty young people who had travelled from Nagorno-Karabakh to Yerevan to take part in the Eurovision Junior song contest. In 2020, teenage Armenian singer Maléna had qualified to represent her country, but had been forced to stay home when the Second War broke out. In 2021, she had rejoined the fray and won—giving Armenia the right to host the junior event the following year. It may only have been the children's version of the competition, but in Yerevan it was like the Olympics had arrived, with Republic Square decked out with lights, a massive stage and television cameras. The troop of aspiring musicians had piled into a minibus and left Stepanakert to join the excitement with a couple of teachers and their instruments. But, the day after, as street sweepers cleared up the streamers, news had broken that they wouldn't be able to return. Not knowing when they might see their parents again, the group—some as young as twelve—sat in a circle in the hotel lobby, playing music from home, clapping as one boy in a bright red sports jacket played a clarinet and his friends accompanied him on the accordion and the *dhol* drum.

"We are close to each other, we will never part," one young girl sang as the other musicians watched on, "Our connection will not be broken forever. Artsakh, Artsakh." One of the teachers excused herself, eyes glassy, as other children joined in for the chorus.

"Your mothers fed me, your fathers have always instilled strength in me," they went on, "my love, Artsakh."

As hotel staff laid out plates of flatbreads, cheese and salads for dinner—luxuries they knew their parents back home would struggle to get hold of—a few of the older boys went out to smoke at the table in the yard, between lines of laundry hung out to dry. Among them was Artur, the clarinet player. "Of course we miss our families," he said, "even if things are hard there, we have to get back." He was seventeen, he explained, and in a year's time he'd be old enough for his military service with the Nagorno-Karabakh Defence Army. For now, he was stuck looking after the younger children, having spent Christmas and New Year in a hotel away from home, just the other side of the mountains.

Having spent an afternoon at the Mirhav with the Eurovision Junior musicians, I wanted to put their case to Baku. The message from the Azerbaijani government was that gun running and gold mining across the Lachin Corridor had to be stopped, but these were children evidently involved in neither. Why couldn't they be reunited with their families? Particularly given that Azerbaijan so often described the local Karabakh Armenian population as their own citizens and insisted it wanted them to live peacefully as part of the country. I picked up the phone to Araz Imanov, a senior official serving in President Aliyev's administration. We'd met on a previous visit to the region and, as well as being an avowed Anglophile, he was a public proponent for peaceful coexistence between Armenians and Azerbaijanis. I wanted to see how he squared the circle with what was going on in Goris, and ask whether his side could give me a quote to justify why these kids were stuck in this predicament, for the story I was working on.

"Children deserve everything," he replied, asking for a few hours to talk to colleagues. The next morning, I got a message asking for the children's details. Azerbaijan, he said, was ready to provide safe passage for them.

The unexpected offer landed me in a predicament—who was I to go around collecting the names and addresses of minors to pass on to a government their fathers and older brothers had fought against? If the Armenian side rejected the offer, even through a strange backchannel like me, I'd be obliged to write that fact in my article, so I at least had to make sure that Yerevan knew about it. I reached out to the Red Cross to find out whether they were following the case and whether they wanted to broker the deal with Baku, but they were determined to avoid getting dragged into anything that would compromise their impartiality—if the two sides agree, they said, we'll facilitate the transfer. An Armenian foreign ministry official, originally from Nagorno-Karabakh themselves, agreed to take on the issue. It proved thorny, however; there were concerns that the children would be returning to a region where war loomed large, and where they'd be an extra mouth to feed in families living under a rationing system. It all boiled down to whether their parents wanted them to come home, or stay somewhere safer.

After a few weeks of diplomatic back and forth, news came that the group would be taken back to Stepanakert by the Russian peacekeepers. However, as the large green military bus they were riding in passed the protesters at the Shusha roadblock, it ground to a halt and an Azerbaijani reporter opened the door, holding out some sweets in his palm and pushing his camera inside. The children sank down in their seats, hiding their faces. Watching the footage in the Azerbaijani media, I recognised Artur at the back in his red sports jacket. The children had made it back to Nagorno-Karabakh, but it was unclear what awaited them once they were home.

As more weeks went by, other ways to run the gauntlet of the Azerbaijani sit-in opened up. Every now and then, after a few days of radio silence, someone who had been in Goris would pop up in Stepanakert unexplained. Down on the Armenian side, at the Kornidzor checkpoint in Syunik leading to the Lachin Corridor, I'd met a young woman waiting by the barrier with a suitcase. "I'm just going home," she said, but clammed up at any further questioning, before climbing aboard a Russian peacekeeping truck and disappearing down the road into the distance. I'd also seen a man hand over a black duffle bag to the Russians, almost certainly to be despatched to somebody waiting for it on the other side. The conventional wisdom was that you could pay the conscripts to take you back to Stepanakert on their regular supply runs for around $350, with the protesters parting for their vehicles to pass. After a few months, the rogue soldiers' money-making hustle collapsed and Moscow's forces began a policy of shuttling civilians more regularly. The Red Cross, meanwhile, was ferrying those who needed medical help out of the region and bringing in as many medical supplies as it could.

There were also other, more dangerous routes into Nagorno-Karabakh. One dirt road that ran through an apparently unpatrolled area of woodland around Shusha allowed a small number of people to circumvent the blockade, driving people and goods back and forth. However, by April, Azerbaijan had launched an operation to capture the hillside overlooking the track, establishing visual control and threatening to open fire on any unauthorised traffic. Another way was to walk: a group of four or five men and women stranded in Armenia made an overnight trek through the difficult terrain to get back to their homes in Nagorno-Karabakh, staying quiet to avoid attracting the attention of the Azerbaijanis. It was so dangerous and difficult that, once they'd arrived, they told anybody who would listen not to try it themselves.

Anger was growing in Nagorno-Karabakh and there was one obvious target for it: the Russian peacekeepers. While their arrival had been greeted with relief in 2020, it had long since faded to fear that the troops weren't doing enough to keep the population safe. With the blockade dragging on, that fear turned into fury. As early as December 2022, Karabakh Armenians had held unprecedented protests aimed at Moscow's troops, marching from Stepanakert to an airfield near Khojaly, where the peacekeeping force had its base. A group of men, women and children clutching Armenian flags walked the distance from the capital to stand outside the chain link fence surrounding the peacekeepers' headquarters. "Putin, keep your word," one placard read, while another asked whether this was the start of "Operation Ring 2," referencing the Soviet Army-backed deportation of Armenians from the region in 1991, just months before the First War broke out. Protest leaders demanded several times to speak with the commander, General Volkov, but were repeatedly told by the rank and file and by junior officers that he could not be found—adding to persistent rumours that he was an alcoholic incapable of doing his job. In a surprise intervention in April, Volkov would be replaced by Colonel-General Alexander Lentsov, a more senior officer with combat experience in Syria, raising hopes that the peacekeepers might play a more active role. They didn't and Lentsov himself would be rotated out in August, in favour of Major-General Kirill Kulakov, a marginal figure who had spent the past few years as the head of a tank training academy in the Russian city of Kazan, even though there were no tanks here in Nagorno-Karabakh to command.

Across the border, too, attention turned to Moscow early on, with a smaller-scale protest held in January outside the Russian army base in Armenia's second city, Gyumri. Dozens of activists were detained by police.[10] The Gyumri base is the largest garrison of Russian troops in the country, and has a dark reputation. In 2018, locals protested after a Russian soldier based there allegedly murdered a fifty-seven-year-old woman, Julieta Ghukasyan, with details of the case effectively hushed up. The incident had echoes of a 2015 massacre that shocked Gyumri, when Russian serviceman Valery Permyakov killed seven members of the Avetisyan family, stabbing their two-year-old baby with a bayonet.[11] He was sentenced to life in prison, and later transferred to Russia—despite demonstrations accusing then Armenian President Serzh Sargsyan of failing to take sufficiently tough action.

Two years prior, two local boys had been killed by a landmine on the base's perimeter, in an area used by residents for grazing animals.[12] And, in 1999, two drunken Russian officers had opened fire with AKs on the local market; they'd been convicted, and later reportedly given early release in Russia.[13] Now, with the situation in Nagorno-Karabakh deteriorating, the entire rationale for Russia's presence in Armenia was falling apart. It was not only the public that felt this way: the peacekeepers, Prime Minister Pashinyan said in late December, were "becoming a silent witness to the depopulation of Nagorno-Karabakh."[14]

"The current standoff is a win-win situation for Baku," Rusif Huseynov, head of Azerbaijan's Topchubashov Centre think tank, told me at the time. "If the eco-activists, Azerbaijani officials and ordinary citizens are allowed into Karabakh and to inspect the mines, it would mean everyone, including the Russian peacekeepers and [the] 'Nagorno-Karabakh Republic' leadership, acknowledges and further legitimises Azerbaijan's sovereignty over the territory. If they are not allowed, then the standoff continues by further deteriorating the situation, psychologically, inside Karabakh; both sides, Azerbaijanis and Armenians, blame the Russian side," which, he added, "seems not to possess enough leverage on Baku and cannot force the Azerbaijani side to unblock the road."

Officially, Azerbaijan denied that it was blockading Nagorno-Karabakh, echoing the activists' defence that they were allowed the passage of supplies via the Red Cross and the Russians, and offering for Baku to supply food, medicine or whatever was needed directly. The real blockade, officials unanimously insisted, was Armenia's thirty-year closure of the road and rail links between the Azerbaijani mainland and the Nakhchivan exclave for the past three decades. Why are we even talking about the rights of Armenians to use the Lachin Corridor, they asked, when Azerbaijanis are barred from using the promised Zangezur Corridor altogether? The fact that Nakhchivan was well-supplied both by air and by an Iranian road to Turkey that ran just south of the Armenian border, and the fact that the exclave hadn't just hosted a major international war, went unremarked upon. But Baku's game plan wasn't to win that argument; rather, to bet that it would face no significant public challenge from anyone it cared about.

The EU's long-suffering special representative for the South Caucasus, Toivo Klaar, was a shy and spotlight-adverse Estonian who had honed the ability to comment on the Nagorno-Karabakh conflict without ever accusing one side or the other of doing anything wrong. He took until almost the end of January to make a statement. "The situation around the Lachin corridor is serious and solutions have to be urgently found," he said in refined diplomatic language on a trip to Yerevan.[15] "I look forward to discussions to explore ways forward," he went on, putting absolute faith in the (very European) notion that there must have been some sort of misunderstanding, it could all be hammered out in a meeting room somewhere, and everyone involved was acting in good faith. It took until February for the EU's gaffe-prone foreign policy chief, former Spanish foreign minister Josep Borrell, to take notice of the issue, calling ambiguously on all parties to "avoid a humanitarian crisis," even as the humanitarian crisis deepened. What would Brussels do to mitigate that risk? Well, not a lot, his office quickly clarified. "Sanctions are only one of the EU's tools to promote the objectives of the Common Foreign and Security Policy and are not being considered in this case," his officials told European Parliamentarians calling for punitive measures.[16] The use of the word blockade was studiously avoided by all. To the shock of those at the helm of the EU, voicing serious concerns didn't immediately translate into food for hungry people.

Securing support from the outside world was the masterplan of Nagorno-Karabakh's leader, Ruben Vardanyan, who had pledged to use his connections to direct international outrage towards Azerbaijan. However, that scheme was looking less and less likely to succeed, while his links to Russia were a distraction from the narrative Stepanakert wanted to get across. On top of that, he'd managed to alienate almost all of the major figures in Nagorno-Karabakh politics, sidelining longstanding leaders like Beglaryan and relying entirely on his own people, while also consolidating his support among businessmen and others who had influence. He was becoming an increasingly unjustifiable threat to President Arayik Harutyunyan who, in February, sacked Vardanyan from government, although he gave him an opaque security role to help him save face. Appointed in his place was Gurgen Nersisyan, a comparatively obscure bureaucrat with little interest in being the face of a struggling nation.

Outside Nagorno-Karabakh, however, there was plenty of grandstanding taking place over the conflict, in the court of world opinion. While international law evidently mattered little to Yerevan in the 1990s or to Baku in the 2020s, in 2023 foreign courts became a key theatre for battle between the two sides. Azerbaijani lawyers filed a series of briefs under key international conventions, stretching the letter of the law in the hope of putting pressure on their adversaries and raising awareness of what they saw as Armenia's crimes during thirty years of occupation. At the start of 2023, they lodged a request for inter-state arbitration with the Council of Europe's Bern Convention, which governs the protection of wildlife and the environment. Both countries were signatories to the agreement, but there was no precedent for it being used as a stick with which one nation could hit another. According to Baku, evidence of massive environmental exploitation had been uncovered in the territories retaken during the 2020 war, including damage to animal species. Now, it was seeking reparations and for those responsible to be held to account. For a petrostate accused of massively polluting the ecosystem, it was clear that this was more about ownership than protection of Nagorno-Karabakh, much like the so-called "eco-protests" on the Lachin Corridor.

In a bid to force Baku to back down over Nagorno-Karabakh, Yerevan had taken the case to the International Court of Justice in 2021, advocating for the rights of a region it didn't formally recognise as independent, in yet another blurring of the line between Armenia and Nagorno-Karabakh. The argument hinged on claims that the blockade constituted "racial discrimination" against the Karabakh Armenians. In an interim ruling in February 2023, the justices issued a series of provisional measures, calling on Baku to ensure, by all means at its disposal, "the unimpeded movement of persons, vehicles and cargo along the Lachin Corridor in both directions." They also asked Azerbaijan to take action on anti-Armenian rhetoric from officials and to punish vandalism and desecration of Armenian cultural sites. However, the court stopped short of backing Yerevan's demands that the protests on the road be ended altogether.[17] The decision, in practice, changed nothing.

This story seemed to repeat itself in the summer, when the two countries entered a "war of legal opinions." Azerbaijan had been spending huge sums retaining legal firms in Europe and the US, accruing plenty of bureaucratic firepower to help shield the blockade from foreign criticism. In an unusually savvy public relations move, Armenia hired Luis Moreno Ocampo, the bombastic first prosecutor of the International Criminal Court, to write an expert opinion in early August, warning that a genocide was underway. Azerbaijan then hired London barrister Rodney

Dixon KC to issue his own opinion a week later, saying that Ocampo was unable to substantiate the claim of genocide, but declining to engage with the broader context of the conflict. The back and forth likely cost tens of millions in legal fees and achieved nothing for either side.

Yerevan's stance on protecting the rights of Karabakh Armenians was ever muddied by its shifting position on the status of Nagorno-Karabakh. In spring 2023, Prime Minister Pashinyan made his most significant overture yet to Baku, using a parliamentary session to "reaffirm that the Republic of Armenia fully recognises the territorial integrity of Azerbaijan." While Yerevan had never recognised the breakaway Nagorno-Karabakh Republic, neither as an independent state nor as part of its own territory, this was the most significant decision any Armenian leader had made about the region's future. "Karabakh is Azerbaijan" was Aliyev's rallying cry—now, Pashinyan was saying it as well.

However, on more practical questions, the two sides were as far apart as ever—Baku insisted that Armenia had to withdraw its troops in the region, which Yerevan maintained were actually just local defence forces who had the right to protect their own communities. Azerbaijan also maintained its demand for the creation of the Zangezur Corridor through Syunik; a decision Pashinyan was reluctant to make, particularly given the prevailing view that the route would have to be controlled by the Russians and would effectively sever access to Armenia's southernmost city of Meghri and the border zone with Iran. Aliyev was becoming increasingly impatient on this front, warning that he was no longer discussing the issue with Yerevan and was taking it directly to Moscow; Armenia might find itself unable to resist if Putin got on board with the plan. Without either of those two concessions from Pashinyan, his unprecedented words on sovereignty were seen in Baku as nothing more than empty rhetoric; pressure would have to be maintained.

ASHES OF OUR FATHERS

In March, Washington became involved in the dispute. Secretary of State Antony Blinken, used a call with Aliyev to "reaffirm the importance of reopening the Lachin corridor to commercial and private vehicles" and warned there was no military solution to the conflict.[18] Aliyev, for his part, resorted to the same semantic flourish the Azerbaijanis had used since the start of the sit-in: that the corridor was not, in fact, blocked because of the passage of aid vehicles and peacekeepers, slightly missing Blinken's point. Any suggestion otherwise, he fumed, was "false Armenian propaganda."[19]

* * *

For those living in Nagorno-Karabakh, the situation felt real enough. The local government had, at least since 2020, maintained a stockpile of dry goods and provisions in warehouses, but these wouldn't last long if they were handed out. Besides, hungry, tired soldiers on the contact line would have to be prioritised in case of a new outbreak of fighting. On a video call while still State Minister, Vardanyan told me that the plan was simply to make it to spring, by which time farmers and villagers would be able to grow fruit and vegetables in the rich black soil. However, as the warmer months came, supplies of fuel began running severely low, hampering the local supply chains that connected villages to the big cities. While people out in the countryside with gardens and livestock had fresh produce—milk, eggs and cheese—getting it to Stepanakert, where virtually half the Karabakh Armenian population lived, was another matter entirely. Like their ancestors before them, the farmers would have to saddle up their horses and carts, although even then the supplies they could haul in were just a fraction of the demand. Water levels were also running low in the massive Sarsang reservoir, because the Karabakh authorities were forced to run the hydroelectric dam around the clock just to keep the lights on.

Warm weather, combined with farmers using the water for irrigation, left it close to critical levels.

Then, in early April, something strange happened. Armenian troops positioned on their side of the border in Kornidzor, overlooking the Hakari boundary river, reported a flurry of activity on the Azerbaijani side. Construction trucks began rolling up to the first Azerbaijani outpost at the start of the Lachin Corridor, past the large Russian peacekeeper base, while cranes unloaded portacabins and materials. The sound of hammering and drilling resounded through the valley. Within days, it was clear what they were building—a border checkpoint, spanning both lanes of the highway into Nagorno-Karabakh. The Armenians were outraged—the 2020 trilateral agreement had put the Lachin Corridor under the control of the Russians, they insisted. Baku, however, disagreed, arguing that Azerbaijan's only obligation under the terms of the ceasefire was to "guarantee safe movement of citizens, vehicles and cargo in both directions along the Lachin corridor." This checkpoint, it said, was needed to ensure safety, and there was no prohibition against Azerbaijan controlling its own internationally-recognised borders.

The US State Department issued a statement warning it was "deeply concerned" by the move, calling on both sides to "to resume peace talks and refrain from provocations and hostile actions along the border."[20] Again though, the critical call fell to Moscow, as the only outside power with boots on the ground. But the peacekeepers stood aside as construction of the border post began, tacitly accepting Azerbaijan's plans and refusing to challenge them despite increasingly shrill protests from Yerevan, calling on the Kremlin to implement its interpretation of the deal.

How the checkpoint would operate remained a mystery; Azerbaijan has a long, unwritten policy of refusing entry to travellers even with Armenian-sounding surnames, and there is no clear visa regime established between the two countries. On top of that, Azerbaijan's land borders had been closed to regular traffic since the Covid-19 pandemic hit in early 2020, remaining shut long after almost every other country in the world had opened back up—a bizarre move that many suspected was making the country's well-connected airline owners unimaginably rich. There was no clear legal framework for how the first and only open border between Armenia and Azerbaijan would function.

On 24 April though, the crossing was declared open. Two banks of passport control booths had been placed under a large roof that covered the road, emblazoned with the flag of Azerbaijan, while troops in body armour and helmets stood guard. The perennially-present television cameras showed the first groups of Karabakh Armenians being forced to stop and show documents to an official in camouflage, as the Russian peacekeepers escorting them hung back. The travellers were the residents of four villages—Lisagor, Yeghtsahogh, Mets Shen and Hin Shen—located west of Shusha on the road into Nagorno-Karabakh, meaning they'd been cut off from Stepanakert and the rest of the region, but still had access to Armenia for food and supplies. Going through the checkpoint was now their only option. And, as the weeks went by, more and more Karabakh Armenians travelling across the Lachin Corridor with the Russians were told to stop, climb down from the buses and present their papers for inspection. Those riding in their own vehicles were asked to open the trunk or the back of their van for a cursory glance, then waved on. The peacekeepers' vehicles in the background of Azerbaijani media footage were blurred out, in an effort to show Karabakh Armenian residents peacefully and willingly cooperating with the Baku government. On April 28, after more than four months, the self-described eco-activists confirmed they would end their sit-in on the Lachin Corridor.[21] Their border guards would do the job now.

However, the Hakari Bridge would soon see violence flare up. In the early hours of 15 June, a dozen or so Azerbaijani soldiers—

seemingly unarmed and some without their heavy flak jackets—emerged from the checkpoint carrying a long metal object. Armenian troops on the hill opposite fixed their scopes and watched as the contingent advanced across the bridge towards them. It was clear now what they were holding: a flagpole. The puzzled Armenians concluded that the Russians stationed by the barrier at their end of the bridge would stop whatever PR stunt this was. Seconds later though, they realised that two armed Russian peacekeepers were actually walking with the group—maybe negotiating with them, maybe escorting them. The Azerbaijanis reached the armoured vehicle parked at the end of the bridge, skirted around the barricades, and began erecting their flag. The Armenians fired shots. The soldiers scattered, taking cover behind the Russian vehicle. Baku said that one of its servicemen was injured in this skirmish, and insisted that maps show the very corner of land at the edge of the bridge to be Azerbaijani territory. Responsibility for the "provocation fully lies with Armenia's military and political leadership," officials said.[22]

The Armenians agreed it was a provocation, but after months of clashes and the ongoing blockade, they pinned the blame on the other side for this entirely needless move. In the aftermath of the incident, Azerbaijan closed the checkpoint altogether—not just to Armenian passengers but also to the Russian peacekeepers and the Red Cross medicines convoys. The official line was that a full investigation was needed, but given Baku had already apportioned blame within hours of the clash, what remained to be investigated was unclear. One veteran Azerbaijani diplomat was more candid when I pushed on the question of why the border was now fully sealed: "it is rather [a] measure to make Armenians think twice next time when they decide to shoot." Nine days after the firefight, on 24 June, a delegation of Azerbaijan's top officials, led by Aliyev's foreign policy chief Hikmet Hajiyev and accompanied by a small number of foreign diplomats, visited the checkpoint for a photoshoot in full view of the Armenian positions.[23] It was apparently safe enough for them, but apparently not safe enough for supply trucks, with a long convoy of heavy goods vehicles—including one full of sweets for the children donated by a local confectionery—lined up on the Armenian side of the border.

If the Karabakh Armenians really needed supplies, Baku said, while casting doubt on the notion there actually were shortages, they'd have to accept them from the Azerbaijani side. The road from Stepanakert to Aghdam, now under Azerbaijani control, had been blocked off since the 2020 war, but could easily be reopened for humanitarian convoys. When I'd put the question to Vardanyan before his sacking, he'd insisted that becoming dependent on Azerbaijan for food and medicine was akin to a total surrender, and that the route could be squeezed any time Baku wanted to put pressure on Stepanakert. Beglaryan went further, publicly: "What would you do if a terrorist blocks your access to a water wellspring in a desert, tortures you for a while, then offers you his urine to drink?"[24]

Speaking to German media in September 2023, Aliyev's special envoy, Elchin Amirbayov, continued to blame Stepanakert for refusing to accept aid from Baku, warning that "genocide may happen" in Nagorno-Karabakh, but "only if this clique of separatists will continue to hold hostage their own population in order to get to their political goals."[25]

Whether you wanted to call it a blockade or not, the empty stomachs and growing fears of conflict spoke for themselves. Before the checkpoint went up, Nagorno-Karabakh had been reduced to accepting handouts from the Russians and from humanitarian aid workers. Any pretence surviving the 2020 defeat that this could be a viable, autonomous state, or more accurately a *de facto* part of Armenia, had already vanished in December 2022. But by the summer of 2023, with supplies not

BLOCKADE

just restricted but virtually ended altogether, there were fears that what remained of Nagorno-Karabakh was now unable even to sustain the lives of its citizens. The trickle of produce that had made its way into the grocery stores from Armenia was abruptly stopped. So too were the medicines, even vitamin supplements for children at risk of malnourishment, and chemotherapy for the cancer patients who hadn't been evacuated to Yerevan. The cut-off was underlined by an accusation from Baku that the Red Cross was engaged in illegal smuggling across the state border, after four local drivers were found to have been carrying mobile phones, chargers, cigarettes, and fuel in their own vehicles to sell in Stepanakert, while displaying the Red Cross logo.[26] There is no evidence that the Red Cross was involved.

Soon, only sick people seeking hospital treatment in Armenia could be taken out by the Red Cross in the occasional pre-approved transfer, a list of names handed to the Azerbaijanis and the Russians. Until, that is, 29 July, when border guards ordered one patient travelling under Red Cross protection out of their white, marked SUV. Photos showed a bewildered-looking sixty-eight-year-old man, Vagif Khachatryan, being detained at the checkpoint.[27] While the Red Cross relied on Armenian drivers to maintain the routes, they were always accompanied by at least one foreign national in case of issues like this—no Armenian would argue with the armed Azerbaijanis or insist on accompanying their Karabakh charges if they were taken into custody. The foreign aid worker escorting Khachatryan demanded to join the patient as he was forced into a military vehicle, one source told me, but was pushed out of it by Azerbaijani troops before they sped off, taking the elderly man off into the unknown. In response to the unprecedented assault on the Red Cross's ability to offer safe passage, the organisation ordered a temporary suspension to all such convoys, with immediate effect. The last lifeline from Nagorno-Karabakh to the outside world had been snuffed out.

The pressures ordinary people were facing rose quickly, and their lives were becoming more and more precarious. Earlier that month, Vera Narimanyan, a single mother from the village of Aghabekalanj, had left home for the nearby town of Martakert, hoping to collect sugar and sunflower oil being handed out to desperate households. She was gone for only two hours but, by the time she arrived back, her six-year-old daughter Gita and three-year-old son Leo had disappeared from the house. The police arrived to help search, pulling security camera footage that showed them walking in the direction of Martakert. Firefighters and the army were called in to comb the area throughout the night, but the children were nowhere to be seen. The next morning, a local man spotted the lifeless bodies of Gita and Leo in his car, which had been parked out on the street without fuel, the doors unlocked. Investigators suspected they'd died of heatstroke.[28]

On 25 July, four days before Vagif Khachatryan was taken at the checkpoint, the Red Cross issued a statement warning that "despite persistent efforts, we are currently unable to deliver aid via the Lachin corridor and other routes, including Aghdam. With these convoys blocked, our concern is that the humanitarian situation will further deteriorate."[29] Life-saving medicines were running desperately low, as were tampons, sanitary pads, baby formula, fresh fruit and vegetables and bread, it said. Staples like sunflower oil, cereals, fish and chicken were unavailable. Locals had explained to aid workers that husks and loose grains were being used to bake a dark-black chalky bread on which many were now subsisting, unless even that was out of reach. The only upside, the Red Cross said, was that two dozen sick patients had been transferred out of Nagorno-Karabakh without incident since the seizure of Vagif Khachatryan.

The statement, while avoiding laying the blame on either party or giving preference to the Lachin Corridor or the Aghdam route, riled Baku—which still maintained there were no real shortages and no risk of famine. That position was getting harder and harder to defend—online, Azerbaijani users scoured social media in an effort to find restaurants that were still operating or weddings still going ahead inside Nagorno-Karabakh, posting adverts for catering companies as evidence all was well. But while life continued to some degree, basic supplies were undoubtedly missing—as a family's only economic lifeline, a cafe might stay open, but it would operate with a drastically reduced menu for the small number of people who could still afford to eat out. The blockade had squeezed key industries, including mining, and many with jobs in the private sector were suddenly out of work and running low on cash.

With attention from abroad slowly growing, France emerged as a major advocate for the Armenians, with President Emmanuel Macron repeatedly calling on Baku to end the standoff. After Russia and the US, France has by far the world's largest Armenian diaspora, and many French Armenians have played prominent roles in cultural and political life, including celebrated singer Charles Aznavour and former Prime Minister Édouard Balladur. During the Second War, France's senate even backed a non-binding resolution calling for the recognition of the Nagorno-Karabakh Republic.[30] In late August, in a show of support likely to go down well with the electorate back home, a contingent of French regional politicians arrived in Armenia to show their solidarity. Led by the mayor of Paris, Anne Hidalgo, and accompanied by influential local leaders from Strasbourg, Marseille and the Hauts-de-France region, the group made a show of escorting a convoy of French aid to the Armenian side of the Hakari Bridge checkpoint. However, once there, the trucks simply parked up behind the ones organised by the Armenians, not even attempting to go through the border station, which would have forced Baku's border guards to reject them. The Azerbaijanis said they hadn't even been notified that the aid was coming, and there was no effort to cross, so the entire exercise felt more like a public relations stunt than anything meaningful.

Privately, Yerevan officials explained this half-hearted effort by saying that the truckers themselves were ethnic Armenians and it would have been irresponsible to put them in danger—but instead of sending drivers, the French sent supplies that would never arrive. Along the roadside, a small football pitch where I'd kicked a ball around with local kids on previous visits had been ploughed over and a large white tent erected as a "humanitarian aid point." But, with nobody who needed aid able to get there, the tent was simply filled with glossy posters offering talking points about the impact of the blockade, as well as a long table for the French delegation's press conference. Good intentions aside, everybody involved was exploiting the crisis for their own benefit.

Tensions in Stepanakert, meanwhile, were boiling over. Early in the morning of 1 August, outside the parliament building in the central square, two men had begun firing into the air with a rifle and a shotgun, insisting that Artsakh President Arayik Harutyunyan do something, anything, to end the blockade. They were arrested. Then, on the night of 17 August, three separate sources confirmed to me that the sidelined Ruben Vardanyan had moved to oust the president, in a bid to have himself installed at the helm. He had come to Nagorno-Karabakh to be in charge, and he wasn't about to give way to other factions in the administration—least of all Harutyunyan, who he saw as a man bereft of ideas and presiding over a massive but inefficient Soviet-style bureaucracy. However, the militia had been sent to defend the parliament, and the putsch soon fizzled out. A few weeks later, with no options left available to him, and under intense pressure both from Baku and internally, a desperate Harutyunyan declared on 31 August that he wanted to step down and serve in the armed forces instead. Elections would be held on 9 September, despite fierce opposition from Azerbaijan, which declared them an illegal provocation that proved the Karabakh Armenians had no intention of accepting rule from Baku. Other countries agreed, with the EU, UK and Council of Europe reconfirming their long stance that Nagorno-Karabakh was Azerbaijani territory and that they would not recognise the results of the vote.

It was bad press that the Karabakh Armenian officials could easily have avoided: in the end, the elections didn't end up taking the form of a popular poll, which would have been nearly impossible with a lack of paper and printer ink for ballots, and fuel to get out to towns and villages. Instead, Harutyunyan's successor would be appointed by the parliament. Vardanyan had been sidelined, and there were only two men who made it known that they wanted the unenviable job. One of them was Samvel Shahramanyan, who had served as director of Nagorno-Karabakh's national security services and in a handful of other top jobs. After his only rival—former Karabakh Defence Army commander Samvel Babayan—was disqualified from the contest on a technicality, support rallied around Shahramanyan. Nearly thirteen years Babayan's junior, he was a figure constantly in the background of the Nagorno-Karabakh administration. He was elected by a vote of twenty-two to one, with ten MPs sitting out the vote.[31] In one of his final acts before leaving office, Harutyunyan had dismissed State Minister Gurgen Nersisyan, a decision that saw long-time official Artak Beglaryan resign as well. Shahramanyan would be taking the helm of an unrecognised state that couldn't so much as feed itself, at a critical point in its history, and without many of the people who knew how its bloated and byzantine institutions worked.

The situation never really registered as a crisis internationally—given the small population at risk, compared to famines where thousands die of malnutrition—but the people of Nagorno-Karabakh were almost universally suffering, and all the more so for feeling that their predicament was being ignored. Among those following the blockade, there were fears that they could soon see Darfur-like images coming out of Stepanakert. It had been scarcely three decades since the First War caused a famine in the Artsakh capital, leaving children with distended bellies and emaciated elderly people lining up for rations. History, it seemed, was set to repeat itself. With Baku having totally ignored the interim ruling from the International Court of Justice, the Armenians called for an urgent session of the UN Security Council, once again putting their faith in the idea that the global community wouldn't stand by and watch a catastrophe unfold. The fifteen-member body agreed, on the condition that Armenia, Azerbaijan and, for some reason, Baku's close ally Turkey, each be allowed to give evidence.

On 16 August, envoys gathered in New York for the session, which opened with UN humanitarian aid official Edem Wosornu cautioning "all parties" involved that "international law is very clear," they must "ensure humanitarian workers have freedom of access" and it was "critical" the Red Cross be allowed to resume humanitarian cargo through any and all available routes, while not politicising aid operations.[32] The debate, however, was as political as they come. A host of rotating members of the council, including Brazil, Gabon, Japan, Ghana, Switzerland and Malta took to the floor, acknowledging the reality of the blockade and calling for a swift resolution, including for all available aid routes to be opened. Albania, which has close ties with Turkey, also used the opportunity to call for the mutual recognition of borders and the opening of the rail link through the proposed Zangezur Corridor.

In reality though, none of their positions mattered—it was only the five permanent members that had real sway. France went first, unabashedly backing Yerevan and calling for "the unconditional restoration of transit along the Lachin corridor in both directions." Paris's support was to be expected; but had the French been able to convince the other major power players to take a stance? China was up next, giving a typically bureaucratic and impartial call for diplomacy to resolve the standoff. Then came the UK, a critical partner for Azerbaijan as the single largest foreign investor in the country since the collapse of the Soviet Union.[33] All of Britain's economic and political interests were in Baku, and none were in Yerevan, so few expected that 100,000 hungry Karabakh Armenians would change that equation. London, said deputy permanent representative James Kariuki, "remains deeply concerned at the ongoing disruption to the Lachin corridor which threatens the supply of life-saving medicine, healthcare and other essential goods and services, resulting in humanitarian consequences for the local population." The International Court of Justice ruling must be respected, he went on, and that meant restoring free movement along the Lachin Corridor. The intervention was a surprise, given Britain's close relations with Azerbaijan; while the French perspective could easily be dismissed, this less so. It was a stance backed by the US, with ambassador Linda Thomas-Greenfield reiterating the call for the restoration of movement through the corridor.

The three Western allies had, it seemed, reached a collective position that they hoped would be impossible for Baku to ignore. But then Russia's deputy representative, Dmitry Polyanskiy, took the floor. Moscow was concerned, he said, by the continuing blockade of the Lachin Corridor. However, Russia's proposed solution was for a double opening of roads: not just the corridor, but also the route from Azerbaijani-controlled Aghdam, as a starting point for the "reconciliation" of Baku and the Karabakh Armenians. The Kremlin, it seemed, was reinforcing the idea that the future of Nagorno-Karabakh lay not as an autonomous unrecognised state protected by landmines and fortifications, but as a connected part of Azerbaijan. It was exactly what President

Aliyev and his envoys wanted to hear, especially from a country that was supposedly a formal ally of Armenia.

The meeting ended without a conclusion. A subsequent French push for a joint statement saw a draft text go through several rounds of reviews, with the language over the humanitarian routes being refined each time. However, it was abruptly killed by a veto from one of the permanent members on the council. Word spread that the UK was responsible, but insiders in Yerevan and London confirmed to me that it was Russia that had blown up the process, despite not having raised any objections earlier.

A month later, as the impending collapse of Nagorno-Karabakh seemed to shudder closer every day, I was at a wedding near Yerevan. The bride and groom were dancing, both draped in rolls of lavash bread, a custom to guarantee they would always have food on the table. As per tradition, they'd fed each other spoonfuls of honey to ensure they'd always have sweet words for each other. And, as the hosts piled the tables with plates of *khorovats*—both barbequed pork and trout fished from the depths of Lake Sevan—the father of the groom asked that the guests respect a moment of silence for those in Nagorno-Karabakh, who would be going to bed hungry. As the newlyweds danced in a rhythmic circle, thumping their heels on the ground while bridesmaids waved coloured handkerchiefs, I was in a corner tapping away on my phone. Moments earlier, authorities in Stepanakert had unexpectedly announced they would accept humanitarian aid laid on by Russia via the Aghdam road, carefully spelling out that all the food and medicine would be Russian-produced, rather than Azerbaijani or Turkish. I immediately reached out to Azerbaijani foreign policy chief Hikmet Hajiyev for confirmation, who told me that "Azerbaijan expressed its consent as a goodwill gesture to ensure simultaneous opening" of the Lachin Corridor to the Red Cross. If it came off, this was

Fig. 1: Karabakh Armenians perform a traditional dance at the "We Are Our Mountains" monument in Nagorno-Karabakh's de facto capital, Stepanakert, 2009. The statues are known affectionately as Tatik and Papik—Grandmother and Grandfather of the nation.

Fig. 2: Mount Ararat, once the jewel of the Armenian homeland, behind the watchtowers and fences marking the Turkish border, as seen from the road outside Yerevan.

Fig. 3: The Azerbaijani ghost city of Aghdam, destroyed during three decades of Karabakh Armenian occupation between the two wars.

Fig. 4: Graves of Azerbaijan's fighters who died in the 1992 Khojaly massacre during the First War, at a cemetery in Aghdam, Nagorno-Karabakh.

Fig. 5: Mural to a fallen Armenian soldier of the Second War (2020) in Yerevan, Republic of Armenia.

Fig. 6: The city of Goris, Armenia, terminus of the highway from Stepanakert. Just over the mountains lies Nagorno-Karabakh.

Fig. 7: Karabakh Armenians leave Dadivank Monastery, days after the Second War in 2020, ahead of the expected handover to Azerbaijan.

Fig. 8: Russian peacekeepers arrive in Nagorno-Karabakh as part of the ceasefire deal ending the Second War, 2020.

Fig. 9: "Dear Shusha, we will revive you!" Billboard of Azerbaijani President Ilham Aliyev, bearing the Azeri name for the city captured from the Karabakhtsis during the Second War.

Fig. 10: Armenian military hardware captured in the Second War rusts in a trophy park under the skyscrapers of Baku, Azerbaijan.

Fig. 11: A guest house hit by shelling in the Armenian Republic city of Jermuk during Azerbaijan's Two Day War assault, September 2022.

Fig. 12: An Armenian paramilitary and civil defence group training in Yerevan just after Azerbaijan's Two Day War, September 2022.

Fig. 13: "CSTO FUCK OFF"—protesters against Russia's alliance of post-Soviet states greet President Vladimir Putin's convoy arriving in Yerevan, Armenia, one week after the Two Day War, 19 September 2022.

Fig. 14: The author interviews Armenian Prime Minister Nikol Pashinyan one week before Azerbaijan's final One Day War assault on Nagorno-Karabakh, 13 September 2023.

Fig. 15: Riot police guard a government building in Yerevan, Armenia, against crowds protesting the fall of Nagorno-Karabakh, the day after Azerbaijan's assault, 20 September 2023.

Fig. 16: Desperate Karabakh Armenians beg Russian forces for help at the peacekeeper airport base the day after the assault, Stepanakert, 20 September 2023.

Fig. 17: A line of cars stretches into the horizon as the mass exodus from Nagorno-Karabakh gains pace, September 2023.

Fig. 18: "If you want to take pictures or something, here are my legs!" The Red Cross tent at the Kornidzor checkpoint, September 2023.

Fig. 19: After a long night on the road, a Karabakh Armenian boy takes one last look at the mountains of his homeland, September 2023.

a hugely significant moment—the blockade would effectively have been ended.

By the next morning, a single truck of aid was driving towards the region along the Aghdam road. After reportedly being held up at the checkpoint by Azerbaijan, it took three days to arrive—and, when it did, it contained only 1,000 small food sets, while space had been given up for bedding and blankets that almost nobody needed.[34] The Lachin Corridor was not reopened, and this truck would be the only one to arrive.

* * *

It was clear to everyone in Yerevan that another war was coming. Russia's security guarantees were now worthless, and they were on their own. On 13 September, I arrived outside the imposing circular government building on Republic Square, where I'd been promised that Prime Minister Nikol Pashinyan would sit down for an interview with me. Despite reporting in Armenia on and off for more than two years, I could count the number of interviews I'd had with senior government officials on one hand and still have fingers left to spare. The Azerbaijanis, by contrast, were much more media savvy, and I'd never had problems setting up meetings with ministers or getting high-level quotes over WhatsApp, and most journalists working on the region received near-daily solicitations from the state's PR companies. Over the border, since the 2020 war Pashinyan had withdrawn from the public more and more, surrounding himself with a shrinking circle of likeminded advisors and with the prospect of another coup constantly looming over him. Just weeks after the Second War ended, his father, Vova, had died aged eighty after years of poor health. The Pashinyan who now governed Armenia was a far cry from the wise-cracking, optimistic revolutionary who had taken power in 2018. It was hard to see him now as anything other than an exhausted, browbeaten man fighting for his political survival, and maybe even the survival of his country.

At the start of the month, three Armenian servicemen had been killed in shelling along the border, close to Sotk. Initially, four fatalities had been reported, but the life of one young soldier, Narek Poghosyan, had later been saved by doctors.[35] According to Azerbaijan, its forces were "taking decisive retaliatory measures" after being targeted by "attack UAVs" from the Armenian side that injured two of its men.[36] In an effort to prevent the situation from spiralling into another round of bloodshed, US Secretary of State Blinken had put in an emergency phone call to Aliyev while travelling in Asia, followed by a conversation with Pashinyan. It was time to open both the Lachin and Aghdam routes for aid into Nagorno-Karabakh, the US's top diplomat had concluded, endorsing a plan first proposed by Azerbaijan and now backed by Russia.

In the week since, there had been reports that Azerbaijan was building up troops on the contact line with Nagorno-Karabakh, and on the border with the Republic of Armenia. Clips posted online by Baku's conscripts, always more interested in impressing friends and family than maintaining operational security, showed troops climbing aboard vehicles and heading westwards from their bases. In their positions along the rocky frontier, hungry Karabakh Armenian troops recorded videos of transport trucks and armour being deployed. More worrying still, the Azerbaijani military vehicles were daubed with never-before-seen markings, like the inverted letter "A." That was reminiscent of the "Z" labels painted onto tanks and armoured personnel carriers by the Russians before they blitzed across the border into Ukraine in February 2022. The diplomatic noise from Baku also sounded like it had been taken from Moscow's playbook. Speaking to me, Aliyev's foreign policy chief Hikmet Hajiyev insisted any troop movements were simply military exercises, while the Azerbaijani foreign ministry said that any claims the country was preparing to launch a new offensive were "part of another fraudulent political manipulation" by Armenia.[37] All of this echoed the Kremlin's vigorous denials that it had any plans to attack Ukraine, right up until the moment it did. This time, the Armenians didn't even bother calling on their "allies" in the Russian-led CSTO for help; they already knew what the answer would be.

Since the invasion of Ukraine, Armenia had become a major destination for Russians escaping conscription or repression back home. Unlike much of Europe, they were able to travel there without a visa, and in fact didn't even need to show their foreign passport on landing. Many were entirely unaware that they were fleeing the consequences of one conflict only to arrive in a country being shaken by another. When Putin announced "partial mobilisation" in September 2022, tickets to Yerevan from Moscow, St. Petersburg and other major Russian cities were going for thousands of dollars as young men raced to escape. In the immediate wake of the invasion there had been a wave of *relokanti*—the Russians didn't see themselves as foreign migrants, in their former colonial hinterland, rather "relocators" or expats—but those who arrived later were far more desperate and significantly less capable of surviving on their own outside Russia. The highly-mobile graphic designers and programmers who could work remotely had long gone, and many of those landing in Yerevan were just young men who had never been out of the country and had never thought to leave until they'd received a summons to the enlistment office. Only a week after Russia had announced that tens of thousands of ordinary men would be sent to the front, there were teenagers sleeping on the streets of the Armenian capital, the hotels and hostels being fully booked. Many had arrived from backwater towns with just two suitcases and their birthday money. Among them though were a number of wanted dissidents and draft dodgers Russia was likely to expect its historic ally to arrest and send back, something the Armenian government had no intention of doing.

Those in Pashinyan's liberal, pro-reform government had never been ideological fans of Putin, but Russia's influence had been accepted and tolerated as an inevitability, so close was Armenia to the southern border of the world's largest country. The job of politicians in the Kremlin's self-declared sphere of influence was to channel that influence and use it to get what they wanted, while always being wary—the bear they were dancing with could turn on them at any time. Azerbaijan had without a doubt won that game, and it was time for Yerevan to look elsewhere for support.

A week before our interview, on 7 September, Pashinyan had dispatched his wife, Anna Hakobyan, to deliver the country's first shipment of humanitarian aid to Ukraine since the start of Russia's full-scale invasion. The contents were ordinary—more than 1,000 tablets, laptops and other devices for Ukrainian schoolchildren. The reaction from Moscow was explosive. The Armenian ambassador was summoned to the Russian foreign ministry for a dressing down. Dmitry Medvedev, the one-time president and deputy-chair of Putin's security council, was incensed. He had transformed from one of the regime's more technocratic, liberal voices to being among the most swivel-eyed advocates of a genocide in Ukraine.[38] Pashinyan, Medvedev said, had "lost a war but somehow managed to stay in post. Now he decides to shift the responsibility of his skilless defeat onto Russia. Then he rejected a piece of territory of his own country. Then he decided to flirt with NATO."[39] The phrasing was clumsy, given that neither Russia nor Armenia actually considered Nagorno-Karabakh to be Armenian territory, but the outrage at the Kremlin having been snubbed was palpable.

Fear of Moscow's reaction wasn't going to deter Yerevan, which was convinced it would survive on the graces of the West or be at the mercy of Azerbaijan, Turkey and Russia. Four days after Hakobyan's trip to Kyiv, Armenia announced that it had begun hosting unprecedented joint military drills with the US, and that eighty-five American soldiers would land in the country to take part in the training.[40] The wargames were the result of months of work between the two sides, and Washington had issued a standing offer for them to go ahead whenever Armenia was ready—that time was now, Pashinyan had decided. The implications were twofold: showing Moscow that it couldn't do nothing to support Yerevan while forever demanding its fealty, but also showing Azerbaijan that the most powerful nation in the world was watching what was going on. The drills, named Eagle Partner, were designed to help Armenian forces play a role in international peacekeeping missions, and would last for the next ten days, giving Yerevan reassurance that an outright attack on its territory was unlikely when the Americans were in country.

However, despite the show of support from the US, the Armenian armed forces were in a dire state. Since the 2020 war, Russia had sold virtually no equipment to the country—in part due to the growing tensions between Armenia and Azerbaijan, but also as a result of severe shortages in Moscow's own arsenal because of the war in Ukraine, which had seen international orders go unfulfilled. Key pieces of Armenian heavy equipment, armour and artillery had also been abandoned in Nagorno-Karabakh after the 2020 war, in the knowledge that open armed protection of the region wouldn't be possible after the Russians took control of the Lachin Corridor. By contrast, Azerbaijan was the second largest customer of Israel's burgeoning defence industry, flying regular cargo plane supply runs from a secluded military runway in the Negev desert, buying vast quantities of ammunition, artillery and missiles.[41] Baku's security partnership with Turkey, meanwhile, didn't just mean access to Bayraktar TB-2 drones, but also to insights and intelligence from Ankara's NATO-trained troops. And, with his distrust of the armed forces, Pashinyan had failed to bring about genuine reforms to a largely Soviet military that still relied heavily on conscription. In some cases, entire garrisons were virtually leaderless, such as in the frontline town of Jermuk, where the search for an adequate commander willing to take charge had already been dragging for almost a year. While satellite imagery showed the Azerbaijanis had reinforced the positions they'd captured around the mountain town following the 2022 offensive, building supply roads up to their positions inside Armenia, the Armenian side had done virtually nothing, and it wasn't even clear who was in charge.

Key lessons from the 2020 war, like how soldiers on foot should move in a spaced-out formation to prevent mass casualties from drone strikes, simply hadn't been instilled in troops on the ground. While Yerevan's soldiers had fought hard in 2020 and 2022, they had been let down by abject failures on the part of their command, military intelligence and the state bureaucracy. That had given rise to a handful of militias and paramilitary groups—usually hardened former soldiers contemptuous of the top brass—that sought to operate outside the army hierarchy, further splintering efforts to coordinate Armenia's forces from the top. Pashinyan had even revealed that he communicated with his top generals by WhatsApp, simultaneously showing how poor command and control was, while raising the prospect that messages were being intercepted. Another war looked set to play out much like the last one, and a week and a half of drills with the Americans was unlikely to change that.

Then, two days after the Eagle Partner drills were announced, came another extraordinary move. Pashinyan confirmed on 13 September that Armenia would ratify the Rome Statute and become a fully-fledged member of the International Criminal Court. Back in March, the Hague-based court had issued arrest warrants for Russia's Children's Rights Commissioner, Maria Lvova-Belova, and for Putin himself for their alleged involvement in the abduction of an estimated 20,000 children from

BLOCKADE

Ukraine, many of whom were still being held in Russia, placed into homes or with foster families and forcibly Russified, taught to hate their Ukrainian identity and embrace the culture of their aggressor.[42] While Russia was not a signatory to the Rome Statute and the arrest warrants stood no chance of being carried out there, countries that had fully ratified it were obliged to enforce them if Putin were ever to set foot on their territory. That had already been causing problems for the Kremlin: over the summer, the Russian president had been forced to stay home while other leaders of emerging economies met for talks in South Africa. A member of the court, South Africa had seen its pleas for an exception denied, despite arguing that having to detain Putin would be seen as a "declaration of war." As a semi-regular visitor to Armenia for CSTO summits and other meetings, with this decision from Yerevan, Putin's world was shrinking by yet another country. Kremlin press secretary Dmitry Peskov had cautioned Pashinyan against it, but the Armenian prime minister was resolute that the decision was about the security of his own country and its ability to be protected by international law, rather than anything to do with relations with Russia.

That same day, I sat down with Pashinyan to ask about the increasingly fractious relationship with Moscow. After clearing security, I was ushered upstairs before coming face to face with about three dozen people who were also there for the interview. Had I been mis-sold on the format, I wondered? If this was actually just a press conference, where I could hope to get in one question at most, I'd have to eat humble pie with my editors to whom I'd promised a groundbreaking exclusive. But no, in the room ahead I could see two armchairs facing each other for a fireside chat. The crowd milling around outside, it turned out, were a mixture of bodyguards, cameramen and audio staff—the interview would be taped and beamed out on Armenia's first channel as soon as we published our story, I was told. That was unusual, and I suddenly wished I'd dressed smarter as a makeup artist brushed powder onto my face and tried to comb my hair for what was probably the first time in my life. The black-suited security officers suddenly stood to attention. Pashinyan appeared through the double doors. A few inches shorter than me, he stood hunched forward, the bald patch in the middle of his greying hair reflecting the studio lights. We shook hands. "*Barev dzez, paron varchapet, shat urakh yem,*" nice to meet you, Mr Prime Minister—I'd been practising my greeting while I waited, certain that I'd get tripped up by the tongue-twisting Armenian language.

Conflict was in the wind, Pashinyan said. "Azerbaijan has started the accumulation of forces along the border of the Republic of Armenia," but the EU monitoring mission along that same stretch of territory could vouch for the fact that Armenia had no intentions of starting a conflict itself. While he had said before that Armenia was prepared to recognise Nagorno-Karabakh as a *de jure* part of Azerbaijan, there had always been constructive ambiguity about whether that recognition already stood, or if it was contingent on some broader peace deal. No, the prime minister replied, Yerevan had committed to respecting Azerbaijan's 86,600 square kilometres of territory, including that inhabited by Armenians. But, "the illegal blockade of the Lachin Corridor and the continuation of the humanitarian crisis in Nagorno-Karabakh is having a very negative influence on the peace process, and the sincerity [of the Azerbaijani side] is becoming questionable." The international community would have to hold Aliyev to account, and Stepanakert would have to work with Baku to resolve the situation—the Republic of Armenia, he made clear, couldn't do much more than it already had.

From watching back previous interviews, it was clear to me that Pashinyan was an expert at dodging questions he didn't want to be asked. I'd expected any direct discussion of the split with Russia to be batted quickly away, to avoid adding fuel to the growing fire. But I was wrong. Armenia, he said, could not be seen as a Russian proxy—it would have to defend its own interests, and that meant it could no longer be quiet about its problems with the CSTO. Talks with the Americans had been going on for a long time, and his wife had a longstanding humanitarian commitment to Ukraine. "We have never declined and we will never decline any agenda of establishing relations with any geopolitical centre based on our state interests. But on the other hand, I and my political team ... are in harmony in this regard, and I think that our society is more and more saying the following: if we want to have a lasting, eternal statehood, first of all we need to take very serious steps to settle our relations with our neighbours." That, he explained, meant not just normalising relations with Turkey but also with Azerbaijan, resolving the three decades of conflict once and for all. "The model whereby we have problems with our neighbours and have to invite others to protect us, no matter who these others are, is a vulnerable model, because these others at any point, for objective or subjective reasons, because they don't want to or they are solving their own problems, may not be here."

Armenia bolstering its sovereignty and fixing relations with its adversaries would be a strategic nightmare for Moscow, which had used Yerevan's precarious situation since the fall of the Soviet Union to take control of the country's borders, and the disastrous 2020 war to insert itself into Nagorno-Karabakh. But, I asked, had the peacekeeping mission failed to stop Azerbaijan taking ground in 2022 and tightening its stranglehold because of Russia's preoccupation with its own war? Or because of simple incompetence on the ground?

"As a result of the events in Ukraine the capabilities of Russia have changed, but on the other hand I think that there is the second factor that you mentioned. In my assessment, both factors exist."

The only way forward, Pashinyan insisted, was direct negotiations between Yerevan and Baku, and acknowledgement of each other's territory. He argued that the West would fill Russia's traditional role, and would not allow Azerbaijan to cross red lines when it came to the local population: "The representatives of the international community are very clear, they are saying that the Armenians of Nagorno-Karabakh should be able to stay in their homes in Nagorno-Karabakh without fear or persecution, they should have the opportunity to live in dignity, security." That faith in the international order was about to be tested.

7

EXODUS

Ruben Petrosyan was getting ready for work when he heard the first explosion. The father of three had a desk in the unassuming office building that housed Nagorno-Karabakh's security services, on the south side of Stepanakert. For weeks, he and his colleagues had known something big was coming. They knew it when their wives came back empty handed after lining up at the shops for rations of bread and sour cream. They knew it when troops on the contact line spotted a massive Azerbaijani build up. And they knew it on Tuesday 19 September 2023, when the war started.

First came the accusations: overnight, Baku said, landmines had destroyed two vehicles killing four of its soldiers and two civilians in the Russian peacekeeping zone. And, in a well-coordinated response to a supposedly sudden and unprovoked attack, the Azerbaijani Ministry of Defence just after midday issued a statement in which it announced it would begin major "local anti-terrorist measures."[1] Just as it was published, Azerbaijani forces began their long-expected assault. A massive wave of artillery shells began pounding the Karabakh Armenian positions around the edge of their breakaway state, while blasts rang out across Stepanakert and several apartment buildings saw their facades shredded by shrapnel.

Ruben's wife, Nouné, had taken their two girls to the dentist. He grabbed his jacket and ran out of the house to go and pick them up. An air raid siren was ringing out all over the city, families were racing to the shelters, shops pulling down their metal shutters. The streets were a picture of chaos and confusion, the roads choked with parents trying to pick up their children from schools and kindergartens across town. Ruben found his family, took them to a shelter under a church next to the security services building, then went into work. They didn't know it yet, but Nouné and the children would spend the next six days there.

While there had been no end of signs that an offensive was about to start, schools had been kept open in an attempt to retain some sense of normality. And so, on that Tuesday morning, thousands of police officers, military staff and government officials like Ruben left their posts in a frenzied rush to get to their children and take their families somewhere safe, just at the very moment the Karabakh Armenians were facing their greatest existential threat since the collapse of the Soviet Union. One Stepanakert resident, a military reservist, had run to his daughter's school the second the fighting began but, when he got there, he found her looking after several younger children whose parents hadn't yet arrived—so he sat and helped distract them until, one by one, they were picked up. Only afterwards did he join his unit and head off to the front.

Minutes before the first barrage began, up in the hills, volunteers and conscripts serving in the Nagorno-Karabakh Defence Army began noticing that the Russians who stood between them and enemy lines were jumping into vehicles and leaving in a hurry. Across the dusty gulf of no-man's-land, they could see camouflage netting being pulled off Azerbaijani military hardware and ambulances lining up on the asphalt roads leading to the positions opposite. Artsakh officers started putting in calls up the chain of command until the message reached Samvel Shahramanyan, the hapless new president of the breakaway republic. He was meeting that morning with the Russian peacekeepers' leadership when he heard the reports that the Azerbaijanis had warned the peacekeepers to take cover, as artillery fire was about to begin. He put the claims to the Russians, who confirmed it—they and the joint Russian-Turkish monitoring centre had been given advance notice. Shahramanyan and his driver turned around and raced back to his office to contact his Azerbaijani counterparts as the shells and missiles began to fall. The military operation, he was told once the call connected, had a specific objective—to take full control of Nagorno-Karabakh—and it would continue until that was achieved.

With the news coming in, Aliyev's foreign policy advisor, Hikmet Hajiyev, insisted to me that the "goal is to neutralise military infrastructure"—Baku's long-held insistence that the Karabakh Armenians must lay down their arms was coming to a head, about to be enforced by the total annihilation of the "illegal formations" on Azerbaijani soil. Local residents, Hajiyev said, had received text messages cautioning them that the operation had begun and asking them to keep clear of military installations. However, the two or three Stepanakert Armenians who answered their phones in the frenzied first minutes after the start of the offensive all told me that neither they nor their families had received any such warning. In a follow-up press release, the most worrying yet, the Azerbaijani defence ministry declared it had established "humanitarian corridors and reception points" in order to "ensure the evacuation of the population from the dangerous area."[2] Did that mean the Karabakh Armenians would be allowed to flee to Armenia? Or would they be directed deeper into Azerbaijan where they could be interrogated and sifted, and those with connections to the state taken away? It was anyone's guess. One prominent local blogger sent me a voicemail summing up the dilemma: "How can I trust them? They will kill me, definitely."

Across town, Azat Adamyan, the owner of Bardak pub, was tinkering in his garage when he heard the explosions. His friend worked as a cashier, but his money counting machine had broken and, without any access to spare parts, Azat had offered to repair it using scrap metal. The bang was just the door slamming in the wind, he thought, and then he heard another. It was the moment everything had been building up to—Azat was delighted, it was finally here, and they could finally do something after months of waiting helplessly. He grabbed a small portable drone with a camera to see what was going on around the city and high up on the hills beyond; but it wouldn't rise above thirty metres, resisting any input from the controller. It was the Russians, he concluded: they had activated their drone-blocking equipment over at the airport, where they had a Krasukha electronic warfare vehicle stationed. Azat and his former comrades had hatched a plan for what to do when the inevitable third war began—they would meet at his campsite in the woods just out of town, where they'd built a little outpost and stored some weapons and equipment. The deal was, they would get their families to the bunkers and basements dotted across the city, then meet. But Azat couldn't wait. With no fuel for the cars, he saddled up his horse with tactical gear and his rifles and rode to the nearby Karabakh Armenian special forces base. Everybody knew who he was, and they remembered fighting alongside him in 2020, so they waved him in.

In the cities and villages closer to the line of contact, the situation was even more frantic. For weeks, internet access and mobile phone service had been cutting in and out, making it hard for those in remote areas to communicate with friends and family in Stepanakert and in Armenia—even when there was reliable electricity and they could charge their batteries. Now, they were going completely dark, with the flow of information cut off. Men lined up, almost all having served in the military and in one previous conflict or another, and local defence units handed out weapons. Women and children were forced to take shelter wherever they could: in one village, a local man had dug a large hole in the ground that several families could hide in as their husbands, brothers and sons went off to fight on empty stomachs.

On the battlefield, it was immediately clear that Azerbaijan wasn't simply trying to gain ground or capture strategic heights. The combat formations that it had concentrated at key points around the front lines—with one pincer pointing towards the northern town of Martakert and another towards the eastern city of Martuni—were elite units of hardened special forces, backed up by artillery units and operators flying advanced drones. In a rare effort to maintain operational security, Azerbaijan briefly suspended access to TikTok, preventing the conscripts bringing up the rear from revealing their locations or documenting the speed of the offensive as they had in previous phases of the conflict. Instead of the regular trickle of triumphant photos and clips posted online, this advance went almost entirely undocumented, leaving those of us on the outside—and even officials in Stepanakert—wondering where the Azerbaijanis were, and where Karabakh Armenian forces were still holding out.

The flustered officials in the security services building where Ruben worked, in the military command centres and in the leadership knew that this was set to be the decisive blow. Those who remembered the First War of the 1990s said the bombardment hadn't been this heavy even then. Their forces weren't just outnumbered, outgunned and outclassed by Azerbaijan's professional army, they were fighting without sufficient reserves of basic food and fuel, and with their communications networks widely disrupted. Simply getting troops from centres like Stepanakert to their positions was proving difficult, as was giving orders to those already dug in on the line of contact. Mobile phones were now effectively useless, and only basic walkie talkies were available, the kind easily intercepted by Azerbaijani signals intelligence. And so, without a clear command-and-control structure, the Karabakh Armenian soldiers went wherever they thought they were needed, held what they could, retreated when they had to and, in many cases, fought to the death where they stood.

Near the poor farming community of Martuni, one of the first targets in the sights of the advancing Azerbaijanis, one key position was reportedly manned by just ten fighters—eight volunteers and two professional soldiers from the local defence brigade. The high ground above them along the side of the mountain range had been lost to Baku in 2020, and the disadvantage was compounded by the fact the Azerbaijanis had deployed tanks and other heavy military equipment. After an hour of shelling and intense sniper fire designed to soften the defences, the enemy advance began. According to the unit leader, Aram Petrosyan, two waves of Azerbaijani troops were turned back with the help of a Russian-made Fagot anti-tank launcher and small civilian drones retrofitted to drop grenades—a technique championed by the Ukrainian army.[3] However, after nearly four hours of fierce fighting, the unit was overwhelmed in close-quarters combat and forced to flee. By then, seven of the ten men in the trench had been killed. That bloody rout was being repeated along much of the front line, with breakthroughs effectively encircling both Martakert and Martuni, cutting off not just the civilian population but also many of the remaining Karabakh Armenian troops on the contact line. There was now little prospect of them falling back or regrouping to join a last-ditch effort to protect Stepanakert. The Azerbaijanis were now pushing towards the capital, having opened a separate front from the Shusha area above the city.

EXODUS

In the panicked corridors of power, the government was losing control. Political flux and palace intrigue had put the reins of state in the hands of a small cadre of comparatively inexperienced officials, far down what would ordinarily have been the line of succession. It had also created a class of immensely powerful former leaders, now outside the conventional power structures, who felt they could manage the crisis better than Shahramanyan—and many had cultivated better contacts with their Azerbaijani opposite numbers during their time in office. Those who could get their hands on a working phone line began reaching out to Baku, generally without bothering to seek permission from their own actual authorities, in the hopes of brokering the most favourable terms of surrender. With members of Nagorno-Karabakh's Security Council, former presidents and well-connected political figures all sending different messages at the same time, Shahramanyan knew he would have to act fast if he was to retain authority and deliver any kind of ceasefire before the fighting was right outside his office. Worse still, there seemed to be no sign of a Russian intervention or a coordinated response from the West.

With the Azerbaijanis on the outskirts of the village of Krkjan, effectively a southern suburb of Stepanakert less than a mile from the city centre, on 20 September the president of the Nagorno-Karabakh Republic decided it was time to formally capitulate. He called a meeting of top security officials to say that the priority now had to be ensuring "the physical security of the population."[4] In practice that meant accepting a ceasefire proposed by the Russian peacekeepers—one that would grant Azerbaijan a blank cheque when it came to specific demands. In exchange, after just twenty-four hours of fighting, the offensive would stop and face-to-face talks between the two sides would be held the following day in the Azerbaijani city of Yevlakh, not far from Ganja.

The pause meant that soldiers wounded in the fighting were being evacuated, but transport was slow without enough fuel to go around, while hospitals and clinics that already lacked sufficient supplies were overwhelmed. Rumours swirled that the Azerbaijanis were already inside Stepanakert, with families too afraid to go back to their apartments and a steady stream of refugees from nearby towns and villages arriving on foot with whatever possessions they could carry. Displaced people were everywhere, sleeping in apartment building hallways and hotels hastily converted into shelters. Electricity supplies had virtually collapsed, with the grid infrastructure seemingly destroyed, and running water had stopped flowing to many homes and buildings. Hunkered down in candle-lit basements, knowing the fighting could resume at any moment, the Karabakh Armenians had a terrifying night in store for them.

Meanwhile, those with nowhere to go began gathering in the parking lot outside the disused airport that served as the Russian peacekeeper base, desperate for someone in authority to tell them where to go and where they would be safe. However, the gates remained closed, and the sentries stationed there were becoming increasingly angry with the desperate crowd.

"Why are you here?" one young Russian demanded, according to those I spoke to. "There's nothing we can do for you."

"It's your fault we're here anyway," said another conscript, pointing at the bleak surroundings, "we have to stand around all day outside and it's freezing."

Russia's apparent indifference to the conflict seemed to know no bounds. That evening, Moscow's Ministry of Defence confirmed that one of its own SUVs had come under small arms fire and several of its peacekeepers had been killed.[5] Among them was Colonel Ivan Kovgan, the mission's deputy commander. The Kremlin said nothing, and President Ilham Aliyev quickly apologised for the incident, vowing to investigate and to ensure the bodies were repatriated.[6]

EXODUS

In Baku, the Azerbaijani leader gave another victory speech. "The process of withdrawal of the illegal Armenian armed units from their positions has already begun," Aliyev said. "They accepted our terms and started handing over their weapons ... We used to say that the illegal junta regime must fold its so-called flag, whose value is no more than a piece of cloth, put it in its pocket, and leave our land."[7] Now, it seemed Azerbaijan had achieved its ambitions by force—putting an end to thirty years of effective autonomy in Nagorno-Karabakh. The capital of the tiny state that so many thousands had died to create and defend was now a city of the dispossessed, its hospitals full of the injured and its residents destitute, fearing for their lives. Turkey congratulated Azerbaijan on the successful operation. However, it came at an unexpectedly large cost for Baku. According to figures released to Azerbaijani media, almost 200 of the country's troops were killed in the offensive, having encountered far stiffer resistance than many would have expected from a half-starved army of volunteers and conscripts.[8]

Privately, I'd believed for a while that another round of fighting had become inevitable as soon as the blockade began in December 2022—Baku, I sensed, wouldn't back down on its key demands. This was a reality few in Stepanakert failed to face up to—officials had quietly confirmed to me that they had begun exploring scenarios for some kind of compromise agreement that might ensure them some autonomy, including control of the local police force and regional administration, while potentially accepting formally being part of Azerbaijan. The pressure on those in power to give up their independence was overwhelming, but even then the process was slow-going. On the other side of the contact line, though, the lack of food and essential supplies had started a timer of a different sort: Azerbaijan wanted to resolve the standoff before there were widespread images of emaciated people and growing numbers of malnutrition-related deaths, knowing the outrage that would cause. By the time the offensive was launched, that prospect was only a few weeks or months off becoming a reality. Meanwhile, in Armenia, there was a palpable sense of shock at what had happened. Bad news from Nagorno-Karabakh had been in no short supply in the past six months, but the effective conquest of the territory in the space of a single day left many people shaken.

As the crowd grew at Stepanakert airport, hundreds gathered in Yerevan's Republic Square. The demonstration had no leaders; as soon as an opposition politician or activist grabbed a megaphone to try and address the crowd—usually to try to pin the blame on Pashinyan—someone in the audience would start arguing back, pointing out the holes in their argument, sparking a back and forth that derailed the addresses. Outside the prime minister's office, riot police in blue camouflage formed a circle around the front of the building, holding metal riot shields in front of them. The night before, as the fighting raged in Nagorno-Karabakh, a smaller crowd had smashed the ground floor windows and tried to storm the foyer, with security forces struggling to hold them back. Today, officials were desperate to prevent worsening violence, especially given how the parliament had been breached in 2020. Almost everybody in the crowd thought Pashinyan should resign: "he's betrayed us," said one man, while a thirty-six-year-old named Van insisted that "the biggest problem is our prime minister because he's doing nothing to save people's lives and Azerbaijan is committing genocide." At the edge of the crowd I met two students. The first, from Yerevan, began animatedly setting out why Armenia's government had become the enemy of the people. The other quietly explained that she was from Stepanakert and hadn't been home in months due to the blockade. Her family were in a basement the last she'd heard, but it wasn't possible to get in touch with them.

"I don't really know what more Armenia could do," she said sadly.

EXODUS

Meanwhile, an opposition MP in the crowd went on at length warning that Baku wanted to drive out the Karabakh Armenians and that Pashinyan was complicit, but struggling to say what Armenia should do differently and who, if anyone, should take control in Pashinyan's place. Having faced a rout at the last election, the opposition bloc had neither the mandate nor the numbers to form even a minority government. If Pashinyan resigned, his most likely successor would be Alen Simonyan, the speaker of the parliament and maybe the only politician in the ruling party more widely disliked than the prime minister. Nobody had any answers, and the protests—defined more by the millions who didn't attend than the hundreds who did—quickly fizzled out.[9] "Internal and external forces want to involve Armenia in the large-scale military operations" in Nagorno-Karabakh, Pashinyan claimed, insisting that his government would "not take any drastic action" in the face of Azerbaijan's offensive.[10]

* * *

Just outside the sprawling village of Kornidzor, the Armenian army had set up a checkpoint on the road leading to Nagorno-Karabakh, up the hill from the Hakari Bridge border crossing. The barrier was down, as it had been for months—apart from when the occasional military jeep raced through to resupply the troops. There was a line of a dozen or so civilian vehicles parked along the Armenian side of the highway. As soon as the bombardment had started on 19th, Karabakh Armenians trapped on this side of the blockade had raced down to the Lachin Corridor, in the hope that their families might be able to get out. Now, after nearly two days of waiting, they were huddling around a small camping stove in the back of a box truck, drinking thick Armenian coffee out of cut up cola bottles and endlessly smoking slim cigarettes. Some had been stuck in Goris, others had been away working in Yerevan, and one man had even flown in from Russia—but most of them had no news from their loved ones.

ASHES OF OUR FATHERS

The most vocal of those trapped in this nightmare situation was David, a middle-aged father originally from Stepanakert. He was short, with wiry hair and a constantly furrowed brow, wearing the thick military jacket that had kept him warm when he fought in 2020. "Nobody is helping us. Not Armenia, not Russia, not the world," he said, instinctively suspicious of foreign journalists but volunteering himself as the spokesman for the group. "What are you doing for us? What is England doing for us? Nothing. We only have ourselves," he went on. One of the group, the one who'd come straight from a worksite in Russia, had virtually collapsed after being told his two brothers had been killed in the fighting, and had been taken back down the hill to Goris. David showed me his dirt-stained hands and his chipped fingernails. "I'm an honest guy, I've worked with these my whole life. Now they're all I have to protect my family. If you want to help us, go to Yerevan, go to London and tell them to give us guns. Maybe they don't want to do it but we'll go across that bridge ourselves!"

Across the mountains, the Karabakh Armenian leadership was in the process of agreeing its unconditional surrender. Having been defeated decisively on the battlefield, with Azerbaijani troops surrounding all major towns and cities, Stepanakert parliamentarian David Melkumyan and deputy security council chief Sergey Martirosyan had been sent to Yevlakh on 21 September with instructions to avoid further bloodshed—military and civilian. The delegation opposite them, led by Azerbaijani negotiator Ramin Mammadov, knew they were in a position to drive a hard bargain. But, even as the conflict entered its final round of diplomacy, fear and panic were spreading through the Karabakh Armenian population. On a call with one Stepanakert resident who had just left a shelter to try and return to her apartment, a series of loud bangs cut through our conversation. "There's gunfire," she said, "very close. I have to start running now." A second local texted to say he'd heard the same and another journalist, on the line with a third person, confirmed their interview had been similarly cut off. The rumours that the Azerbaijanis were entering the city cut through the crowds of huddled civilians almost instantly, with at least some groups of officials urging people to leave their homes and head for the basements.

In a message posted on social media, Artak Beglaryan accused the Azerbaijanis of immediately violating the ceasefire behind the backs of the Yevlakh negotiators and resuming their push towards the capital. Within an hour though, what was left of the Karabakh Armenian leadership was denying the claims as "fake news," insisting there had been no shooting, and urging calm.[11] Quite how they'd know either way wasn't clear, holed up in offices struggling to get reports from an increasingly small pool of officers and officials who hadn't yet left their posts to flee with their families towards the centre of the city, where things were said to be safer. After several hours, the delegation's black SUVs left Yevlakh for Stepanakert, guaranteed safe passage back to the city. Everybody knew the outcome already: Nagorno-Karabakh's armed forces would have to turn in their weapons, and the priority would now be "reintegration of the Armenian population of Karabakh." In return, Baku acknowledged the requests for power and heating to be restored to buildings like schools and hospitals, where displaced people were sheltering.[12] But there was no news on what would happen next—and would those fearing for their lives be allowed to leave?

The prospect of a mass exodus had haunted all discussions of Nagorno-Karabakh for months, with many believing the blockade alone would be enough to make people want to leave their homes for safety in the Republic of Armenia. But the official opinion in Yerevan was that this was far from inevitable; even as Stepanakert descended into anarchy, Pashinyan took to the television channels to say that the "situation is stable." Facing criticism for a lack of preparedness, he said thousands of hotel rooms had been booked as emergency accommodation if needed for the fleeing Karabakhtsis. On the ground though, there was no evidence this was in any way true. In Goris, the closest city to the Lachin Corridor, none of the major hotels had received government bookings and they all had rooms to spare.

At the town hall, Goris's deputy mayor, Irina Yolyan, confirmed that suspicion. There were no plans to accommodate large numbers of refugees, she told me. "We're not talking about this at the moment. We are hoping a humanitarian disaster can be prevented." Preventing a humanitarian disaster, however, was well outside the remit of the deputy mayor of a small border town—whereas preparing for one might have been a better use of time. Meanwhile, an increasingly embittered Pashinyan was beginning to see Nagorno-Karabakh not as a crisis to be managed but a political storm to be weathered; as the scale of suffering deepened, he turned his ire on the protesters in Yerevan. In his address to the nation, he accused students "with connections to high-ranking circles of Nagorno-Karabakh" of fomenting unrest, and he promised that anyone trying to overthrow the government would be met with the full force of the law. Almost 100 people were arrested on the streets of Yerevan as the government sent in the notorious red beret riot police, a feared instrument of the old regime for cracking down on protests—like the ones Pashinyan himself used to organise. It would be a great tragedy, I thought, if Armenia's loss of Nagorno-Karabakh cost it all the progress it had made since the Velvet Revolution as well.

On 23 September, four days after the start of the offensive and ten months since the blockade first began, a steady stream of humanitarian aid trucks got the green light to cross the bridge and travel down the Lachin Corridor into Nagorno-Karabakh. The Armenian and French cargo vehicles that had been waiting in line for months still wouldn't be allowed to cross the border, but Red Cross vehicles would be. And behind them, throwing up dust as they ripped through Kornidzor, Russian Army flatbeds and fuel tankers followed. At the same time, Azerbaijan confirmed it had sent trucks carrying petrol to Stepanakert along the Aghdam road—the simultaneous opening of both routes had been Baku's demand, and it had been achieved despite the objections of the Karabakh Armenians who saw it as akin to accepting dependence on their enemy. Insofar as Artsakh had ever been an independent state, it clearly was no longer one. If Azerbaijan revoked its agreement for deliveries like these, the population would have no way of even feeding itself, and local leaders knew that the goodwill could end at any time. In a sign of things to come, Davit Babayan, a long-time official serving as an advisor to Stepanakert President Shahramanyan, said that "99.9 percent of our people" would flee their homes as a result of the sudden conquest.[13] "Ethnic cleansing," he declared, was underway—and those responsible "will have to answer to God for their sins."

With his previous address having failed to reassure anybody at all, Pashinyan reluctantly made a second speech, shortly after the first, in which he praised the access for humanitarian organisations but acknowledged that, if the Russian peacekeepers weren't going to uphold their security guarantees, there might only be one safe option for the Karabakh Armenians—to leave. The Armenian government, he insisted, wouldn't be a "traitor" to its own people and would support them however it could in either case. The challenge now, he said, wasn't the independence of Nagorno-Karabakh but the independence of Armenia itself.[14]

Almost as he finished speaking, Stepanakert announced that the first evacuations from the war-torn region would begin under the protection of the Russians. Only those who had lost their homes, had small children or were injured would be helped to leave, officials said, playing down the preparations for a mass humanitarian evacuation. Suddenly, the small group of men waiting on the Armenian side of the Kornidzor checkpoint were joined by a crowd of new faces, those who had heard from loved ones inside Nagorno-Karabakh that they might be able to get out. One young man, Artur, was checking his phone every few seconds and scanning the horizon. He explained he was waiting for his sister, Rima, and her two children to arrive, having received a message that they were passing through the checkpoint on the bridge. There was a flurry of action from the police, pushing the crowd of waiting families back up the road to the edge of the village, as officials worked to convert the humanitarian aid tent from an empty public relations prop to an actual reception point. And then, after what seemed like an age, a small convoy of cars appeared from over the hill—old Ladas and Zhigulis laden down with suitcases, entire families of seven or eight people squeezed into the narrow back seats. Among them was Rima—she'd hitched a lift with another driver and was lifting her children out the car, hugging Artur and beaming with joy. In the back of her brother's people carrier, she unwrapped chocolate bars he'd brought for her three-year-old and one-year-old—a luxury they'd done without for months.

For almost a year, I'd been trying to get as much information out of Nagorno-Karabakh as possible, speaking to as many people as I could while the region was effectively on total lockdown and suffering regular internet blackouts. I'd never been to Stepanakert while it was under Armenian control, with the Russian peacekeepers having closed off access to foreigners after the Second War. But I'd spent over a year building up the most comprehensive picture I could of what life was like there when no outsiders were allowed in, obsessing over what food was available and what wasn't, how people were living and what they were feeling in a place I couldn't travel to. I'd driven to the Kornidzor checkpoint half a dozen times, interviewed those stranded in Goris and chased down Russian peacekeepers. Now, here in front of me was someone who'd lived through the food shortages, the panic and the fighting I'd tried so hard to get first-hand information on, but for some reason I couldn't think of any questions to ask her. The circumstances of the conflict seemed far away from the suffering of someone affected by it. "We made it," Rima told me through tears as I sat beside her on the edge of the passenger seat in silence.

* * *

Through the twenty-four hours of fighting, and the four days of chaos and uncertainty that followed, those in the Nagorno-Karabakh security services had tried to do their jobs as best they could, coordinating the response and tracking the enemy troops getting closer and closer to the capital. Now they'd done all they could. Ruben Petrosyan had left the office to try and gather what he could from his house, in a suburb where there had been sightings of Azerbaijani forces. There was a suitcase by the door, stuffed with all the pictures Nouné had taken down off the walls, along with documents and some essentials for their children. It had been there since after the 2020 war. Now, friends, cousins and colleagues were ringing around desperately trying to work out how to make their escape. The Facebook pages and message groups that they'd used to swap scant supplies during the blockade suddenly lit up again.

"Doesn't anyone have two litres of petrol? That's how much it should take to get to Kornidzor."

"Who has a truck that can carry furniture? I can pay."

"Is anyone from Berdashen village? My mother lives there and I can't get in touch with her."

With fuel trickling in via Russian and Azerbaijani aid convoys, the number of cars on the roads began to rise. Families crowded outside apartment buildings, loading their most precious possessions into car boots, filling bags with clothes and heirlooms and loose bedding, comforting crying children and abandoning whatever they couldn't carry in the street before they set off for the border. One man was carefully positioning a massive jar of homemade vodka into an old Soviet Zil truck. Another, a petrol station owner, had managed to unbolt his pumps and load them onto the back of a vehicle—obviously hoping he wouldn't have to start his life again entirely from scratch. Everyone I spoke to said the same thing: "We know we aren't coming back." Shops were emptied out and shuttered. The priests up at Dadivank chanted their final prayers by candlelight before packing their things. In a video posted online, a woman from the village of Chartar, close to the contact line, climbed a hillside to take a final look around the place she'd called home.

"This is the worst day of my life," she said through tears. "I'm listening to the wailing from the cemeteries. Forgive me, my homeland, I don't want to abandon you. I want to live here, to breathe your air, to eat the fruit from your trees, to drink the water of your streams ... I don't know if I'll ever be back to feel your embrace ... Forgive us for not being able to protect you."

People said goodbye to their homes, to their mountains, and wept as they set off towards the Lachin Corridor for what they knew could be the very last time. Stepanakert's iconic central square outside the parliament building had always been spotless, with locals boasting their city had the cleanest streets in the South Caucasus; now, it was filled with discarded prams and abandoned chairs dragged over from nearby cafes so that those with nowhere to go could at least sit down. The speed and scale of the unfolding exodus choked the roads. What was usually under a two-hour journey was now taking twelve, eighteen or twenty-four hours, people sleeping in their cars in gridlocked traffic on the way out of the city. At the Hakari Bridge, the Azerbaijanis were carrying out cursory inspections of the vehicles—while state media filmed soldiers handing out Azerbaijan-branded water and sweets to the terrified passengers. Most took a sweet with a wary smile, holding on to it for the remainder of the journey as a grim souvenir, and as proof that, no matter how hungry they were, they wouldn't be reduced to that.

By the second day, 25 September, the number of people fleeing via Stepanakert was already in the tens of thousands, pictures snapped and sent to me by those getting out showed. But only a fraction of them had actually made it across the border because of the traffic on the roads, with city streets in gridlock and cars queuing bumper to bumper on the highway. Some had decided to try and wait out the rush, putting their lives in order as best they could before leaving, while others decided it would be safer to at least get going before the situation deteriorated further. The biggest obstacle for most was still petrol, which had largely been used up during the blockade: that evening, hundreds descended on an army fuel station just outside the capital's northern suburb, with crowds frantically trying to fill up jerry cans and containers, using a pipe from an underground fuel tank, so they could get their families to safety. Without reliable supplies and with the constant fear of the Azerbaijanis moving into the city, there was panic in the air. Men hunched over the spout, while others opened the cover and dropped buckets directly into the pool of fuel. People jostled for space, several smoking cigarettes as petrol splashed on the ground. A fireball lit up the night sky, sending searing hot flames and broken metal fragments through the forecourt. At least 218 people were killed and over 300 were injured with burns that would go septic long before they reached Armenia.[15]

Officials and volunteers sent ambulances, private cars, anything with enough fuel to get to the blast site and back in an effort to save the lives of the survivors, carrying them to the Republic Medical Centre, Stepanakert's modern hospital. But the medics there were almost instantly overwhelmed. For days, they had been treating wounded soldiers and civilians hurt in the shelling, scraping together what few medical supplies they had left. Now, doctors who had worked non-stop shifts had gone home to pack up their apartments—and many were already on the road to Armenia. Burned bodies lined the corridors as nurses tried to treat as many patients as they could, even asking local volunteers to wash their hands and help give injections.

Without urgent support, dozens or maybe even hundreds more people would die in agony. In an unprecedented move, Azerbaijan announced that it would allow medical helicopters to fly into Nagorno-Karabakh to evacuate the injured—the same helicopters it had threatened to shoot down during the blockade. The sound of beating rotor blades could be heard in Goris, in Kornidzor and in half-empty Stepanakert, carrying the worst affected to Yerevan for treatment. In and of itself, the fuel depot blast would have been devastating for the Karabakh Armenians. But coming when it did, on top of the defeat and death and uncertainty, it was enough to break just about anyone. After a blockade, a war and a mass displacement, Nagorno-Karabakh was being forced to deal with a mass casualty event. In practical terms, it stretched what remained of the state's limited resources and complicated an already entirely uncoordinated flood of refugees. And, for individuals, the consequences were almost impossible to comprehend.

In most cases, it was the husbands and sons of each family who had been sent to collect fuel, and who had burned alive or wound up disfigured on a hospital gurney, crying out for their mothers and wives. Getting in touch with loved ones was already a tall order, and finding people in the sea of shattered lives around Stepanakert was even harder. The window to leave before the Azerbaijanis inevitably took control was closing. How long do you wait for your son to come back before you flee? What do you do when you can't find your nephew in the hospital? Who will be around to give these boys a decent burial if you leave now?

EXODUS

These were the questions hundreds of families were now facing, in addition to everything else. One woman, Berta Shahramanyan, was forced to leave her home with only the portraits of her husband, father and two brothers, who had died in the blast—instead of their bodies.

As the hours passed, fewer and fewer people were around to fulfil basic roles. Volunteers made bread in the bakeries using the small quantities of flour brought in as aid, feeding those who hadn't had proper meals in weeks and ensuring that some of those about to spend long nights on the road would have something to sustain themselves. It was volunteers who tried to restore power to the water pumps and who rang around their network of contacts to see if anyone had space in their car for those with nobody to take them. Ruben and his family had managed to find fuel and had packed up the car but, like many, many other families, had to leave behind their beloved dog because of a lack of space. And so it was also volunteers who fed the abandoned pets now wandering the silent streets. Until even those people left.

By now, the Kornidzor border had been overwhelmed. Dozens of people had turned up to help the refugees, many of them young diasporans who had travelled from Yerevan to hand out bags of baked goods, bottles of water and sweets for the children. The concept of a handout was unfamiliar to the Karabakhtsis: "how much is it?" was the most common response. The reception point had initially served to tell groups of new arrivals where to go but, even with a dozen computers and Red Cross staff working around the clock, there were just too many people. Within the first forty-eight hours, almost 15,000 Karabakh Armenians had reached the checkpoint out of an estimated population of around 100,000. A tired-looking official at the checkpoint gave me an updated count every few hours and I scribbled it each time in my notebook, watching the numbers go up each time. At first, it was women and children—men, almost all of whom had fought in one of the wars, were reluctant to deliver themselves directly to the Azerbaijanis to be arrested. But now, so many people were coming through that they were being asked to drive on to Goris to avoid congesting the only road down the hill.

The Armenian authorities had initially been careful to downplay the scale of what was going on. A government source, furious that Yerevan wasn't being up front about the numbers waiting to cross over, sent me a photo from the tightly controlled military position looking down across the Lachin Corridor. A river of shining vehicles snaked around the hills and into the horizon. Now, with the numbers soaring, there was no point pretending this was anything other than a total departure from Nagorno-Karabakh. While the pack of journalists who had flown in to cover events were initially asked to stay behind the barricade and not speak to anyone, those rules quickly collapsed, and the muddy intersection became a media circus. As officials waved the press in for the first time, photographers swarmed the buses carrying people on the worst day of their lives. Some tried to shield their faces, others shouted angrily as the flashes went off. One woman collecting water and snacks for her daughters after spending the night in a car was accosted by a Russian photojournalist, who snapped away as she tried to tell him to stop in three different languages. I pushed his camera away. He rounded on me, angry I'd blocked his shot. What were we even doing here?

For a year, these people had been living under a blockade that the world, and the media, had virtually ignored. They had held press conferences, they'd started online action groups, they'd tweeted at journalists and policymakers begging for coverage in the sincere belief that if the world paid attention, it would do something. It didn't. Now that they had lost everything, we were going to put them on the front page. We were going to scribble down their saddest words and photograph the most harrowing scenes we could, and our editors were going to thank us for getting such great "colour" into our stories on the conflict. And then we were going to leave and go back to our homes and our families somewhere safe, while the people we wrote about worked out what to do next, how to rebuild their lives. In the Red Cross tent, an elderly man had come to the same conclusion—"where were you all when we were in Karabakh?" he demanded of the journalists milling around. "If you want to take pictures of something, here are my legs!" He lifted his trouser sleeves to show dark yellow bruises extending from his ankles up his calves, with clean new plasters put over them by the doctors on call. He shook his head in sad bemusement as the circle of journalists photographed him, lowering his head and folding his hands around his walking stick.

Outside, there were scenes unfolding that hadn't been seen in Europe for decades—not since the collapse of Yugoslavia, the war in Kosovo, or the First Nagorno-Karabakh War. As well as the cars and buses filled with suitcases, there were now trucks and open-top construction vehicles coming through, filled with people unable to find a more comfortable mode of transport. One large dumper truck was filled with children, some disabled, and a handful of worried parents; they'd spent the night under a tarpaulin strung up above them. A group of men, cold and sitting in silence, came through on the back of a trailer being pulled behind a tractor. Some people had family in Armenia waiting to meet them, but others had nobody. One elderly woman standing on the roadside, clutching her possessions in carrier bags, asked me where she should go next—"with all my things here, I'm worried people will think I'm a refugee."

But, in the village of Kornidzor itself, a grid of interlocking lanes and houses built by hand, one family was preparing for a party. Karina Kafyan had made it to her relatives' house, just a stone's throw from the border. She and her husband had lived in the village of Aygestan, just north of Stepanakert, but she'd turned up alone—he had still been on the front lines near Lachin, holding his position, when he'd called to tell her to leave. They'd built two homes, bought three cars and had a herd of cattle to tend—but she'd left with just two bags, she said, smoking a cigarette in her relatives' sitting room. Leaving wasn't a decision Karina would ever have made lightly; she'd fought in the Karabakh Defence Forces in 2016 and in 2020 as a sniper, one of the few combat roles women were allowed to fill. She hadn't heard from her husband since and she was worried he would be stopped by the Azerbaijanis at the checkpoint and detained—for months there had been persistent rumours that Karabakhtsi traitors had sold the entire military enlistment database to Baku for a price. She'd left her passport and her mobile phone in Nagorno-Karabakh just in case, so that she wouldn't have any identifying documents with her when she left. Downstairs, a plump furry pig had been beheaded for a barbecue in honour of Karina's arrival. Its dismembered head sat in a pool of blood in a bowl on the floor as an uncle hacked up its carcass for *khorovats*. With so much suffering in their history, Armenians never fail to celebrate whatever little good they can find.

Meanwhile, down the hill in the Soviet-built Hotel Goris, others were trying to find a place to stay for the night while they worked out where to go. A flustered-looking receptionist was trying to help an elderly deaf couple, while someone had done a run to the nearest pharmacy with a long order of prescription medicines for those in need, handing out little bottles and tubes from a cardboard box in the foyer. Upstairs, I met forty-three-year-old Parkev Agababyan and his wife, Anush Aghajanyan, sitting with their three young children. They too had left everything they had, and Parkev's eyes watered as he talked about the tomatoes and cucumbers he'd grown in his garden in Askeran.

He'd made a living off his land, coupled with occasional work as a labourer—what would he do now? He'd served in the armed forces, but he'd had no problems getting out, having been told that as long as they didn't bring weapons or military uniforms, they'd be fine.

I excused myself and slipped into the empty hotel ballroom to call Baku. The calm, clipped voice of foreign policy advisor Hikmet Hajiyev answered the phone. The government, he said, regretted that the Karabakh Armenians didn't trust its assurances that they would be safe as citizens of Azerbaijan. However, it would "also respect the individual choices of residents. This is free movement of the population—they have a choice." And, he went on, a mechanism would have to be put in place to ensure that those who had left would have the right to return. In the end, Baku would launch a website with an Armenian-language option to register the details of those who wanted to stay. None of the Karabakh Armenians I've spoken to viewed it with anything other than derision.

While the Azerbaijanis were waving through almost everyone, it was clear there were a small number of targets still for arrest. On 27 September, Baku's special forces captured former state minister Ruben Vardanyan, who had been trying to leave along the Lachin Corridor. Despite being in power for less than six months and only ever holding a civilian role, he was probably Azerbaijan's public enemy number one given the fury he had sparked during his time in office. A photograph showed him being helicoptered to Baku, his handcuffed hands blurred out and two officers posing alongside him. The following day, former foreign minister Davit Babayan turned himself in, recognising he was on the wanted list. Within a week, former presidents Arayik Harutyunyan, Bako Sahakyan and Arkady Ghukasyan appeared in Azerbaijani custody, as well as former security officials Levon Mnatsakanyan and Davit Manukyan. The latter group were rumoured to have been handed over after seeking refuge at a Russian base, despite promises of protection—but their supporters said they understood that their incarceration was the price they would have to pay for everyone else being able to leave freely. The leaders who had effectively been clients of Putin's Kremlin were now reduced to begging the Russians to help them, and being turned down time and time again. They were being left to their fate.

One former government official, a well-off businessman who had served as the culture minister in Stepanakert, held his breath as he handed his passport out the car window. His wife and two daughters were sitting alongside him in silence, watching as the Azerbaijani soldier ran his eyes over their documents and praying they—like the cars in front of them—would be quickly waved through. The soldier paused, turned, and walked over to a cabin with his passport. Minutes went by. They imagined the special forces with their face masks running over and hauling him out of the car, whisked away to what would have felt like certain death. The soldier returned, handed back the passport.

"And how is cultural life in Karabakh?" he asked, as he stood aside and allowed them to drive on.

Near the Hotel Goris was the city hospital. While the injured soldiers and the airlifted burns victims had all been taken to Yerevan, the local clinic had been left to deal with civilians suffering from a whole host of illnesses and injuries as a result of the exodus. One man had brought his wife in after she gave birth just before they fled; they'd spent a day and a night on the road. She was too weak and malnourished to breastfeed and there was, of course, no baby formula. He'd been convinced both of them would die, right up until the Armenian border guards came into view. Both mother and baby were now doing fine. In another *kabinet*, as the shared rooms in Soviet-built hospitals are called, sixty-five-year-old Anush was looking after her husband. They were from outside Martuni and, after recovering from a stroke a few years ago, he had been looking forward to spending his final years with his garden and with his friends in the village. When the assault started, he'd had a heart attack and was now laying quietly under a thick blanket as his wife tried to coax him into drinking water. In a third room, a couple were chatting away from beds opposite each other, while in the corner a tiny woman was contorted in a nest of blankets and cardigans like an injured bird, her rasped breathing escaping an open mouth filled with gold teeth.

"She's been unconscious since she came in," a nurse said. "She arrived with the Red Cross and we have no idea who she is. But she doesn't seem likely to live very long."

A few moments later, the woman sat bolt upright and looked around. The matron came running over with a glass of water and, finally, she gave her name and address. Well into her nineties, she was from a village where someone else knew the local football coach. Calls were placed and her brother, who was blind, was contacted.

Back up at the Kornidzor checkpoint, officials were preparing for a VIP visit. Samantha Power, the US's former UN ambassador and now President Joe Biden's head of the United States Agency for International Development (USAID), was arriving as part of a major show of support for Armenia. After her convoy of black SUVs pulled up, she walked around the makeshift refugee camp, speaking to those passing through and those lining up for help. Embassy officials had asked reporters to form a semicircle around the spot where she would speak—conveniently, right in the middle of an access road being used by emergency vehicles. In a pre-prepared statement, she announced that Washington had signed off on $11.5 million in humanitarian assistance to fund critical supplies as well as psychosocial support for those who had fled. Azerbaijan, she said, had "created excruciating humanitarian conditions," while "the attacks of last week have made a dire situation even worse." But the conference was, inevitably, interrupted by an ambulance trying to get through. When it resumed, we were told there would only be two questions allowed; moments before the start I'd bent a consular officer's arm to ensure I would have one of them. Crouched on the rocky roadside to keep out of shot of the television cameras, my arm raised in the air to keep my dictaphone up, I shouted out the best one I could think of from Power's knee-height.

"You quite literally wrote the book on ethnic cleansing," I said, referring to her 2002 Pulitzer Prize-winning *A Problem from Hell: America and the Age of Genocide*. "Surrounded by people who've fled their homes, are you prepared to say that's what this is?"

Her book had concluded that, in the long history of massacres and forced displacements from 1915 to the 1990s, American leaders had failed to stand up against genocide or call it by its name for fear of the consequences. With a face of almost infinite empathy, Power began her answer, insisting "we need to ensure that the international community gets access into Nagorno-Karabakh. There are still tens of thousands of ethnic Armenians living there in very vulnerable conditions," she said, pointing out that testimonies were being gathered and it was clear there was genuine fear among the Karabakhtsis about living under the government of Azerbaijan. From somewhere outside the ring of reporters, a heckler cut her off.

"Sanction Azerbaijan or go back to your own country! We don't care, stop the lies!"

Ultimately, Power will have been on a short political leash from the White House, and it was impossible to expect her to make pronouncements off the cuff, but there was still an irony in her transformation from genocide scholar to tight-lipped administrator.

By the time the flow of vehicles came to a halt, nearly two weeks after the start of the offensive, more than 100,000 people had fled Nagorno-Karabakh, accounting for almost the entire population. Those who stayed were often the most elderly, feeble and isolated, but even they can't have amounted to more than 100 or so. At the reception point in Goris, a middle-aged man approached me begging for help.

"My mother is eighty-three," he said. "She's an ethnic Russian and she said she would never leave her home. But yesterday she called and said she needed to leave right away. We think maybe she left with the peacekeepers or the Red Cross, but we can't find her. Have you seen her maybe?"

The humanitarian aid point in Kornidzor had been closed after just a few days in favour of registration centres around Armenia's southern Syunik province, where people could sign up for financial support or request rehousing. International aid organisations were on the scene providing everything from clothes to SIM cards. In a development that surprised many, some Russian émigrés who had fled the consequences of the war on Ukraine had even set up a group to try and help people in their country of refuge. Before the week was out, a group of police officers who'd been on shift at Kornidzor for days had taken over a tent to use as a cafeteria, and someone had brought barbecued pork from home along with crispy roasted potatoes and vegetables fired on the grill. From a water bottle being passed around, they took quick shots of homemade spirits. On the roadside, I saw David, the unofficial spokesman of the guys who had been there from the start. He looked very much like a man who'd been sleeping outside for a week.

"I've just found out two of my family died in the explosion," he said. "I don't feel anything. My heart has turned to stone."

"This is why Komitas went mad," he said, referring to the Armenian priest who'd been confined to a psychiatric hospital after the 1915 genocide. "Not because of what the Turks did—but because of the indifference of everyone else."

PART THREE

THE AFTERMATH

8

THE WORLD WATCHES ON

In July 2022, just five months after Russia had launched its all-out invasion of Ukraine, Ursula von der Leyen landed in Azerbaijan. The European Commission president was on a mission to manage the crisis that the war had created and, in doing so, weaken Moscow's hold over the continent.

Putin's decision to launch his "special military operation" had already proven disastrous, with poorly-led Russian forces, hollowed out by decades of corruption, failing to overwhelm those defending their homes in Ukraine. It was obvious that this hadn't been part of the Kremlin's plan, which was that, within a matter of days, it would conquer Kyiv, destroy its independence and detain or drive out anyone who stood in Russia's way. By the time the West was able to respond, the annexation of Europe's second-largest country would have been *a fait accompli*—and, ultimately, world leaders might rant and rage, but wouldn't do anything to harm their own economies if it had no chance of changing the situation on the ground. This hunch had proved correct in 2014 when Russia's "little green men" invaded Ukraine's Crimean peninsula and, with only cursory sanctions, faced almost no real consequences for the illegal annexation. But this time, with Ukraine turning back the tides and defying all predictions by taking the fight to the Russians, the West's calculus had quickly changed. Now, Kyiv's allies were set on trying to stem the flow of cash into Putin's war chest, while Moscow did its best to coerce European capitals into backing down.

To do so, it had one weapon at its disposal: energy. Since 2014, the continent had continued its reliance on Russian fossil fuels, making it vulnerable to the weaponisation of energy supplies. While Brussels had set an ambitious embargo on Moscow's oil shortly after the invasion of Ukraine, it continued to buy large volumes of natural gas from Russia, for everything from heating homes to powering heavy industry. Germany in particular had built its economic strategy on the assumption that cheap gas from Siberia would never stop flowing, with its massive chemicals sector reliant on the discounted fuel pumped through the cross-continental Yamal pipeline and the subsea Nord Stream pipelines. Putin knew this and, in June, had begun turning off the taps to the EU, reducing the volumes reaching the bloc and sending prices soaring, triggering an energy crisis. Now, with the colder months on their way, there were fears that industrial shutdowns, biting recessions and even an inability to keep homes warm could be on the cards for winter. One Russian propaganda film predicted that Europeans would be forced to huddle around stoves and eat their pets, gloating at the damage the Kremlin could do as a result of its massive share of the EU's energy imports.[1]

Preventing a winter fuel crisis was the sole reason for von der Leyen's visit. Azerbaijan had been synonymous with oil and gas for over a century, fuelling the Red Army in the Second World War. Adolf Hitler famously had designs to conquer Baku to shore up the Nazi army's access to diesel, even being presented with a cake that showed a map of the then-Soviet republic, complete with an oil derrick. Now, Brussels hoped, the country could be the answer to Russian aggression. For months, officials had been working on a flagship gas deal that would see Azerbaijan double its exports of gas to the twenty-seven-member bloc by 2027, making it a supplier of growing importance and offering it more than €15 billion in revenues for the first year of the plan alone.[2] There was, however, one catch—von der Leyen would have to go to sign the memorandum of understanding herself, after Baku rejected suggestions that one of the commissioners who handled energy security would attend in her place.

And so, the stern-faced former German defence minister jetted across Europe for a triumphant ceremony celebrating the agreement, and heaped praise on her hosts. The EU, she said, had "decided to diversify away from Russia and to turn towards more reliable, trustworthy partners. And I am glad to count Azerbaijan among them."[3] Baku, she said, is "a crucial energy partner for us and you have always been reliable." Standing beside her, President Aliyev beamed as she spoke. Azerbaijan wasn't just about fossil fuels, he said in his welcoming statement, pointing out that the territory taken in the 2020 war would also help Europe keep its lights on. "In the liberated areas of Karabakh and Eastern Zangezur, the potential of solar and wind power plants is 9,200 megawatts," he boasted. This was the exact sort of legitimisation, the bestowing of prestige from a major power, that Aliyev so craved and that Azerbaijanis viewed as proof that their dark decades as an irrelevant, humiliated nation were over.

However, the deal didn't come without criticism. From one corner, energy experts were furious with the EU's decision to go out and strike supply deals for gas on their own, rather than leaving it up to market traders to purchase energy from wherever they saw fit. Elsewhere, there was concern that Brussels simply hadn't learned its lesson about becoming dependent on belligerent autocracies: in opposition to the agreement, over fifty French politicians penned a cross-party letter warning against substituting Russia with Azerbaijan. "Not only is it ruled, for the past three decades, by the same caste of people that indulges in every possible human rights abuse, but it is also desperately seeking to finance arms being used to exterminate Armenians in Nagorno-Karabakh and in the Republic of Armenia," they said.[4] However, the protest fell on deaf ears, overridden by the simple logic of supply and demand, and the fear that Europe could be left without the gas it needed.

At the same time as von der Leyen was shaking hands with Aliyev, the EU's other leader—European Council president Charles Michel—was trying to take on the role of mediator in the conflict over Nagorno-Karabakh. The mild-mannered, bearded Belgian, an ex-prime minister, was theoretically in charge of the bloc's foreign policy but, in practice, spent his time picking individual issues to weigh in on. For nearly two years, whenever journalists reached out to Michel's office with queries about some aspect of European affairs, they were batted away with a simple answer: he was busy trying to prevent a war in the South Caucasus. Eyeing the power vacuum created by Russia's strategic collapse in its former imperial hinterlands, this was an opportunity for the EU to step up, bolster its influence and replace Moscow's brutal realpolitik with values-based humanitarian considerations. And so the Brussels track for peace talks was born, stepping in to fill the gap left by the Organization for Security and Co-operation in Europe (OSCE) and its defunct Minsk Group, which had brought together diplomats from Moscow, Paris and Washington since 1992 to negotiate a resolution to the Nagorno-Karabakh crisis. The 2020 war had made it increasingly apparent that there wasn't enough real diplomacy being done, and Russia's war on Ukraine had created a power vacuum.

Along with its outreach and border monitoring mission in Georgia, this would be a major foray for the EU into an issue well beyond the bounds of continental Europe, and a key test of

THE WORLD WATCHES ON

whether it really could exert the kind of influence that it should be able to wield as the world's second largest economy. In May 2022, Michel hosted President Aliyev and Prime Minister Pashinyan to agree on a roadmap for future talks, clinching an agreement from both sides to commit to working together and resolving issues peacefully. A Brussels-backed joint commission on border demarcation was also established in the hope that actually determining where the frontier lay would put an end to territorial disputes. The move was hailed as a success by almost everyone involved; Armenia was desperate to bring in Western powers, given the unreliability of Russia, while the Azerbaijanis were confident Brussels' mediation wouldn't stand in the way of them getting what they wanted. Besides, it was the Russians who had helped broker the ceasefire that had carved up their territory after the First War, and who, at least on paper, had been protecting the separatist republic since the end of the Second War, so Baku was more than happy to see Moscow's dominance challenged.

Even the Kremlin was seemingly impressed, with press secretary Dmitry Peskov hailing the "very positive" moves towards resolving some of the thornier issues. However, Maria Zakharova, the angry mouthpiece of Russia's foreign ministry, would take a tougher line as the 2020s rolled on, insisting that "we see persistent attempts by the EU to intervene in the process of trilateral agreements at the highest level."[5] The Europeans, she blasted, should stay out of Moscow's sphere of influence—no matter what the sovereign countries inside it might want themselves.

Michel and his special representative for the South Caucasus, Toivo Klaar, spent months building bridges with both sides and, by the summer of 2023, Aliyev and Pashinyan had convened for EU-mediated talks nearly half a dozen times.[6] The sharp uptick in multilateral summits was seen by the hosts as a shot in the arm for regional diplomacy. If Armenia and Azerbaijan were talking, the Eurocrats concluded, at least it meant they weren't shooting at each other. But, in reality, they were doing both. The near-daily clashes claiming hundreds of soldiers' lives along the line of contact continued unabated, and EU officials, determined not to lose their role as impartial facilitators, refused to comment on who was to blame. Whenever there was even a hint of criticism aimed at Baku, Azerbaijan's most prominent commentators would loudly warn that the EU was losing its perceived neutrality.

Armenia's envoys were desperate to keep the process on track, fearing that if the diplomacy collapsed, Azerbaijan would yet again pursue a military solution; but Michel and Klaar were constantly aware that if Baku lost faith in them, its diplomats would simply walk out of the room. As a result, instead of insisting on concessions from both sides to broker a compromise, they ended up allowing Aliyev not to give an inch, while encouraging Pashinyan to acquiesce more and more in order to keep talks going—with the unwavering belief that dialogue, no matter the result, had to be a good thing, and that a comprehensive solution was around the corner. This strategy was unaffected by the possibility that Azerbaijan was engaging in coercive diplomacy, setting out its conditions for peace around the table in Brussels while simultaneously threatening to overrun the Armenians on the border and in Nagorno-Karabakh. The mediators were convinced the belligerence was intended for Azerbaijan's domestic audience and/or was a negotiating tactic—similar to how many European officials had seen Putin's threats against Ukraine prior to the full-scale invasion.

Even naming the region where the conflict was playing out proved tricky for the fence-sitting team; "Nagorno-Karabakh" had long been opposed by the Azerbaijanis, while "Karabakh" alone seemed too pro-Baku. Most of the time, Michel settled on "the former Nagorno-Karabakh oblast," a strange Soviet definition that neither reflected the totality of the territory being discussed nor was used by anyone with any knowledge of the area.

THE WORLD WATCHES ON

Wherever possible, he and his team studiously avoided using place names at all, so as not to have to decide whether to call the capital Stepanakert or Khankendi. Every few months, as a gesture of goodwill and an incentive for Yerevan to keep backing down on core demands, Azerbaijan would agree the release of Armenian prisoners of war—young men who had been captured in 2020 and held for years in Baku's prisons, where NGOs warned they were subject to torture and psychological abuse.[7] Armenia, meanwhile, progressively softened its position: from demanding autonomy for the Karabakh Armenians to recognising Azerbaijan's sovereignty and simply asking Baku to respect their human rights. Even that was unacceptable to Aliyev, who insisted the treatment of these de facto Azerbaijani residents was a matter for Azerbaijan alone. Where, after all, had Yerevan's concerns been for the wellbeing of Azerbaijanis forced out of their homes or even killed during the collapse of the Soviet Union?

To speak to officials in Brussels was to enter a parallel universe where everything was moving in the right direction. Careful diplomacy was the only way to prevent misunderstandings, they had opined in 2022, when Azerbaijan launched its Two Day War against Armenia. The talks were really promising, they insisted a few months later, as the blockade began and people started to starve. Peace, they concluded, had never been closer—just as it seemed more than ever like another war was on the cards. Every move Azerbaijan made to bring about the inevitable showdown shifted the frame of reference for diplomacy; they might have imposed the blockade but they've at least now agreed to let the Red Cross operate, so that's a positive development, the thinking went. Baku was taking three steps forward and winning plaudits whenever it moved a millimetre back.

At the heart of the problem was that the people in the room simply weren't qualified to deal with the conflict they had waded into. Wars in and around Europe for almost the entire post-Second World War history of the continent had been dealt with either by individual member states, by the US or, more recently, by NATO. There simply wasn't the institutional knowledge or understanding of how to do foreign policy among officials in the European Council or the EU's External Action Service. In the arena of Western politics where they'd cut their teeth, the worst imaginable outcome was that a poorly phrased missive might rile a member state or upset an industry lobby group. Now, they'd inserted themselves into a bitter ethnic dispute where the worst thing that could happen was somebody burning down your house and cutting your head off. That was simply unimaginable for career diplomats who put total faith in the idea that no problem was too big to be sorted out over a plate of sandwiches in a Brussels meeting room. And while the EU had been represented in talks over other international crises, like the Dayton Accords that ended the Bosnian War, it had played second fiddle to more serious diplomatic services like those of the US, France and Britain. Now, Brussels thought it had what it took to run the show.

That paradigm counted doubly for Michel. His team constantly talked up his credentials as the former prime minister of Belgium. But being at the helm of a tiny Western European nation with no notable foreign policy conflicts or international disputes does not instantly turn a lifelong centre-left politician into a titan on the world stage. Worse still, he wasn't even a titan in his own office. As European Commission president, Ursula von der Leyen wielded far more practical power than Michel did in his largely symbolic role. And she was set on doing her gas deal with Baku, no matter whether it compromised Michel's ability to act as a mediator or not. The pair had a famously fractious relationship, both vying to position themselves as the true owner of key issues like foreign affairs. In 2021, during a joint meeting with Recep Tayyip Erdoğan, von der Leyen was visibly shocked when her Belgian colleague darted in to grab the only available chair opposite the Turkish president, relegating her to a nearby couch.[8]

As much as she might have seen herself as Europe's real leader, von der Leyen herself was far from a visionary. She'd been hand-picked in a closed-door agreement by the leaders of member states as a compromise candidate, who wouldn't ruffle feathers on any side of the political aisle. But the biggest sighs of relief had come from some in Germany's national politics who were eager to see the back of her. "Von der Leyen is our weakest minister. That's apparently enough to become Commission president," said ex-European Parliament President Martin Schulz in an extraordinary put down on social media after she was anointed.[9] As Berlin's defence minister from 2013 to 2019, she had overseen a startling deterioration in the state of the armed forces, consistently presiding over procurement errors, equipment shortages, recruitment shortfalls, overspending with slick consultancies and even managing to offend generals.[10] Her tenure made it far harder for an already-reluctant Germany to provide Ukraine with the weaponry and equipment it needed to defend itself in the weeks and months before the war and, while London and Washington were dispatching anti-air and anti-tank launchers to Kyiv as the invasion loomed, Berlin only offered an insulting 5,000 helmets.[11] It didn't bode well for Europe's ability to handle a crisis.

The leadership of the EU simply wasn't taken very seriously by the countries that were part of it, who were confident that on the most important questions, they would be able to get their way by twisting arms and making their positions known. Officials like Klaar came under fire from Armenians for eternally failing to take a real stance on events but, in reality, these Eurocrats had no actual mandate to do so—when they spoke, they were in effect representing the positions of twenty-seven separate countries including both pro-Yerevan France and Baku-friendly Hungary and Italy. Somehow they had to find a way of not upsetting any of their members, even if it meant dismaying the Armenians. People like Michel and von der Leyen were seen more as a secretariat for the bloc than actual decision makers in their own right. And so, Europe was about to enter the most dangerous period of upheaval since 1945, with third-rate politicians at the helm.

The Brussels track of negotiations was kept separate from occasional talks hosted in the US and in Russia. However, when the blockade worsened and the prospect of Azerbaijan launching a military campaign soared, the three powers came together to hold secret discussions in an attempt to prevent another war. On 17 September 2023, Klaar flew to Istanbul to meet with Louis Bono, Washington's point person for the South Caucasus, and Igor Khovaev, Putin's special envoy for relations between Armenia and Azerbaijan. The face-to-face was initially kept secret until its existence was confirmed to me by officials weeks later—and marked a rare moment in which Moscow and the West appeared to be on the same side since the start of the war in Ukraine, seemingly all agreeing on the need to get humanitarian aid into Nagorno-Karabakh and end the siege.[12] Two days later, Azerbaijan attacked.

After the offensive triggered the mass exodus from Nagorno-Karabakh, Michel dropped what had been his flagship issue faster than anyone could have expected. Apart from an initial call for restraint and respect for the rights of the Karabakh Armenians on Twitter, he almost never again commented on the issue publicly.[13] The responses were incandescent—"you did this," wrote one EU parliamentary staffer in reply. Foreign Affairs chief Josep Borrell, meanwhile, took two days to even put out a statement on the subject.[14] And, in private conversations, their advisors were stubbornly convinced that they had done the right thing, even if the results had been catastrophic. The conclusion they came to was that despite their best efforts, Moscow had done a deal with Baku behind their backs and pulled the rug out from under everybody else involved.

"I think this could not have happened without the active complicity of Russia," one senior EU official told me in the aftermath, speaking on condition of anonymity. "Just from the very basics: they've got peacekeepers on the ground and Russia, if they had wanted to, could have in normal times stopped this and provided security guarantees to Armenia that they have long marketed as their unique contribution."

EU analysis confirmed, the official told me, that those peacekeepers had pulled out of their positions after being given ten minutes notice—an agreement this top official suspected had been concluded with Putin when Aliyev flew to Moscow for talks in May.

"The timing was absolutely not incidental: there were American troops on a joint training mission and, if you look at what happened, there were local elections in Armenia where Pashinyan did not come out of those elections in a strong position."

Russia, the official concluded, had given its tacit consent for Azerbaijan to take what it had been determined to regain for thirty years, destroying the EU's efforts at the same time, and there was nothing anyone else could do about it. However, Brussels refused to acknowledge it had been played. In an interview weeks after the exodus, Klaar told me that the outbreak of war in Nagorno-Karabakh did not mean the peace process had collapsed, because, no matter what happened within the breakaway region, there was still an active track designed to prevent further conflict between Azerbaijan and Armenia. Baku's troops were occupying Armenian territory in areas near Jermuk and Sotk and in Syunik, so a solution would have to be found to resolve that. But would Aliyev face any consequences for flipping over the negotiating table?

"We expect that when we have commitments, those commitments are upheld. We continue to expect that."

However, the EU's timid executive branch was becoming increasingly out of touch with its elected representatives. As far back as 2015, the European Parliament had voted in favour of resolutions calling for sanctions to be imposed on Aliyev's inner circle in response to alleged human rights abuses and crackdowns on political opponents.[15] The measures had never been implemented by the EU's appointed leadership, but the calls had only intensified as the standoff over Nagorno-Karabakh worsened. In October 2023, as the dust was settling at the Kornidzor checkpoint, MEPs overwhelmingly backed a resolution condemning the "forced exodus," alleging that it "amounts to ethnic cleansing" and calling on Brussels to reconsider its energy partnership with Azerbaijan. Stingingly, the text approved by parliamentarians expressed "deep dissatisfaction" at the fact that regular calls for action from the parliament were being ignored by von der Leyen and Michel, as well as demanding that the bloc's diplomatic service "replace dedicated staff"—widely interpreted as a barb aimed at Klaar.[16] As usual though, the demands from the EU's main democratic institution were ignored by the bloc's unelected managers.

The outrage from the parliament had been factored in by Baku, which knew that all twenty-seven member states would have to sign off on any proposed punishment. According to Rusif Huseynov of the Topchubashov Centre, the military offensive "was designed to be very speedy before the whole international community mobilises against Azerbaijan." Aliyev wouldn't make the same mistake as Putin had in Ukraine. "At some point there has been a slight fear about possible sanctions or action by Western capitals against Azerbaijan but this probability was always considered low, especially at an EU level, because Azerbaijan likes to have strong bilateral relations with different EU member states—Italy and Hungary most importantly—and at least one or two will always help us avoid any kind of huge barriers or sanctions."

THE WORLD WATCHES ON

There was a clear understanding in Baku that while the EU publicly advocated democratic values, an issue as important as foreign policy wasn't going to be left up to lowly MEPs. That meant Azerbaijan could comfortably express its contempt for the European Parliament without fear of consequences. Responding to a motion that condemned Azerbaijan's closure of the Lachin Corridor, Azerbaijan's parliamentary foreign affairs committee hit back at the European Parliament, accusing it of having been manipulated by "Armenia and the Armenian diaspora, long since a cancerous tumour of Europe."[17] Then, in June 2023, a delegation of European parliamentarians flew to Armenia to visit Kornidzor and denounce the ongoing blockade of Nagorno-Karabakh. Responding to the news, Vaqif Sadiqov, Baku's ambassador to Belgium and head of mission to the EU, wrote online that the MEPs had been wise to stand far back from the Azerbaijani positions. "They know what they are doing to protect themselves," he said. "The Istiglal IST-14.5 anti-materiel sniper rifle produced in Azerbaijan has the effective firing range of about 3,000 metres. Guys, keep clear of Azerbaijani state border."[18] Calls for him to be stripped of his credentials or declared persona non grata in response were ignored, although the president of the European Parliament and Borrell condemned the apparent threats.[19] The rhetoric from official Azerbaijani channels was drawing obvious parallels to states that had committed terrible acts of ethnic violence, but officially Brussels was still convinced Baku was a "reliable partner," and that the peace talks were going to be a success.

Humiliatingly, while the Europeans had been desperate to ensure negotiations continued no matter what egregious violations they had to overlook in order not to offend Baku, Brussels was quickly sidelined following the conquest of Nagorno-Karabakh. After the September offensive, the EU hoped to get both parties together, to try and work out humanitarian guarantees for the Karabakh Armenians and to prevent the situation from spilling over into an inter-state conflict. But, at short notice, the best it could get was the attendance of senior advisors to the leaders—Michel, per diplomatic protocol, was unable to meet with them properly, instead just dropping in and leaving his own aides to drive the conversation. After a herculean effort, his team was able to get another round of discussions in the diary for October at a meeting of the European Political Community in Granada. With the importance of the issue growing, EU member states concluded that Michel couldn't be left alone to handle it—France's Emmanuel Macron insisted on sitting in as a supporter of Armenia while Germany's drab chancellor, Olaf Scholz, was brought in as a lukewarm supporter of Baku. At the last minute though, Aliyev announced he would pull out, accusing the French of derailing the process.[20] There was a sneaking suspicion that the decision was actually taken because Baku had wanted Erdoğan to join the session to back Aliyev up, but the Turkish president had been forced to pull out as a result of illness. Either way, with confusion and a scramble for control of the talks underway, Brussels had lost its role as the most promising mediator.

* * *

While the EU failed to combine the necessary diplomatic niceties with harsher words, or even real-world consequences, the US has never struggled to make it clear that its priorities will be backed up with action. However, Joe Biden's White House had far less time for foreign affairs than previous presidents had been happy to spend. Dealing with Moscow was already a full-time job for the State Department and, since the 2010s, much of its focus had been drifting towards East Asia as China became an increasingly difficult adversary. That shift spooked European capitals, where for years a strain of anti-Americanism had pre-

THE WORLD WATCHES ON

vailed, in the belief that the continent could look after itself without the need for a global policeman. The war in Ukraine, and the EU's initial inability to face up to the economic or military challenges that came with it, had proved them wrong. Without the support sent by the US, and to a lesser extent the UK, the result on the battlefield could have been very different. Now, went a popular refrain among defence analysts, Europeans weren't worried about America going in, they were worried about America getting out. In Armenia, that was doubly true.

Nancy Pelosi's September 2022 visit created an expectation that Washington wouldn't stand idly by if Azerbaijan did the unthinkable. But Washington's position on the core issues was far from united, with Kristina Kvien—a first-time ambassador posted to Yerevan in February 2023—hinting that Nagorno-Karabakh's future was as part of Azerbaijan. The Karabakh Armenians, she argued, could live safely and securely under Baku's rule.[21] Yet the week before the mass exodus, Acting Assistant Secretary of State for European Affairs Yuri Kim told the Senate Foreign Relations Committee that the US "will not countenance any action or effort—short-term or long-term—to ethnically cleanse or commit other atrocities against the Armenian population of Nagorno-Karabakh. The current humanitarian situation is not acceptable."[22] I spotted Kim a fortnight later down at the checkpoint in Kornidzor.

"Will there be any consequences for Azerbaijan, Ms. Kim?" I shouted.

She looked up as though she wanted to answer, then looked down at her feet, as her bodyguard stepped between her and my dictaphone.

Days after the mass exodus, US Secretary of State Antony Blinken held a conference call with American lawmakers, including some of Armenia's most hardline supporters, who challenged him on whether Washington had finally gained a handle on the situation.[23] Officials, he said, were now closely monitoring whether the fall of Nagorno-Karabakh could be followed by an assault on the Republic of Armenia itself. Baku was insisting it had no intentions to invade, but many were suspicious, given the combination of extreme anti-Armenian rhetoric, Azerbaijani militarism, and having been lied to before about the supposed lack of plans to attack Nagorno-Karabakh. With the conversation confirmed by two people on the other end of the line, a colleague in Washington and I published it as an exclusive—one wildly misinterpreted by many as a prediction that Azerbaijan would launch an all-out attack on the Republic of Armenia. In a symptom of the perennially-confused communications that characterise South Caucasus diplomacy, the State Department issued an opaque rebuttal that it refused to make public, despite not having raised objections to our story when approached. A top-level official in the department later reached out to explain that they had been spooked by the response to the headline, and had had no objection to the facts of the piece. As part of an interview offered to rebuild bridges after this foul-up, the official went on to explain Washington's plans in the region—now that the Nagorno-Karabakh conflict had ended in bloodshed and exile.

"We've had to be very clear with Azerbaijan that this is not business as usual and there are consequences for their actions," the official said. "There have been quite a few high-level engagements that we've had to cancel."

Aliyev, who had always seen relationships with foreign powers as a tool in the struggle against Armenia, would probably rather have had Stepanakert than a friendly photo-op with an American ambassador. But there was also one step the US had taken that would be met with at least some concern in Baku.

Back in August, in response to the blockade, the Biden administration had pressed pause on the renewal of a key piece of paperwork, one that had granted Azerbaijan millions of dollars in military assistance since 2002, when President George W. Bush had championed the use of Azerbaijan as a launchpad for troop movements into Afghanistan. Under the terms of the Freedom Support Act, introduced as a result of Armenian-American lobbying in 1992, Azerbaijan was barred from receiving US military aid, making it the only post-Soviet country to be blacklisted. However, as Azerbaijan became an increasingly important ally in the War on Terror, the Bush administration had introduced a so-called Section 907 waiver suspending that provision. Now, in October 2023, the senior State Department official who spoke to me confirmed suspicions that the process of renewal wasn't going to move forward any time soon. Azerbaijan had undermined the progress it had made towards becoming a significant American ally.

Ultimately though, Azerbaijan had all the weaponry it could ever want. It had spent hundreds of millions of dollars purchasing advanced Israeli hardware over the previous decade, including the drones and missiles that helped it retake Nagorno-Karabakh.[24] And, two months after the offensive, Azerbaijani media reported the country had splashed $1.2 billion on a Barak MX missile system, which its manufacturers say can take out enemy missiles and aeroplanes simultaneously.[25] Much of the cost of procurement over the years had been offset by energy sales, with Azerbaijan providing around forty per cent of Israel's oil, and working with it to explore its most promising gas reserves.[26] The two countries had formed an unlikely partnership; Azerbaijan is a secular nation, but Muslim-majority, and the more religious among the population were still sceptical of an alliance with the Jewish state.

That partnership only became harder to sell to the public after Hamas's attacks on Israeli civilians on 7 October 2023, and Israel's immediate response, which saw hundreds of thousands of homes in Gaza levelled and tens of thousands of innocent people killed in the year that followed.[27] These events were unfolding just weeks after Azerbaijan's conquest of Nagorno-Karabakh, immediately distracting global attention from what was going on in the South Caucasus, and further reducing Western capitals' interest. However, there were parallels between the two assaults; while the scale of death and destruction was far greater in the Gaza Strip than it was in Nagorno-Karabakh, Israel's political rhetoric closely resembled the messaging put out by Baku. The inhumanity of the attack Israelis had suffered, officials said, gave them licence to do whatever it took to right the wrong and eliminate the threat to their nation, no matter the human cost. The international legal grey zone around both Gaza itself and the sovereignty and self-determination of a Palestinian state complicated outside efforts to intervene, while senior Israeli ministers and officials described the Palestinians as "human animals" and talked of erasing their communities from the face of the earth.[28] Outside the Israeli embassy in Baku, people laid flowers for the victims of Hamas's attack, while one lone Azerbaijani woman who held up a Palestinian flag in public was detained.

That policy put Aliyev's government at odds with its closest partner, Turkey, where President Erdoğan was pushing to position himself as the champion of the Islamic world, turning fire on Israel and accusing it of being a "terror state."[29] Ankara, he said, would support South Africa's appeal to the International Court of Justice, accusing Benjamin Netanyahu's government of embarking on a genocide. Azerbaijani state media, which usually picked up any and all comments from Erdoğan, was under strict instructions not to broadcast his criticism of Israel. Meanwhile, Israeli Foreign Minister Israel Katz hit back with an astonishing counterclaim, accusing Turkey of being "a country with the Armenian genocide in its past."[30] While Israel has never formally acknowledged the killings and displacement of 1915, the message was clear—if you smear us, we'll smear you. There was evidently little regard for what weaponising history or politicising human tragedy would mean in the longer term.

On paper, it's hard to conceive of two nations with more in common than Armenia and Israel; both societies were defined by the genocides they endured, both saw their security situations as existential in the face of neighbours they believed wanted to wipe them out. But there were no values in this foreign policy. Azerbaijan was more useful to Israel than Armenia was, and Armenians had a long history of sympathy with the Palestinians. Palestinian militant groups operating in Lebanon had even trained Armenians who would go on to serve as commanders in the First Nagorno-Karabakh War, including the American-born Monte Melkonian, credited with capturing Kalbajar and Aghdam, and reviled by Azerbaijanis for victories that forced tens of thousands from their homes. The fractious relationship between Yerevan and the State of Israel showed no sign of being repaired thirty years later, despite shared experiences—Armenia is of such little relevance and interest that the Israeli ambassador, Joel Lion, also serves as ambassador to Moldova and, like his predecessor, remains living in Jerusalem despite his posting.

Ironically, Armenia's peril is a cautionary tale for Israel: having failed to resolve longstanding disputes with its more populous neighbours when it was materially stronger, Yerevan now faces what it sees as an existential conflict and, having disregarded international laws and norms itself when it came to borders and territory, it can't suddenly take refuge in those same laws and norms now that it feels under threat. Likewise, Israel's survival offers lessons for Armenia, predicated as it is on having allies that count. But the consequences of pursuing security at all costs, inflicting huge suffering on civilian populations with the resulting isolation on the world stage, offers a worrying lesson for Aliyev as well.

* * *

Not all partnerships have been as resistant to change in the face of global events as the one between Azerbaijan and Israel. The war in Ukraine has precipitated a major realignment of regional dynamics, with an increasingly paranoid and desperate Russia driving the flux. In the 1990s, it was seen as a major priority for Russian border guards to secure what had been the Soviet Union's only border with NATO—the Armenia-Turkey frontier—in order to ensure Moscow's continued hold on the region. In 2020, putting peacekeepers in Nagorno-Karabakh fulfilled Russia's decades-long ambition to extend its foothold there, guaranteeing that it would remain, unassailably, the most important partner to both Armenia and Azerbaijan. After 2022, however, the almost 2,000 servicemen based outside Stepanakert represented manpower and equipment that Russia could otherwise deploy to plug the holes in its lines in eastern Ukraine. And while the thousands of troops at the notorious Gyumri base had once been a convenient way to put pressure on nearby Georgia, Moscow now had better relations with Tbilisi than it did with Yerevan. By the time Baku took Nagorno-Karabakh, the Kremlin's calculus of friends and adversaries had changed, and not just because of Pashinyan's pivot to the West.

Turkey was also an important part of the equation. Although a NATO member, Ankara had refused to impose Western sanctions on Moscow in the wake of the full-blown invasion of Ukraine—although it has supplied both its Bayraktar TB-2 attack drones and humanitarian aid to Kyiv. In a deft political move, Erdoğan has sought to portray his country not as a party to the conflict but as a mediator for it, hosting occasional and unproductive talks between Ukraine and Russia, while also managing to profit from the war. With the Turkish economy crippled by years of stagnation that saw inflation reach nearly sixty-five per cent, and Erdoğan's refusal to raise interest rates on Islamist grounds, access to Russian and Ukrainian markets was a must to prevent further price rises.³¹ With its control of the strategic Bosphorus Straits that link the Mediterranean to the Black Sea, Turkey has been able to act as a hub for imports of grain from Eastern Europe's two major agricultural nations, helping manage domestic food prices. Ankara also struck deals with Putin to import cheap Russian gas and oil, as well as getting help from Moscow to build a major new nuclear power station in the hope of bringing down bills for struggling households. In return, a blind eye was allegedly turned to vessels helping Russia evade sanctions. Turkey has also exercised its right to prevent foreign warships from entering the Black Sea, under the Montreux Convention governing the waterway. As a result, British naval minesweepers weren't donated to Ukraine, with Turkey standing in the way of the transfer.

Erdoğan needs Russia but, by the same token, Erdoğan is capable of hurting Russia. This dynamic has meant that, in history's latest back-and-forth in Russo-Turkish relations, Ankara went from adversary to critical partner in a matter of months. Unlike almost any other state in the world, Turkey had enough leverage on Russia to treat it as an equal, with the Black Sea, sanctions enforcement and support for Kyiv as buttons it can press if and when it wants to. The Kremlin has been loath to alienate the country. So too are Washington and other Western powers, who know that Turkey has a pivotal role to play in the security of important Black Sea trade routes, which help to prevent global food prices from soaring. The West also hopes to charm Ankara into taking a firmer stance against Putin. Erdoğan is the man nobody can afford to upset.

Aliyev too is a man who matters more in Moscow as a result of the war in Ukraine. Struggling to find customers for its fossil fuel exports amid Western divestment, the Kremlin struck a deal to sell Azerbaijan as much as a billion cubic metres of natural gas between November 2022 and March 2023 alone.³² Baku was frosty about why it wanted to purchase a commodity it already had plenty of, saying only that the deal would help to meet domestic demand so that Azerbaijani gas could be exported to the EU. Critics suspected that the Azerbaijani regime was simply serving as a laundromat for sanctioned Russian energy, shipping it onwards under the pretence it was its own—a suspicion bolstered by reports that Azerbaijan was planning on exporting higher volumes of gas than it was capable of producing.[33] But even if the exact molecules of gas that ended up in Europe weren't from Siberia, the arrangement made a total mockery of von der Leyen's deal and its hopes of hitting Russia's revenues.

The growing importance of Baku and Ankara in the eyes of the Kremlin also took the legs out from under Moscow's peacekeeping mission: what had started as a show of force, with the promise of protecting the Karabakh Armenians, ended in farce. After Russian troops retreated and allowed Azerbaijan to capture the entire region, the head of the State Duma's Defense Committee, Andrey Kartapolov, said that its servicemen had had no choice but to stand aside. "As long as the peacekeepers themselves are not threatened, they have no right to use weapons," he said.[34] That certainly wasn't what Stepanakert or Yerevan had expected of the armed mission, and it raised the question of why they'd been there in the first place. But, after all, the Armenians had far less to offer Russia.

Moscow's mission wasn't to protect the Karabakh Armenians, or even really to maintain its military presence in the region. It was to try and prove that the West was a paper tiger, and that any country seeking to escape Russia's self-declared sphere of influence would find nobody really prepared to help it with anything more than platitudes—not the EU, not the US. With former Soviet republics like Armenia, Moldova and Kazakhstan turning their backs on over a century of domination by the Kremlin—which expected total loyalty in exchange for total antipathy—get-

THE WORLD WATCHES ON

ting that message across was more important than any other outcome. Brussels and Washington had had a genuine opportunity to help Armenia extricate itself from Russia's grasp, but they'd struggled to see that failure to do so would make it harder for other nations in the neighbourhood to turn their back on Moscow, and would instead underline Putin's central thesis: that the Western-led, rules-based global system and its lofty democratic ideals matter little when you have a gun in your hands.

Armenia's historic ties with Russia put it on the wrong side of another emerging military and political power, Ukraine. Kyiv's open backing of Azerbaijan in the Nagorno-Karabakh conflict was reinforced by Moscow's massive violation of its own territorial integrity in 2014 and 2022. The sham referendums of the 1990s, and the talk of self-determination in a territory from which hundreds of thousands had been forced to flee, simply had too many parallels with Ukraine's own struggle against its former imperial overlord. And, despite being a symbol of democratic resistance himself, President Volodymyr Zelenskyy had formed close relations with Aliyev; Yerevan dispatching humanitarian aid would do little to fundamentally change that. A senior advisor to the Ukrainian president even used a television appearance during the blockade of Nagorno-Karabakh to suggest that the Armenians were lying about the extent of the humanitarian disaster—claiming that there were only 40,000 people living there, that the consequences were being exaggerated to distract from the war in Ukraine, and that Russia was considering illegally annexing the breakaway territory, as it had with Crimea.[35] "Russia one way or another wants to return its dominant position" and "demonstrate that only it can mediate to resolve conflicts like this," he argued. But Russia didn't seem to be doing much mediating, and its once-absolute position of dominance was in rapid retreat.

* * *

Energy aside, Azerbaijan also holds another key appeal on the world stage. Its historic antipathy towards neighbouring Iran has made it a vital regional partner for the West. Ensuring that Baku had the weapons it needed to deter the theocratic Islamic Republic from military provocations on the border has always been a major justification for arms sales and military assistance from Washington. After relations failed to take off between the two Shia countries following the fall of the Soviet Union, with Azerbaijan choosing Turkey and secularism over Iran and theocracy, an air of mutual distrust developed. Somewhere between ten and twenty-five million ethnic Azeris live in Iran, many of them in and around two regions named West and East Azerbaijan, close to the border.[36] Their community has for decades faced discrimination and suppression of its language at the hands of the regime, which wants to see total assimilation of Iran's minorities, and is instinctively cautious about the prospect of Baku igniting ethnic tensions within Iranian territory by building cross-border Azeri ties.

Armenia, meanwhile, counts Iran among its most important partners—despite their religious differences and the obvious tensions between a liberalising democracy and a murderous theocracy. There are more than 100,000 ethnic Armenians in Iran, a historic and well-integrated community that is given special treatment by the government and held up as a model minority.[37] The *parskahayer*, or Iranian Armenians, are granted rights that Muslims are not; including the ability to hold private club nights and concerts where alcohol is regularly consumed. In turn, Armenia itself serves as a respite for ordinary Iranians, where they can drink, shop and party over the border without fear of the morality police; along the southern highways dozens of cheap, seedy bars and strip clubs have sprung up to service Iranian truckers. Even the authoritarian elites aren't immune from temptation: once, at a lunch, I was introduced to an Iranian state prosecutor with a cigar in one hand and a large whisky in the other, which back home was an offence that could see the defendants in his court room receive eighty lashes—or even the death penalty after a third offence.

"Once you're in Armenia it's fine," he said with a laugh, "Allah can't see through the mountains."

Armenia also acts as a vital thoroughfare for Iranian overland trade. In 2020, Azerbaijani troops took control of a major international highway that ran along the north-east side of the shared border with Armenia, even crossing the loosely-demarcated line at various points. Reports that the soldiers were harassing motorists and closing the road with no notice led to it being abandoned as a safe route, and Iranian trucks that used to head up towards Georgia, Turkey and Russia via the Syunik border town of Meghri were now forced to trundle along the narrow roads further into the province's interior. Armenia has also served as a hub for illicit supply chains too, with banks acting as middlemen for Iranian businesses that would otherwise be shut out of the global financial system by sanctions.

As a result of this close economic partnership, Iran publicly committed in 2022 to defending its northern neighbour against what it saw as imminent Azerbaijani aggression.[38] It also viewed NATO member Turkey, and by extension Azerbaijan, as part of a US-led adversary bloc that wanted to up its presence in the region. Following the Second Karabakh War, Tehran consistently warned it wouldn't tolerate any changes to its border regions as a result of Baku's plans for the Zangezur Corridor. "If there is an effort to block the border between Iran and Armenia, the Islamic Republic will oppose it because this border has been a communication route for thousands of years," Iran's supreme leader, Ayatollah Ali Khamenei, told Erdoğan, showing just how involved in the dispute the great regional powers had become.[39]

As fears of an invasion of Syunik loomed following the Two Day War in September 2022, Iran made the unprecedented decision to open a consulate in Syunik's provincial capital, Kapan.

The small former industrial city along the riverside was within spitting distance of the border and the Iranians quickly put up a giant flagpole to ensure the Azerbaijanis in the hills above could see the green, white and red banner. This was hotspot diplomacy at its most acute, making it clear that Tehran wouldn't countenance a sudden annexation, which would have seen Azerbaijan and Turkey take control of Iran's entire northern frontier. Then, in a massive show of force that October, the Iranian Revolutionary Guards Corps said it was beginning colossal-scale exercises along the Aras river that marks the border with Azerbaijan, practising bridging techniques and launching missiles. The wargames, one Revolutionary Guards commander explained, were designed to send a message of "peace and friendship" to countries nearby.[40]

In response, in November 2022, Aliyev decided to ratchet up the rhetoric and play on Iran's fears about its Azeri citizens. According to the president, Baku was going to step up its efforts to ensure the rights and security of its cousins across the border, and "we will continue to do everything to help the Azerbaijanis who have found themselves cut off from our state."[41] State media, meanwhile, began featuring prominent exiled activists persecuted by Iran for calling for Azeri-majority regions to secede, and posters began being put up around one such Iranian city, Tabriz, hailing Aliyev as "our president." The hostilities culminated in January 2023, when a gunman walked into the Azerbaijani embassy in Tehran and opened fire with an assault rifle, killing a guard and injuring the head of security. While Iranian police sealed off the area and quickly detained the attacker, who they said was motivated by personal rather than political animosity, Baku blamed Tehran's security services and demanded action. Still, neither side was ready for an all-out confrontation and, as 2023 wore on, both sides embarked on efforts to fix troubled relations—a series of high-level meetings between officials was followed by the reciprocal accreditation of state media journalists,

THE WORLD WATCHES ON

the construction of new shared infrastructure and promises that the events that unfolded at the embassy would never be repeated. Aliyev parked the rabble rousing when it came to ethnic Azeri Iranians, and Tehran slowly but surely softened its line when it came to Azerbaijan's Armenia policy.

Iran had been the first country to stand up to Azerbaijan's pressure tactics in public—and, unlike the soft and cautious approach championed by the West, or the complete lack of interest exhibited by Russia, it appeared to have achieved results. Following the assault and mass exodus in September 2023, Tehran volunteered itself as a host for bilateral talks between Yerevan and Baku, wresting the role of mediator from the West with Russia's approval, while the Brussels track ground to a halt.

There were limits to the potential for Iranian advocacy, however: Armenia's pivot to the West was hardly welcome in Tehran, and would put an inevitable strain on the partnership. The only other partner Yerevan had hoped to count on was India. Once again, the South Caucasus was being treated as a proxy issue for geopolitical tensions far larger than the issues on the ground. India, which became a staunchly anti-Muslim, Hindu nationalist state after 2014 under authoritarian-populist Prime Minister Narendra Modi, viewed the conflict as a religious one. Its longtime rival, neighbouring Pakistan, has historically gone above and beyond to support Azerbaijan on Nagorno-Karabakh, while Baku and Ankara have backed Islamabad in its own dispute with India over Kashmir. So committed is Pakistan to the Nagorno-Karabakh issue that it is the only country in the world that refuses to recognise Armenia as a country at all, never having established diplomatic relations after the fall of the USSR. In that context, it seemed only natural that Modi's government would take the opposite side, seeking to check Pakistan's influence as well as that of Turkey.

However, the history also runs deeper: India has had an Armenian population for centuries and, despite virtually the entire demographic having moved to the Republic of Armenia in the post-Soviet decades, India still plays host to an Armenian school and churches that serve the local Indian population. Meanwhile, Armenia has recorded a sharp influx in Indians arriving in the country at least since late 2023, if not starting further back: more than 50,000 people, many from Christian areas in the south of the country.[42] While some are tourists, the vast majority are looking for work, taking advantage of a liberal visa system and an incredibly strong currency that makes working as a food courier, taxi driver or construction worker significantly more lucrative than back home. And, with deliveries of Russian military supplies to Armenia paused or slowed down, New Delhi has also taken the opportunity to cash in on Yerevan's desperate need for new hardware. From 2022, a series of deals have been signed covering a whole host of imports, including anti-tank missiles and multi-barrelled mobile rocket launchers designed to fire and move before they can be struck down by Azerbaijani drones. But this support was never going to be enough to save the Karabakh Armenians: while India had a political interest in supporting Armenia and a commercial interest in selling it arms, Modi's government was incapable of really projecting Indian power, with a poorly-developed foreign policy and a lack of levers to pull outside of its home region.

With Russia entirely unreliable, Brussels and Washington failing to grasp the seriousness of the situation and Iran eager to step back from its standoff with Azerbaijan, Armenia—or, more to the point, the Karabakh Armenians—were in practice left on their own as the security situation worsened. When Baku delivered its critical final blow in Nagorno-Karabakh, no outside force was ready or willing to stop it—nor, after more than 100,000 people lost their homes, to hold anyone to account. Azerbaijan had simply played better in the game of geopolitics. Aliyev had achieved in Nagorno-Karabakh what Putin couldn't in Ukraine.

9

A NATION UNITED

Behind a layer of bulletproof glass, Vagif Khachatryan was weeping. The sixty-eight-year-old had been whisked away from the Red Cross and arrested by Azerbaijani authorities while crossing the Hakari Bridge checkpoint to receive medical care in Armenia. Now, he was sitting in the dock of the Yasamal District Court in Baku as a judge explained he was being charged with mass murder.

The trial, which began in October 2023, just a month after Khachatryan's family were forced to flee their homes in Nagorno-Karabakh, was an Azerbaijani media frenzy. Photographers for state outlets contorted themselves to get the perfect shot as the defendant rubbed his balding head and put his hands up to cover the tears. A translator occasionally turned to the glass box and muttered a few sentences that sounded nothing like any Armenian I'd ever heard, while court officials sat sternly scratching away at documents, determining his complicity in the killings of civilians during the First Nagorno-Karabakh War. As the judge took a brief recess, an older man appeared from the back of the room and approached the cage.

"Do you remember me, Vagif?! Do you recognise me?"

Khachatryan, who maintained he never took part in the fighting, slowly shook his head and then looked away as the Azerbaijani man continued shouting. Outside the court room, I asked the heckler, who identified himself as having been one of those displaced from Karabakh, what he'd meant.

"He was my friend and he threw a grenade into my house. He killed people. He's a beast, the Armenians are beasts!"

While some details of the story seemed to change depending on who it was told to, the man seemed certain that Khachatryan was, without doubt, the monster who had inflicted upon him all manner of miseries over three decades ago.

The legal proceedings were a strange affair. Khachatryan had been assigned a lawyer named Natiq Baybalayev, a small man with large glasses askew on his face who, according to state records, had been practising law for just three years. I requested an interview, expecting him, like all defence lawyers, to want to take the opportunity to declare the innocence of his client, who was refusing to plead guilty as part of the high-profile trial.

"At the moment I'm very busy, but if I have free time I'll inform you," he wrote back, explaining that the Karabakh Armenian wasn't really his client, having been assigned to him by circumstance rather than by choice. Days later he dropped Khachatryan, claiming he had to excuse himself from the process on health grounds.

Prosecuting historic crimes is, even under the best circumstances, exceedingly difficult; trials in major international courts like The Hague often come up against the fog of war, hazy memories of survivors and a lack of tangible physical evidence. However, in the space of a month, the Yasamal District Court proved to its own satisfaction that the defendant was involved in the killings of around twenty-five people in the village of Meşəli in 1991. Instead of forensic evidence, historic photographs put up on plasma screens or testimony from experts, a procession of former residents were brought in to denounce the man in the glass box. "Vagif and his brother were there," said Cherkaz Mehraliyev, who had fled the fighting. "They hated Azerbaijanis. They said that the land and the village were theirs and we had to leave… they slaughtered our cattle in the meadow."

The judge banged a gavel and Khachatryan was sentenced to fifteen years in prison, virtually a life sentence for a man of sixty-eight. The conviction, in November 2023, marked Baku's first successful prosecution of a Karabakh Armenian arrested after the start of the blockade that previous December. It was clear there would be others, with high-ranking officials like former Artsakh President Arayik Harutyunyan and former State Minister Ruben Vardanyan languishing in cells somewhere nearby in the city, awaiting war crimes tribunals.

It wasn't just Armenians feeling the full fury of the state—the total control handed to Aliyev's government in the name of securing victory spelled injustice for Azerbaijanis as well. In the weeks that followed the mass exodus from Nagorno-Karabakh, Baku's security apparatus moved to arrest opposition figures, academics and journalists who had been critical of the regime, the latest in years of purges. From 20 November, scores of media workers like Mahammad Kekalov, Nargiz Absalamova, Hafiz Babali, Ulvi Hasanli and Sevinj Vagifgizi were held on opaque and spurious charges like smuggling, or simply without a charge being given at all. Then, in December, veteran pro-democracy politician Tofig Yagublu was detained on charges of fraud and forgery, which organisations like Human Rights Watch said were transparently invented.[1] A judge ordered him to be kept in prison without prosecutors producing any evidence to support the charges. The crackdown was widely condemned by groups like Amnesty International and the Committee to Protect Journalists, to no avail; Aliyev and the system he had created simply didn't care what the outside world thought of its tactics, safe in the knowledge that those tactics had allowed it to prevail in the conflict with Armenia.

Earlier that year, prominent scholar and research fellow at the London School of Economics, Gubad Ibadoğlu, had been driving along the side of a canal to his summer house just outside Baku when the police rammed his car. The dazed fifty-two-year-old was pulled from the vehicle and quickly disappeared into Azerbaijan's labyrinthine prison system, facing charges of fraud and counterfeiting that human rights groups said were "spurious."[2] Denied access to medical care, his condition quickly deteriorated. The fact that he held a UK residency permit did little to help him, and British consular officials in Azerbaijan, who could normally count on friendly relations with their counterparts, came up against an unrelenting insistence that they were meddling in Baku's internal affairs when they tried to advocate on his behalf. Ibadoğlu had been one of the strongest critics of the EU energy deal, arguing that "the only viable way for the country to fulfil its obligations to Europe by 2027 would be to purchase additional gas from Russia," effectively rebranding Moscow's exports as its own.[3] The Economic Research Center think tank for which he worked had also publicly claimed that companies involved in demining and restoration work in Nagorno-Karabakh were closely linked to the regime's inner circle.[4] That, his family feared, was why he had been targeted.

As if any further proof was needed that the self-declared environmental protests that had blocked the Lachin Corridor and cut off supplies to Nagorno-Karabakh were a farce, it was delivered in the summer of 2023. Armenians had been quick to point out that Azerbaijan's own domestic environmental record was appalling, with oil and chemicals seeping into the ground from the heavy industries that lined the pockets of the elite. Even as the supposedly committed green activists blocked the road to

A NATION UNITED

Stepanakert in June and July that year, put up in hotels and showered with praise by Aliyev, the government was brutally cracking down on a genuine environmental movement. Villagers in Söyüdlü, in the west of the country, had come out to protest against plans to build an artificial lake to hold runoff from a gold mine, with locals fearing it would become a toxic sink for cyanide and other chemicals used in a lucrative venture that would enrich those in Baku while they lived with the consequences. A crowd of protesters—mainly elderly women wearing headscarves—were confronted by riot police in heavy protective gear. The residents waved homemade placards and told reporters of how they were forced to put up with a permeating stench from the mine, operated by Anglo-Asian Mining, a company alleged to have close links to Azerbaijan's ruling family.[5] In stark contrast to the government-sanctioned activists, these unlucky eco-demonstrators, fighting to protect their homes, were sprayed with tear gas and reportedly beaten by the security forces.[6]

After weeks of tense protest, Aliyev himself was forced to face the issue, simultaneously blaming his own environmental protection officials and "a foreign investor contaminating our nature," bemoaning the fact that nobody had listened to the "legitimate voices of protest."[7] In the same breath though, he vowed to hunt down "provocateurs" who clashed with police, even if it meant tracking them down abroad. "Chaos, arbitrariness and provocations in Azerbaijan ended in 1993," he said.

Against that backdrop, the mood in Baku didn't feel jubilant: the capture of Shusha in 2020 had brought huge crowds onto the street, waving flags and chanting the name of the commander-in-chief, but the total destruction of the Karabakh Armenian state in 2023 didn't lead to an outpouring of public joy. If anything, ordinary people seemed unsure of what to say about these events that had shocked the outside world. Even the officials and experts I spoke to were equivocal on the issue; for years, they had insisted that their country bore no ill intentions towards those living in Nagorno-Karabakh, and that peace and coexistence were just around the corner. Azerbaijan was a secular, multicultural state; they'd lived alongside the Armenians before and they'd do it again. One senior government official, among the first to enter Stepanakert as the exodus was still going on, exasperatedly told me the story of how he, his driver and his assistants had come across an entire family with three vehicles at the side of the road.

"Do you need any help?" they called out in Russian.

"Yes, we don't have any fuel for the cars. We need a few litres to get where we're going."

With their own car full, the Azerbaijani group offered to take the family patriarch, a grandfather in his seventies, and leave one of their own behind with the others while they picked up petrol. Once inside, the official leaned round from the front and offered the Karabakh Armenian a cigarette. He sat quietly in the back seat, smoking and looking out the window as they drove to a petrol station. Back at the roadside, his children and grandchildren asked the waiting Azerbaijani: "So, are you going to bring him back, or will you kill him?"

Where did all this distrust come from, the official laughed, to the point that the Karabakh Armenians were convinced even a small group of civilian administrators offering to help them were actually out to murder them?

It's true that there were no verified reports of widespread civilian casualties or massacres as some had feared there might be when the final offensive began—it was clear that, unlike in the past, troops had been ordered to show maximum restraint with civilians. But the Azerbaijanis had managed to convince themselves that the takeover had been a limited operation with no impact on regular people, that the nine-month blockade hadn't really existed, that the documented war crimes, beheadings and executions of 2020 had been faked. Like the Turks who Hrant

A NATION UNITED

Dink said denied genocide "because they think that genocide is a bad thing which they would never want to commit," many Azerbaijanis simply refused to believe their country was doing anything wrong. As a result, they didn't understand why these people were so scared. If history showed anything, they felt, Azerbaijan had more to fear from Armenia than the other way around. While Armenians had been on the receiving end of more bloodshed in recent years, the memories of the 1990s still loomed large in Azerbaijan.

Even Yerevan's military cemetery, Yerablur, which was now the final resting place of so many innocent boys, had also played host to unimaginable cruelty inflicted on the enemies of their fathers' generation. In his book on the conflict, Markar Melkonian, the brother of famed Armenian commander Monte Melkonian, recalled the fate that had befallen a young Azerbaijani soldier as war engulfed the region following the fall of the USSR. Syed had been taken prisoner by a comrade of Monte's named Kechel and chained up in a cottage in Yerevan for over a month. As Markar writes, Kechel, his comrades and a police officer dragged their captive to the top of Yerablur, the burial hill near Yerevan. There, Markar alleges, "they kicked Syed to his knees under a spreading tree next to the grave of a fellow fighter named Harut. Then Kechel, a father of three children, began cutting Syed's throat with a dull knife. At first Syed screamed, but after a while the screaming gave way to moaning and gurgling. Finally, when Ardag could no longer listen, he pushed a knife into Syed's chest, putting an end to it."[8]

Monte's grave is now a virtual shrine in Yerablur, topped with flowers and touched for good luck by visitors. And yet, few Armenians are truly ignorant of what their side did in the First War, even if the full extent of massacres like Khojaly were minimised by politicians. They know what was done in the name of their security, and know it could be done to them by their foes for the same reason. They'd seen it in the Second War, and none wanted to stick around to find out what would happen in the aftermath of a third.

In the weeks that followed the mass exodus, Azerbaijani leaders struggled to work out how to spin what had unfolded, even to themselves. At the same time, the international condemnation left many feeling furious and alienated, unable to comprehend why, in their view, the world had been silent when their people were victimised in the 1990s, only chiming in when Armenians were on the receiving end. In reality, of course, the condemnation was superficial and came without any meaningful consequences, but it was still seen as much of the world siding with Yerevan. The narrative that came to prevail in elite Baku circles was that the Karabakh Armenian leadership had ordered its citizens to leave in a dramatic show to spite Azerbaijan.

Having met some of them, men who would die for their homeland and women who visited their children's graves every day, having seen the desperation with which civilians had against every instinct abandoned everything, I didn't buy that. Besides, during the First War the Azerbaijani military had warned Azeri villagers to flee before the advancing Armenians arrived—and this communication from the state hadn't detracted from the scale of the tragedy, or changed who was ultimately responsible for it. The Karabakhtsis living in Hadrut and other areas captured by Azerbaijan in 2020 had, in turn, been booted out of their homes, and Baku had done nothing to suggest that the rules had changed between then and now.

Despite its insistence that it wasn't seeking to force out what it called the "ethnic Armenian residents of the Karabakh economic region," Azerbaijan had never so much as published a real or credible plan for integrating them. If Baku had put a fraction of the effort it dedicated to military supremacy into state-building and forging trust with those on the other side of the contact

A NATION UNITED

line, catastrophe could conceivably have been avoided. But instead of using the period after the Second War to build mutual understanding, Aliyev and his inner circle had doubled down on their extreme rhetoric: there would be no special treatment. In 2020, days after he said that the Karabakh Armenians would have better lives as part of his country, Aliyev had gone on to add that "they have neither conscience nor morality. They do not even have a brain."[9] The "ugly and savage enemy" would be driven out. It was little surprise, to outsiders at least, that people in Stepanakert didn't view his advancing troops as those of a benevolent leader with their best interests in mind.

At first, many Azerbaijanis who'd dreamed for decades of regaining full control over Nagorno-Karabakh didn't seem sure how they were supposed to feel, now that they'd done it. But that changed on 15 October, when Aliyev gave an uncompromising victory speech, effectively ignoring the humanitarian cost.

He was supposed to have been the first to raise the Azerbaijani flag in Stepanakert, but the month before one eager official had beaten him to it within hours of reaching the city, at the iconic "We Are Our Mountains" statue—balancing the flag on the red stone faces of Tatik and Papik that watched over the local population, icons of tradition and resilience. The image had shocked Armenians at a time when Stepanakert officials still maintained that the Azerbaijanis weren't inside the city. In a sign of just how seriously Baku took symbolism, the official responsible had been dismissed for jumping the gun—officially because of the distress it caused local residents. Aliyev was relegated to flying the flag there for the second time in history when he staged his moment. Once again inexplicably wearing camouflage fatigues, he strode into Nagorno-Karabakh central government building on 15 October, wiping his boots on a Karabakh Armenian flag placed on the floor. "The counter-terrorism operation last month was inevitable," he declared.

"Unfortunately, the mediators dealing with this issue wanted to freeze the conflict, to perpetuate it. They wanted this wound to fester. The people and the state of Azerbaijan could never come to terms with this situation. I have often said that we will never accept this situation; we will never allow a second Armenian state to be created on our land," he went on, declaring victory in the three-decades-long conflict.[10]

The speech, and the crackdown on the opposition and civil society, came ahead of snap presidential elections called by Aliyev for early in the new year, capitalising on his resounding triumph in Nagorno-Karabakh to seek a fifth consecutive term. The vote was far from competitive—even Aliyev's supposed challengers lavished praise on him in a television debate that he himself didn't bother to attend, and they set out either no alternative policies, or ones that would be so conspicuously unpopular as to rule themselves out of the race. On the day of the poll, 7 February 2024, the president and his family, all immaculately dressed in black, travelled to what had been the capital of Nagorno-Karabakh to cast their votes in an empty city. This was where for thirty years the Karabakh Armenians had built their lives and their societies, this had been the place they loved above all else and had risked their lives to defend. Now it was abandoned, nothing but boarded up houses, ransacked apartment buildings and trash piled in the street. It was Khankendi now.

By March 2024, construction machinery was tearing through the iconic domed parliament building on the central square, razing the main symbol of Karabakh Armenian democracy to the ground. In a speech that month to mark the holiday of Nowruz, a year on from his belligerent address pledging to end the autonomy of Nagorno-Karabakh, Aliyev stood in Khankendi's central square, in front of a painted mural showing his raised right fist— the iron fist that had been brought down on the city.

"Where I am standing the separatists had built a so-called parliament building. As you can see, there are no buildings here anymore," he said, describing the democratic seat as a "devil's nest." Both the Artsakh national assembly here and the building in Shusha that Harutyunyan had hoped to move to had been torn down. The bonfire now lit in the centre of the former Karabakh Armenian capital, Aliyev added, would "do the final cleaning."[11]

Unsurprisingly, Aliyev was, according to the official account, re-elected with over ninety-two per cent of the popular vote.[12] A small number of observers from countries like Italy and Georgia hailed the process as having been competitive and orderly, while the chairman of the Russian Federation Council's foreign affairs committee, Grigory Karasin, said that the election's organisation had been so effective in achieving its result that it should be an inspiration for Putin's own re-election process later the same year.[13] However, trained election monitors from the Organization for Security and Co-operation in Europe were quick to point out that the vote "took place in a restrictive environment," lacked any sense of pluralism and "was marked with the stifling of critical voices."[14] Freedom House, meanwhile, which gives Azerbaijan an almost unrivalled zero out of forty for political rights, simply said: "since the early 1990s, elections have not been considered credible or competitive by international observers."[15]

In a mark of just how far relations had deteriorated, monitors from the European Parliament were not invited to observe the election, effectively blocking them from taking part in the process. And yet, apparently undeterred by the total failure of his approach to negotiations over Nagorno-Karabakh, European Council President Charles Michel issued a statement congratulating Aliyev on his re-election and said he was hoping to bolster co-operation in key sectors like transport and energy.[16] Weeks later, the EU's Energy Commissioner, Kadri Simson, flew to Azerbaijan for talks over gas exports and the green energy transition. I texted her team ahead of the summit to ask whether they planned to raise the case of Gubad Ibadoğlu, himself an energy expert and an analyst whose reports on alleged Azerbaijani laundering of Russian fossil fuels might have given Brussels pause for thought. Ibadoğlu's family had told me they were coming to terms with the fact that, without access to diabetes medicine, on a restrictive prison diet and barred from being seen by the Red Cross, he was likely to die behind bars, sooner rather than later. I got no reply from Simson. Aliyev hadn't just beaten Armenia, he'd beaten Brussels as well. Or at least carved out an Azerbaijan-shaped exemption for its values-based foreign policy.

* * *

At the heart of the Azerbaijani state was a divide between the civilian bureaucrats, many of whom were on some level in favour of reforms and democratisation, and the militarists in the armed forces, who put strength and decisiveness above all else. Part of Aliyev's governing style was to split his image between the two: sometimes he was the besuited statesman discussing new wind farms in the Caspian, at other times he was the macho generalissimo in uniform, taking personal command of troops on the ground. Ultimately though, the bureaucrats had been given their chance to resolve the Nagorno-Karabakh conflict through lobbying, litigation and international diplomacy—but it was the guys with the guns who'd managed to achieve what the civilians couldn't, and they were the ones who would reap the rewards when it came to shaping the future of the country.

Several government employees in civilian roles had told me over the years that Aliyev's cast-iron grip on power was a necessity while the Armenian threat loomed large, given that political chaos and instability had led to the loss of the First War. Once Nagorno-Karabakh was resolved once and for all, they argued, Azerbaijan could finally start thinking about loosening its tight restrictions on free speech, and modernising its political system in the same way it had modernised its economy. All the signs pointed to them having made a catastrophic miscalculation about who Aliyev was and what he had in store for the country next. While Armenians were furious with the West's tacit acceptance of Aliyev's rule and its absolute refusal to call it what it was, the development was even more worrying for Azerbaijanis who hoped to see their country pull back from the brink of total despotism. In the course of the decade prior, and without ever really attracting stiff denunciations from foreign capitals, the government had succeeded in banning, prohibiting or forcing out almost all of the independent Western NGOs in addition to homegrown civic groups—leaving pro-democracy Azerbaijanis entirely without support.

Faced with complete abandonment by the exact people who claim to support the democratic cause, Azerbaijan's opposition activists are now forced to choose between three paths. There are those who have gone into exile to continue their fight abroad; those who have quietly dialled down their activities, coming to terms with the fact there is little they can do; and those who have continued, and expect to be arrested. One young trade unionist told me two months after the mass exodus that at least four or five of his friends were in prison or awaiting trial at any given time. Nagorno-Karabakh, he went on, was its own issue, and it was up to individuals to decide whether the military offensives had been right or wrong—but the way it had become an all-consuming mission for Azerbaijan had suffocated domestic politics. For this activist, the Nagorno-Karabakh mission allowed Aliyev to distract from the fact that many ordinary people were living in squalid conditions, with a GDP per capita that was actually lower than resource-poor Armenia, despite the vast wealth of Baku's elites. Dependent on fossil fuel revenues, growth had slowed dramatically in recent years, achieving the lowest rate among nearby former Soviet states like Russia, Armenia, Moldova, Kazakhstan and Tajikistan in 2024. Meanwhile, ever-increasing military spending, accounting for more than seventeen per cent of the budget, took resources away from public services like health and education.[17] But, without legitimate political parties or a free press to make this case to the public, Aliyev's appeal to patriotism and victory appeared to have a hold on the population.

Even those who directly benefited from the recovery of control over Nagorno-Karabakh and the surrounding area weren't necessarily without complaint. On a visit to the town of Lachin just weeks after the fall of nearby Stepanakert, local Azerbaijanis who had returned were eager to show me their freshly-built homes, replacing the ones that had been allowed to crumble or inhabited by Armenians during the thirty-year occupation. The school and the apartment buildings around the central square were what the government wanted journalists to see on state-organised trips. This was all very nice, my colleague pointed out, but there didn't seem to be anyone who actually lived in Lachin. We'd struck out asking people milling around the centre if they were returnees, with small groups of men waiting outside a canteen there shaking their heads and identifying themselves as workers brought in for the construction. Incensed by the insinuation that this was all for show, one older man insisted we climb into his SUV and go off in search of real Lachinlilar, authentic residents of the village. But, off the main streets, the quality of construction visibly dropped: many of the new buildings had already lost much of their paintwork or developed cracks, despite being constructed just a year or two before, after the handover of the village in 2022. At a row of badly whitewashed houses, returnees who had fled the region as children came out of their houses to meet foreign reporters on a state-organised trip. As they gathered around, shaking hands and offering cups of tea inside their homes, I got talking to a family on the edge of the group. Their two-bedroom house overlooked a muddy hole in the ground where construction machinery still sat dormant.

A NATION UNITED

The father, who was originally from Lachin himself, told me that while he was grateful to Aliyev for the chance to come back, he had given up reasonably-paid skilled work in Baku to do so, and now couldn't find a job in Karabakh at all. "Nobody gives us any money for anything," he said, "we can't even afford groceries or clothes for the children. It's terrible." None of the labourers tending the well-manicured green spaces in the village or working on building restoration were living there, though they were working for nameless contractors that stood to make hundreds of millions from the projects. As a formerly internally-displaced person in his fifties, it was unclear what this man would be able to do even if he retrained—the pastoralist lifestyle his parents had lived before the First War would no longer pay the bills and, besides, many had forgotten those ways of living off the land during the long years of exile. These were the people that all the violence and authoritarianism had supposedly been for, and now they too were being left alone.

There was nobody to represent those concerns to the government—no think-tanks, residents' organisations or opposition politicians—and any questioning of the regime's approach was akin to treason. These were the people who, in theory, it was all for: the victims of the very injustice the modern Azerbaijani state had been built on, the very proof it pointed to in defence of its crackdown on enemies foreign and domestic. It was hard not to draw the impression that their undoubtedly genuine tragedies had been weaponised for something far larger than them and, when the photo ops were over, they'd be left picking up the pieces of their lives once again. These former refugees, like the elderly women protesting the gold mine near their modest homes, belonged to one Azerbaijan—the security officials, businessmen and members of Aliyev's inner circle, with their chauffeurs and glitzy Baku apartments, belonged to a different one altogether.

By contrast, the state had invested significant time and resources into manufacturing its own civil society organisations to promote its interests. The one receiving the most attention since 2022 was the so-called Western Azerbaijan Community, an influential state-funded group that represents the ethnic Azeris who were forcibly displaced from Armenia during the 1990s. Their rhetoric, although rooted in a genuine grievance that would be familiar to many Armenians who'd fled Soviet Azerbaijan, was openly irredentist and conspiratorial—driven by pro-government figures who constantly propagated claims that the Armenians weren't indigenous to the region and that the territory of the Republic of Armenia was "rightfully" Azerbaijani. For months, outside interlocutors like the EU had dismissed this group as no more than a pressure tactic; these campaigners were simply there as leverage in Baku's demand for concessions in Nagorno-Karabakh, and to point out that a wider conflict would be catastrophic for Yerevan. But what if they weren't just a negotiating tactic?

Following the exodus, the group only became more prominent. The next demand was the surrender of three enclaves inside Armenia—by international law they were Azerbaijani territory, but had been under the control of Armenia since the fall of the Soviet Union. This was an unthinkably thorny issue for Yerevan, given the practical challenges of opening the borders for transit to and from these forlorn villages, ousting their residents and welcoming in the very armed forces they had so recently fought tooth and claw to defend against. But the ferocity of the propaganda against Azerbaijan's neighbouring country went even further. While not openly calling for the complete destruction of Armenia, this propaganda consistently advocated for the return of displaced Azerbaijanis to their former towns and villages, as well as to Yerevan, which had been largely Azeri until the 1900s. In support of that cause, Aliyev famously declared in 2023 that "Armenia is a country of no value... a territory artificially created on ancient Azerbaijani lands."[18] On its own, the right to return could have been a peaceful ambition, but coupled with the con-

A NATION UNITED

spiratorial belief the Armenians were foreign occupiers, and with the support for the government's military actions, it created a far more disturbing discourse—one that reinforced fears that the military phase of the conflict wasn't actually over.

Despite a deal with Iran that had seen new infrastructure being built to reinforce the road link between Nakhchivan and the mainland, Baku's insistence on the Zangezur Corridor through Syunik hadn't gone away. The project, which Aliyev had previously said would "unite the whole Turkic world," was still a major priority, despite—or possibly because of—the Russian forces (who, under the terms of the 2020 ceasefire, would be in control of it) having proven themselves to be entirely useless. This demand from Baku is the only surviving aspect of that 2020 trilateral agreement, with almost every other provision, such as the Lachin Corridor and the Russian peacekeepers protecting the Karabakh Armenians, having disappeared from reality.

In response, in October 2023 Yerevan unveiled an alternative plan that officials had spent weeks drawing up to turn Armenia into "the crossroads of peace."[19] Using existing road and rail infrastructure, as well as building new highways from east to west, the country would open its borders to both Azerbaijan and Turkey after three decades of reciprocal closure. The move, just a month after the fall of Nagorno-Karabakh, was a major departure from anything any previous government would even have considered. It was partly designed to shift the conversation away from Azerbaijan's version of the Zangezur Corridor, with transit taking place under existing sovereign borders and without handing yet another mandate to the Russians. And partly it arose from an understanding that it was impossible, in the long term, to govern a prosperous and safe country if both its eastern and western borders were shut, flanked by neighbours it had no productive relations with. "If we are trading, there's a small chance we won't be shooting each other—and that's worth trying," one

Armenian foreign ministry official told me. But Baku was utterly disinterested in the idea, with its favoured experts saying it had no appeal and Pashinyan eventually being forced to admit that Azerbaijan was unlikely to go for the idea. Normalisation with Turkey looked on the rocks as well, with a border-post opening having been hotly-anticipated for years without ever actually coming to fruition. In May 2023, Ankara even temporarily suspended the right of Armenian flights to cross its airspace, after a monument was unveiled in Yerevan in memory of those who took part in Operation Nemesis to assassinate the architects of the 1915 genocide.

While Azerbaijan has faced few if any material consequences following its conquest of Nagorno-Karabakh, the fighting, the crackdown on the opposition and its continued standoff with Armenia have hurt its standing in at least some international organisations. The Parliamentary Assembly of the Council of Europe, once the chief hunting ground for Azerbaijan's caviar-bearing lobbyists, resolved in January 2024 not to ratify credentials for the country's diplomatic mission, arguing that Baku had "not fulfilled major commitments" made as part of its membership of the international body.[20] "Very serious concerns remain as to [Azerbaijan's] ability to conduct free and fair elections, the separation of powers, the weakness of its legislature vis-à-vis the executive, the independence of the judiciary and respect for human rights, as illustrated by numerous judgments of the European Court of Human Rights," a report to the assembly warned, and the punitive motion was voted through by an overwhelming majority with only ten dissenting votes, despite the decades-long charm offensive by Baku's diplomats.

But prestige was showered on Azerbaijan elsewhere, and from an unlikely partner: Armenia. In December 2023, Pashinyan and Aliyev issued a joint statement in the wake of Nagorno-Karabakh's catastrophe. Baku would release thirty-two prisoners of war, many of them having spent three years in jail since the 2020 war, while Yerevan would withdraw its application to host the all-important COP29 United Nations climate talks in 2024.[21] There had been a general consensus that the summit, which gathers world leaders from across the globe, should take place in Eastern Europe—but Russia had been actively vetoing any EU country from hosting. The two remaining candidates were Armenia and Azerbaijan, which had been vetoing each other, so Yerevan's decision gave Baku a lock on the nomination, allowing it to play a key role in bringing together thousands of diplomats and experts to tackle the existential challenges facing humanity. In November 2023, the conquest of Azerbaijan's breakaway territories had been presented by envoys at COP28 in Dubai as a win for the climate; the Karabakh economic region, emptied of most of its inhabitants, had been the first in the country to reach climate neutrality, a sign on the Azerbaijani stall proudly proclaimed. The region had bountiful renewable energy resources, including hydroelectric stations (for example, at the Sarsang reservoir), potential for wind power, and some of the highest ultraviolet radiation in the country, making it a promising site for new solar farms that international firms would be more than happy to help build. COP29, Baku said, would be a "COP of peace," aimed at resolving conflicts across the world.[22] It was hard to conceive of better optics for Aliyev, at the centre of the global community, shaking hands with presidents and prime ministers, leading the way on clean energy and selling fossil fuels at the same time, preaching peace after having vanquished his rivals.

"We did not allow the Karabakh subject to be erased," Aliyev said a month after the mass exodus.[23] "Many countries and forces wanted to instil this in us, saying we must come to terms with the situation and start cooperating with Armenia. Many reiterated that there was no military solution to the conflict. We have shown that there is and have shown it again recently. This topic is now closed! The subject of the Karabakh conflict is closed once and for all! The book of separatists is closed once and for all!"

10

A NATION NO MORE

It had been scarcely two weeks since the mass exodus from Nagorno-Karabakh, and the road from Stepanakert to the Armenian border was littered with abandoned suitcases, discarded petrol cans and the now-extinguished campfires that escaping Karabakhtsis had huddled around to keep warm while spending the night in their cars. A month before, in the chaotic week following the Azerbaijani offensive, it had taken people more than twenty-four hours to get out along this highway. Driving from Shusha to the Hakari Bridge checkpoint through Azerbaijani-held territory now took just forty minutes, and ours was the only vehicle on the road. A thick fog had descended in the mountains, making it impossible to see more than ten or fifteen metres ahead. Every few minutes, out of the mist would appear a reminder of what had taken place here: a broken-down car, a soaking wet pile of clothes abandoned when the passengers were forced to hitch a ride in a passing bus or construction vehicle.

About halfway to the border, an old blue Soviet ZiL cargo truck sat by the side of the highway, its hood caved in from a collision, unable to finish its final journey. The force of the impact had thrown its contents into the air; whoever had been driving had wanted to take their plush dining room chairs, a cut-glass chandelier and their bathtub, prised out of their home and placed carefully in the back. The top had been covered with a makeshift tarpaulin, made of banners strung together from a local football stadium; one read Artsakh Football Federation, while others showed glorifying images of Armenian soldiers fighting in the First Nagorno-Karabakh War. It seemed a dangerous thing to take through the Azerbaijani checkpoint, but I guessed they simply couldn't find anything else to keep their things dry from the rain. A stack of women's shoes had been piled up next to the rear wheel, where someone had obviously sorted through them and decided which pairs they really did need to take and which would have to be left behind. A box of crystal champagne glasses sat nearby, shattered in the accident.

I'd seen the crowds of desperate people coming across the border, but I'd never really seen the place they'd come from, at least not up close. In the couple of years I'd been covering Nagorno-Karabakh, the Russian peacekeepers had prevented outsiders and foreign reporters from entering the region to report on the situation; they hadn't, however, prevented the entire Karabakh Armenian population from fleeing. Now, I was looking at the same rugged landscape that had been their final view of their homeland. I wondered what they'd felt as they were leaving, the people I knew, who I'd spoken to every day during the blockade, or had met since. People like Karina, the sniper who had risked her life for Artsakh, or Bardak-owner Azat, who had poured everything he had into his bar in Stepanakert, or security official Ruben who was leaving behind his job and his property to start again from scratch with a young family. Azerbaijan maintained that they'd chosen to leave—but it was self-evidently a choice nobody should ever have to make. Would they know whose jumper this was on the side of the road? Would they recognise the family in these photographs at the bottom of a discarded suitcase? And what would the people in the photos do now?

Up in the hills around the former capital, the fighting positions were in the process of being de-mined. One outpost on the road down from Shusha was just a camouflage metal container with some netting stretched over it, protected by a barrier of earthworks and corrugated iron. The volunteers stationed here hadn't surrendered or retreated until the ceasefire was signed; only then had they taken what they could and walked the few miles down to their homes in Stepanakert, as their wives wondered whether they were still alive. Even if they'd wanted to get out earlier, their yellow minibus parked just behind the position had been hit and destroyed, laying sideways on the grass as a mangled wreck. Now, out of the trenches cut into the ground, a large *gampr* came bounding towards me, an Armenian sheepdog that the former occupants had obviously fed and looked after, wondering where everyone had gone.

Further down, on the second line of defences, a massive bunker had been built into the hillside, constructed from reinforced concrete. It had vast rooms for weapons storage, barracks with beds and for command and control; there were large gates at the back big enough for a tank to roll through, as well as a covered firing position from where you could see both the tower blocks of the capital and the archways of Shusha. The once-impressive vehicle storage hall was filled with wasps that had built lattice nests high up among the rafters. On the floor was an Armenian camping stove and the uneaten remains of the last meal a soldier had cooked there—green beans in a tomato sauce. It was a dish I'd seen both in Armenia and in Azerbaijan. The boy who'd made them may well be dead, I thought. Tradition will have demanded that his family hold a party when he went off to do military service—maybe they wouldn't ever have one to celebrate him coming back. And, if that was the case, then unlike those who buried their children and brothers at Yerablur, they probably wouldn't even get to recover his body.

I remembered posters I'd seen in Karabakh Armenian villages, declaring that a strong army meant a safe homeland. I remembered the young boys I'd met, now refugees, who'd spent their summers at military camps learning to strip an AK-74, to detect and disarm landmines, playing with their friends and vowing that they would be the bravest soldier Artsakh had ever seen. I thought of a poem I'd read once.

> To every man upon this earth
> Death cometh soon or late.
>
> And how can man die better
> Than facing fearful odds,
> For the ashes of his fathers,
> And the temples of his gods.

It was by a nineteenth-century British war minister, Thomas Babington Macaulay, and part of that genre of patriotic verses that poured praise on the kind of suffering ordinary people were expected to do for their country. Macaulay was a hardened believer that European culture was far superior, nobler and more honourable than the ways found in the "Orient." I wondered whether he'd consider this mountainous corner to be the Orient, and whether he would have been able to find something admirable in the decades of fighting over Nagorno-Karabakh—an existential, total war that ended with one side victorious and the other vanquished. Sheltering in a wasp-infested bunker as explosions blew dust down from the ceiling might not have been what he was imagining when he wrote those words, but it would be hard not to see that both Armenians and Azerbaijanis were prepared to sacrifice everything—their lives, their possessions and their freedoms—in the defence of their mosques, their churches, their graveyards. But what had it got them? A land of ashes and empty hearths. I thought of those sad mothers I'd seen in Yerevan's Yerablur cemetery and Baku's Martyrs' Lane.

Around the outskirts of what was now Khankendi, the houses closest to the contact line had been abandoned in a hurry. In one, a pot of macaroni sat on the table, now covered with a thick layer of black mould, next to a cup of tea the owner never got around to drinking. Outside in the yard, someone had been cutting onions on a workbench when the offensive began. The Azerbaijani troops who had got there before me had pulled over wardrobes and sifted through drawers, but it was still clear to me that this had been a house a family had done their best to make a happy place, even after 2020, when their enemies had arrived almost on their doorstep. A warm jacket emblazoned with the insignia of the Artsakh Emergency Ministry had been hung on a peg in the garden, as though taken off momentarily while picking the fresh herbs in the flower beds.

For the people living further into the city, who'd had more time to prepare for their departure after the assault began, the question of what to do with their homes had been a divisive one. Some had put the shutters across their windows, locking every door and holding onto their keys in the hope they could deter looters and one day return. At the Kornidzor checkpoint, a family had virtually torn apart the car they were in, looking for a house key that had been dropped down the back of a seat somewhere along the way. Others had left their front doors open, thinking it would spare them from being kicked in by the troops when they arrived. One woman had left out washed, folded bedding for the Azerbaijani soldiers or workers who she thought would inevitably end up garrisoned in her building. Yet others had smashed everything they thought could be of use or value, to deprive the advancing army of plunder; one woman tore apart her entire apartment, before being forced to spend the night in the shattered ruins of her former home after her planned exit was delayed.

* * *

No matter what they chose, the refugees from Nagorno-Karabakh were almost unanimously convinced they'd never see their mountainous motherland again. Once in Armenia, they were sent to towns and villages where there were buildings for them to stay in—sometimes these were school gymnasiums converted into barracks, shared by dozens of traumatised people. More often though, they were given disused village houses out in the regions, abandoned or left uninhabited as part of the population drain that had seen entire communities relocate to Yerevan over previous decades. Many were in a dismal state. In November, I visited Ruben, the security official, and his three children. They had taken up residence in a village about an hour's drive from Yerevan, in a small farm building that belonged to the relative of a comrade of his from the Yeghnikner commandos. They'd bought some chickens and tried to patch up the holes in the window frames that let the wind whistle through the wood. Things would be better in spring, he told his family, when fruit and vegetables would grow in the garden. Over the peeling wallpaper he'd stuck a drawing by his eleven-year-old son that showed the family in the house they'd left behind, accompanied by Artsakh flags and the ever-present Tatik and Papik from the "We Are Our Mountains" monument, smiles drawn onto their Easter Island-style stone heads. On a nearby shelf were toys the boy had made himself from plywood: a tank and a carefully carved Russian Sukhoi fighter jet.

At least two other houses in the tiny village were now home to refugees. There was the young bride living with her in-laws, making coffee as her husband's mother reminisced about their farmhouse and vegetable patches back in Nagorno-Karabakh.

Just down the street were the middle-aged sisters whose husbands had died, and the teenage son who dreamed of becoming a professional martial arts fighter after he'd finished his military service. "When the first person goes back to Artsakh," his aunt said through tears, "I'll be the second." But so far no-one had. While Azerbaijan talked publicly about a right to return for those who'd left, the details hadn't been set out—the land borders were closed, Armenians couldn't exactly fly into Baku and, besides, even if they wanted to take up the offer of Azerbaijani passports, they'd have to give up their Armenian ones, because their new nation staunchly refuses to accept dual citizenship. Nobody believed Aliyev was serious about letting them return, so they made the best of the situation they could.

However, the new arrivals had more than just practical challenges to overcome. While individual Armenians, from students to diasporans to local mayors, raised funds and ran errands to help the displaced Karabakhtsis, the political response to the exodus was mired in confusion and controversy. Those living in Nagorno-Karabakh had been treated as Armenian citizens since the fall of the Soviet Union, and almost all had Armenian passports, but Pashinyan's government was within weeks calling their citizenship into question, arguing that the documents had been issued for travel rather than as proof of nationality. These people, Yerevan attempted to argue, were stateless—and therefore entitled to specific protections and access to support from international organisations. Those with passports issued in Nagorno-Karabakh or with registrations there were banned from applying for new ones in the Republic of Armenia, and ruled ineligible to hold jobs in state bodies reserved for citizens, despite Karabakh Armenians having previously served in every role, from the security council to the presidency. Those who decided to keep their refugee status would not have the right to stand in elections, or even vote in them, effectively disenfranchising the victims of a conflict that Armenian officials maintained was a battle between democracy and autocracy.

There had been fears in some corners of the political elite that the anti-Pashinyan protest movement, which had struggled to articulate its aims when Baku moved on Stepanakert, would be revitalised by the wholesale arrival of much of the Karabakh Armenian political class, as well as tens of thousands of veteran military men and women, who could forcibly seek to remove the government they blamed for their dire situation. Those concerns hadn't materialised: the people who'd come over the mountains to Armenia were more concerned with finding somewhere for their families to live and putting food on the table than with starting to organise in any meaningful sense. Even once they were settled somewhere safer, many suffered with mental health problems, night terrors, gastrointestinal issues that had started during the blockade, and a general sense of exhaustion and total defeat.

Under the terms of the ceasefire signed by President Shahramanyan in September 2023, the Nagorno-Karabakh Republic was dissolved in its entirety at the end of the year. But the question of whether to continue it as a government-in-exile was soon being asked. The unrecognised state's final president had been allowed to exit with his family, presumably thanks to his compliance in accepting the surrender demands. His supporters now argued that he was the only legitimate representative of the Karabakh Armenians, even if he'd never been directly elected by the people. Apart from Artak Beglaryan, who had managed to slip out through the Lachin Corridor without being confronted by Azerbaijani border guards, all of Shahramanyan's would-be competitors were now languishing in a prison in Baku. But it was unclear what a government-in-exile, with no meaningful prospect of returning to the place it had governed, could actually offer its former citizens. The obvious demands were for a right of return, on which no progress was being made and none was even

A NATION NO MORE

imaginable; or alternatively for the Karabakh Armenians to be compensated by Azerbaijan for the properties and assets they'd left behind, which seemed to have little chance of being agreed bilaterally. Without their own official state administration, it would be down to Armenia—a country which now refused to claim the refugees as its own full citizens—to represent them in international legal proceedings. Armenia had also ended its subsidies for the Nagorno-Karabakh government since the fall, meaning that its funding was now uncertain and it would be unable to retain its entire cabinet of ministers in exile.

With no plan or purpose set out, in October, a month after they'd arrived in Armenia, a large crowd of Karabakhtsis gathered in Yerevan outside the State of Artsakh representative's office to demand answers from their leaders. The elite, they said, were living in the large houses they'd bought in Armenia with the profits from corruption and shady business deals, while regular people struggled to afford bread. In a bid to defuse the situation, the stateless state officials invited a small number of men as representatives to come in and speak to Shahramanyan. But the crowd surged forward, trying to push into the foyer, scuffling with police and even punching one of Shahramanyan's senior advisors.

Another challenge was that the authorities in Yerevan didn't have a strategy on how to preserve Karabakh Armenian civic life. Families who had lived together in villages for as far back as anyone could remember were now broken up, spread across towns and cities throughout the country. Skilled farmers had no real way of acquiring arable land or livestock, and resorted to seeking work as taxi drivers or handymen. Whereas after the First War Azerbaijan had set up specific schools for Karabakh Azeris in order to help preserve their culture and sense of identity, those things were dissolving in real time in Armenia. Some had advocated that settlements be built to keep communities together, potentially around abandoned villages in the Syunik region. But when I asked, Armenian officials would only say that the country had a long history of integrating and rehousing refugees after the First War. The fate of the Karabakhtsis looked set to mirror that of the Baku or Nakhchivan Armenians who'd left in that period of conflict: total assimilation into society. Without intervention, their unique traditions, customs, mentality and dialect will fade. The wide-eyed children who came through the Kornidzor checkpoint in September 2023 could well be the very last generation of Karabakh Armenians.

The problem is compounded by the fact that many didn't feel much safer in Armenia than they had in Nagorno-Karabakh. In the year after they fled their homes, as many as 10,000 of the region's former residents didn't stop there, choosing to move abroad.[1] The bulk went to Russia where they could travel without a visa and where many had family. Their professional skills and military experience will now benefit the country that abandoned them to their fate. On top of that, the conflict with Azerbaijan has shown no sign of easing up. In February 2024, almost six months after the fall of Nagorno-Karabakh, four Armenian volunteers were killed in a firefight near Nerkin Hand down in Syunik. Despite being inside Armenia's borders, the village was effectively surrounded by Azerbaijani troops from four sides, with a single road in and out supposedly protected by the Russians. The army didn't even want to station troops there any more, in case they were cut off in the precarious encirclement, and the men who died were revealed to be in their fifties and sixties—fighters with the Yerkrapah volunteer corps left to protect their homes on their own.[2]

Under continuing pressure from Baku, Pashinyan has committed himself even more resolutely to trying to avoid being dragged into another war, by acquiescing to more and more of Aliyev's demands. Chief among them was that Armenia change its constitution and declaration of independence to remove provisions calling for "reunification" with Nagorno-Karabakh. According to Baku, this was proof that Yerevan was a revanchist occupying power and, Pashinyan reasoned, there was no realistic prospect of it ever happening so it may as well be dispensed with. In the ultimate reversal of his earlier claims that "Karabakh is Armenia," and his dancing on the cliffs at Shushi, the Armenian prime minister in June 2024 declared he had been wrong—and that instead of his jubilant visit to Stepanakert in 2018, he should have admitted that Karabakh was Azerbaijan.[3] He was ready to make any concessions to Baku up to the point they infringed on Armenia's internationally-recognised territory, he said: only the guarantees of international law would offer Armenians protection.

Ultimately, the symbolic importance of the statement mattered more than its legal reality, and for many Armenians—already furious and disappointed with how unceremoniously the conflict had ended—it was the final proof that Pashinyan was a fool willing to run away every time Baku barked. Criticism of his government had previously been largely confined to the circles of wealthy urban Armenians who had prospered under the previous regimes, to pro-Russian cranks and to diasporans who had never experienced the realities of autocracy and corruption before Pashinyan came to office. Now, the opposition was far more widespread, even among those whose lives had materially improved thanks to the Velvet Revolution. It wasn't that people had changed their minds about the government's aims when it came to tackling corruption, seeking closer ties with the West or striking a better status quo with neighbouring countries: they were just no longer convinced that a bitter and stubborn Pashinyan was the man to do it.

Just as in 2020, though, there was no obvious replacement, leaving those who wanted a change in leadership without a change in political ideology lost for what to do next. Misunderstanding the very people who had taken to the streets to bring them to power in 2018, Armenian ministers wrote off the criticism as part of a Moscow-made information operation—the Kremlin was certainly trying to sway people away from their chosen path, through state-owned international media, Telegram channels and provocative statements, but these methods had never been as effective among Armenians as total defeat in Nagorno-Karabakh was proving to be. The paranoia in Yerevan even led to senior government figures complaining about media organisations and NGOs that it said were "pro-Russian," even when they were funded by Western capitals and actively sought to further the democracy and reform agenda.

Another deeply unpopular move was the effort by Pashinyan's party to remove Mount Ararat from Armenia's crest and other national symbols. The exaltation of the iconic peak that could be seen from the streets of Yerevan was a reminder for many of Armenia's past, where its people had come from and what they had been through. In Turkey though, the obsession with Ararat has often been framed as a direct territorial claim—notwithstanding the fact that the Armenians are hardly likely to invade their NATO-member neighbour to retake it, or the active denials by Yerevan officials of any claim to what was once Western Armenia. It has been a bone of contention since the Soviet era, when Ararat was featured on the Communist state emblem. During talks with Ankara when the issue was raised, a Soviet Armenian negotiator is said to have asked his counterparts whether, just because Turkey has the crescent moon on its flag, it therefore had a territorial claim on the moon. But Yerevan couldn't afford to mock or ignore the complaint any longer. Normalisation with nearby countries had now become a national security issue for the leadership. And so, after decades of children being taught that Ararat is an Armenian mountain, by spring 2024 officials were sent around schools to check that posters of Ararat weren't being hung on the walls, as internal discussions began on designing a new national symbol. If they were looking for inspiration, Pashinyan said, they should look at the tallest mountain actually inside their own country—Mount Aragats, a significantly smaller four-peaked volcano just north of the capital.[4]

If you were to read between the lines, it seemed that Pashinyan was presenting the collapse of Nagorno-Karabakh as an opportunity for Armenia. No longer would Yerevan be locked into a conflict that it couldn't win, divided from its neighbours because of the standoff. Now that the issue had been settled by Aliyev once and for all, the government could put prosperity and peace back on the agenda, where previously the overriding priority had been guarding against an inevitable war. Saving the core of the Republic of Armenia had meant sacrificing the Nagorno-Karabakh Republic, or at least admitting he was powerless to prolong it. Faced with a revanchist nationalist enemy, Pashinyan was prepared to give up territory, cede political capital and now even dismantle the Armenian national identity in the hope that he could appease Aliyev and put an end to the conflict once and for all. Having embarked down that path, he was unable to turn back or revise his strategy, desperate as he was to prove it could lead to peace.

It was a strategy virtually unique in history, and it was hard not to conclude that Pashinyan, like so many international mediators, had himself become a hostage to the negotiations with Aliyev. It was clear, though, that Yerevan saw its future lay with the West, even if it had been treated with apathy in the past, and Pashinyan had recognised it was time to shut the door on Russia for good. If this strategy worked, it would free another generation of Armenians and Azerbaijanis from following in the footsteps of those who came before them, and close the cycle of violence and hatred. What would happen if it failed didn't bear thinking about.

But the future hardly felt bright or promising for those who had left their homes in Nagorno-Karabakh and now waited to see whether their apartment would be next to appear in footage shared online of soldiers smashing up furniture and stepping on picture frames of their slain relatives. There had been faith in Stepanakert that the Russians would prevent this catastrophe from ever unfolding but, since the start of the full-scale war in Ukraine, it had become clear this faith was misplaced. Still, the West, Armenians had believed, wouldn't allow a mass exodus to take place, not after they'd stepped up their presence in the region. Now, in their disappointment, it was Brussels and Washington that more often took the blame from displaced Karabakhtsis. You couldn't really be surprised when the Russians sold you out to the higher bidder, but being let down by the very politicians who talked about the importance of democracy and human rights stung more. And worse still, it had played right into the Kremlin's hands, despite the fact it was the Russian peacekeepers who stood by as the offensive began and turned their backs on the desperate people gathering outside their headquarters. The failure of Washington and Brussels reinforced Putin's insistence that the West, despite its warm words, wouldn't do anything either.

As a result, Armenia's pivot to democracy risks being an abandoned revolution: it is a country that has genuinely done the hard work and made sacrifices in the name of joining a liberal world order, but that is now struggling to get any attention or support from those it is trying to emulate. A trickle of one-off deals will do little to change that. In 2024, the EU pledged to despatch around a quarter of a million dollars to help shore up Yerevan's economy against the impacts of a break with Russia. A separate ten-million-dollar plan to support its armed forces was reportedly blocked by Baku's close ally Hungary, which argued Azerbaijan should receive funding as well. In a bid to help

A NATION NO MORE

address the imbalance between the two countries, an imbalance Aliyev made masterful use of to squeeze out concessions, France moved to step up military co-operation with Armenia, shipping self-propelled artillery and other hardware. As well as Paris, India and Greece stepped into the void left by Russia as an arms dealer. Unsurprisingly, Baku has said the move risks destabilising the region. "We cannot just sit idly by," Aliyev said in April 2024, "if we see a serious threat, we will have to take serious measures."[5] Balancing the scales would be bad for Baku—which has maintained that the only version of peace is the one it wants to impose on its rival at bayonet-point.

Faced with this geopolitical pressure, and with the government intent on trying to use the end of the Nagorno-Karabakh conflict to normalise relations with its neighbours, the collapse of this tiny nation state went virtually unmarked, even in Armenia. The plight of refugees was seen as sad, but almost inevitable, by most. And, unlike Azerbaijan in the wake of the First Nagorno-Karabakh War, the government of Armenia saw the defeat as a threat to its hold on power, rather than a chance to tighten it, and so there were few commemorations of the state that had existed for three decades.

At Tsitsernakaberd, Yerevan's Armenian genocide memorial complex, an eternal fire burns, shaded by a ring of twelve giant dark stone slabs—each representing one of the historic Armenian-inhabited regions inside modern-day Turkey that had been lost. Nobody was prepared to add a stone to the circle for Nagorno-Karabakh.

* * *

The sun was going down on the evening of 9 May 2024 when Archbishop Bagrat Galstanyan shuffled into Yerevan's central Republic Square. Dressed in white robes, a crucifix hanging around his neck, he walked at the front of a column of supporters. They'd come a long way—the clergyman had for days led a march from the border region of Tavush to the capital in protest at the imminent handover of four villages technically inside Azerbaijan's internationally-recognised territory, but held by Armenia since the fall of the Soviet Union. As the procession snaked through the dusty lanes of the Armenian countryside, it was joined by hundreds of ordinary people and more than a few hardened opposition activists. Now it had arrived and it seemed like half of Yerevan had turned out to hear what he had to say.

Shoes covered with dirt from the road, Galstanyan—who had taken up the role of primate in Tavush after years preaching to the diaspora at a church in Canada—took to the stage. The thronging crowd joined him in singing the national anthem and reciting the Lord's Prayer, a marriage of patriotism and religion that I'd never seen from any other Armenian politician. Then, with a magnetic charisma that seemed to only pull more people onto the square, he began his speech, railing against unilateral concessions, praising the people of Tavush and insisting he had no political agenda other than to champion their fears and wishes.

The excitement built. Six years ago it had been Pashinyan marching across the country to hear the concerns of ordinary people; now, he was the isolated leader shuttered away while riot police set up their shields in front of the government buildings. One woman in the crowd spotted my EU press card hanging around my neck, pointed to the little flag and repeated *"shat vat e!"*—"very bad." I asked her what she meant, and she began regaling me with a confusing tale of how a government office had kept her documents in some kind of bureaucratic mix up, and how she blamed Pashinyan and his new friends. It was a bad sign for the government that they were taking the flak for all the gripes and grievances and injustices, just as his predecessors had before being ousted. The EU, she went on, should worry less about the Armenian border and more about illegal migrants crossing the Mediterranean into Italy. It was a strange thing for an Armenian to care about, and seemed to echo a line directly from Russian propaganda.

On stage, Galstanyan was becoming more and more animated, buoyed by the massive turnout and joined on stage by opposition activists with ties to the old regime. His insistence he was apolitical was quickly dispensed with, and he called for Pashinyan's resignation, giving the embattled leader an hour to step down. An hour came and went, with television cameras filming the clock ticking. The archbishop and his allies seemed unsure of what to do next—they gave Pashinyan another fifteen minutes. Unsurprisingly, nothing happened and the deadline again expired.

"As he has not reacted, he has shown he despises and rejects those who elected him," Galstanyan told the crowd. "We will force him to do it."

The ultimatum was a mistake. The call for an end to unilateral concessions was overwhelmingly popular, and had the would-be revolutionaries stuck to it they may well have forced Pashinyan's hand, receiving support from both the pro-Western Sasna Tsrer political group and the pro-Kremlin Union of Russian Armenians.[6] But Galstanyan's stunt—which his aides privately confirmed to me had not been pre-planned—made it easy for officials to write him off as a puppet of the former government. Kicking the prime minister out of office would prove harder than expected: over the weeks that followed, Galstanyan's supporters clashed with the police, throwing objects and receiving tear gas cannisters and flash grenades back in return. One photo showed a flashbang exploding in a rank of assembled news crews, while one protester who attempted to throw back a projectile had it explode in his hand, requiring the amputation of three fingers.[7] A tent encampment was set up outside the parliament, blocking traffic, while supporters flooded intersections elsewhere in the city.

But, as time went on, support for the movement waned and the archbishop's rhetoric only became more and more extreme. Turning his ire on the government, his official Twitter account issued an ominous warning: "no matter where you try to escape, we will find you and come. If necessary, we will come alone; if necessary, we will come with others. We will come on a donkey or by metro if needed." Officials, he said, needed to repent, while he put himself forward as this pure bastion of morality and traditional Armenian values. The message was simple: this was no longer patriots versus traitors, but saints versus sinners. Pashinyan's authority may come from the ballot box, but Galstanyan's came from God, so how could any man stand in his way? He soon declared himself the movement's candidate for prime minister, despite the fact that as a Canadian dual national he was ineligible to stand. The increasingly theocratic nature of his campaign earned him the mocking nickname of Hayatollah, a pun referencing Iran's Islamic leadership.

At the same time, he preached a geopolitical view for Armenia. Speaking to reporters, he called for "normalisation" with Russia and bemoaned that relations with the CSTO were in decline.[8] "Revenge," he said in one interview, was the only way to "restore the home that you have lost." Quite whether he wanted another war with Azerbaijan, or how he imagined he might win it, was unclear—but while the rhetoric alienated ordinary Armenians, it fired up his base. Chief among them were diasporans, particularly from the US, with influential groups based outside the country wasting no time in offering him their support. Many had families who had come to America via places like Syria and Iraq, countries they saw as having suffered under Western foreign policy. Others simply saw the Russians as the saviour from the Turks, given their families had suffered under the latter but never the former. Hayastantsis (those living in the Republic of Armenia itself) were under few such illusions, having seen the realities of being ruled from Russia both before independence and afterwards. It was those living in the country that had seen their incomes rise, their roads repaired, their corrupt mayors kicked out of office, and it was them who would wave their sons off to a war of revenge if one was declared. Without them on board, the movement soon fizzled into the background. But it left the sense that Armenia's democracy, its pivot towards the West, was on shaky ground.

"This conflict is a battle between democracy and autocracy," one Armenian official once told me.

"That's nonsense," I replied. "Even in the freest and fairest election, the most popular thing an Azerbaijani politician could do would be to take a hard line on Nagorno-Karabakh." Just because Azerbaijan was an autocracy doesn't mean it isn't one with legitimate grievances.

"No, no," the official said, "it's a battle between democracy and autocracy—in Armenia. We've told everyone that the West won't let anything happen to us. If that fails, it becomes harder to argue against the voices that say that only Russia and the old regime can save us."

EU and US officials were right to see Armenia as a rare opportunity to help a country escape Moscow's oppressive orbit, but it came with risks as well—and getting it wrong was a win for Russian propaganda. Despite that, the myth of Moscow as a protector has also shattered for good among the bulk of the Armenian population, and particularly among the Karabakh Armenians I spoke to. Those who had been failed by the promises of protection had simply concluded that nobody was going to save them. Aliyev had been able to enforce the terms he wanted, and even questions of protections or self-determination for the Karabakh Armenians found few supporters abroad. While many resented the contrast with the support and attention Ukraine has received, they often overlooked the fact that its fate and Armenia's are tied together: if Russia's imperial ambitions are realised in Eastern Europe, the handful of countries trying to break out from under Moscow's shadow in the South Caucasus and Central Asia will find their task far harder. If the West fails to give Ukraine what it needs to defend itself, what faith can countries on Russia's Eurasian fringe have that they won't be standing alone against Moscow? Putin's invasion triggered a second collapse of the Soviet Union, and this one looks set to be even bloodier than the first.

* * *

The fate of Nagorno-Karabakh, however, was probably sealed not in 2023 but in 1990. The fury that Armenians and Azerbaijanis unleashed on each other then turned into a vicious cycle, and the victory of Yerevan and Stepanakert triggered a chain reaction in Baku. The failure of leaders like Levon Ter-Petrosyan and Aliyev's father, Heydar, to reach a lasting agreement over the future of Armenian-inhabited Nagorno-Karabakh and the surrounding territories may have meant the conflict was put on ice, but ice thaws. The threat posed by Azerbaijan's neighbours gave the Aliyevs—first Heydar, then Ilham—enormous power over their own citizens and justified just about anything the state did in the name of regaining control of its borders.

Ethnic hatred had built up and bubbled over in the early 1900s, had simmered quietly during the Soviet Union, and has been carefully nurtured, fed and channelled by both Armenian and Azerbaijani leaders since. Pashinyan's efforts to dial down the tension came too late. By the time he came to power in 2018, two peoples once able to live side by side no longer could, and the power disparity between them had been reversed. The shifting geopolitical landscapes gave Baku the chance it needed to settle the conflict by force, and Aliyev knew the power imbalance was as great as it ever was going to get. The Azerbaijanis now

A NATION NO MORE

returning to the ruins of their Soviet-era homes can only hope that the pendulum never swings back in the opposite direction—that the cycle doesn't repeat itself again, with their children suffering at the hands of children they watched being driven out.

History, however, means little to those suffering through it. The families now living in draughty Armenian shacks, cooking their *zhingyalov hats* around stoves in the yard and leaving a place at the table for a missing son or brother, can't take any comfort in the knowledge that theirs is just the latest in a long line of tragedies. One family I met found a place to live on the outskirts of Yerevan near the airport, where they had to comfort their young son whenever aeroplanes roared overhead. Living in Stepanakert, every time he'd heard a plane it had meant everyone running for cover. To show him there was nothing to be scared of, his father took him down to the runway to sit on his shoulders and watch the passenger jets taking off and landing.

He, like Ruben's and Azat's children, are almost certainly the last Armenian generation to be born Karabakhtsis. They may get to grow up in relative safety with parents that love them, but they will likely never know the place they called home, the place their parents fought for. They'll never get to buy pickles in the central market or go for a drink at Bardak or spend time sitting on the grass beside the "We Are Our Mountains" monument, looking up at the stoic faces of Tatik and Papik. They'll never taste the wine produced on the land for generations or drink the mulberry vodka made by its villagers. For that unique society has now been extinguished by those who said it was worth nothing, having once been told the same about their own. Like the Azerbaijanis forced out in the 1990s, they had now been shut out of the land that defined them and shaped them, let down by everyone they had pinned their hopes on. And so the Karabakh Armenians have ceased to be Karabakh Armenians. They had been their mountains. What would they be now without them?

ACKNOWLEDGEMENTS

There are well over 100 people without whom this book would not exist. Some are those I'm privileged to call friends. Others were just passing acquaintances and friendly (or not-so-friendly) encounters. In each case though, the trust that people put in you when they share their stories creates an enormous responsibility, and it's one I've tried my best to live up to.

At times when access was closed off by the Russians, or as a result of the blockade, it would have been impossible to get news out of Nagorno-Karabakh without the efforts of dozens of people who, no matter how hungry, tired or fearful they were, went to charge their phones and keep those of us on the outside up to date. In particular, I want to thank Marut Vanyan, Siranush Sargsyan, and Nina and Lilit Shahverdyan, among a long list of others.

In Azerbaijan, I have been fortunate enough to hear the testimonies of tens of internally displaced people, former soldiers, analysts and activists. Specifically, I'm grateful to Vasif Huseynov, Rusif Huseynov, Orkhan Amashov and Adnan Huseyn for their perspectives and updates on the conflict, and to Araz Imanov for his constant troubleshooting and insights, as well as to my one-time fixer Ramiz for help with translations and avoiding landmines.

ACKNOWLEDGEMENTS

In Armenia, Astrig Agopian was invaluable in making the reporting in this book happen and gaining unparalleled access during 2023's mass exodus. Anna Naghdalyan has also given me far more help than I was ever comfortable asking for. I owe a debt of gratitude to Karena Avedissian for her insights, her help with brokering interviews and driving Ladas up and down the country to conduct them.

I am also immensely grateful to the editors who gave me the freedom over the years to write about a conflict that few of their readers had heard of and that other outlets were often uninterested in: particularly Jan Cienski, Cory Bennett, Christian Oliver and Ali Walker at POLITICO, as well as the teams at *The Spectator*, *Foreign Policy*, *TIME Magazine* and others.

At Hurst, I'd like to thank Lara Weisweiller-Wu, Alasdair Craig and Michael Dwyer—this book may have found its way into existence without them, but it would have been much the worse for it.

Special thanks go to Laurence Broers, whose encouragement, keen eye for detail and indispensable work on the region have improved both my understanding and my writing.

Finally, to my parents, Jane and Simon, for their support and love.

LIST OF ILLUSTRATIONS

1. Karabakh Armenian traditional dance and "national" monument, Stepanakert, 2009. Photo © Scout Tufankjian.
2. Mount Ararat & Turkish border photographed from Armenia. Photo © Gabriel Gavin.
3. Aghdam, Azerbaijani ghost city. Photo © Gabriel Gavin
4. Graves of Azerbaijani victims of the 1992 Khojaly massacre. Photo © Gabriel Gavin.
5. Mural to a fallen Armenian soldier of the 2020 Second War in Yerevan. Photo © Gabriel Gavin.
6. Goris, Armenia, over the mountains from Nagorno-Karabakh. Photo © Gabriel Gavin.
7. Karabakh Armenians leave Dadivank Monastery after the 2020 war. Photo © Scout Tufankjian.
8. Russian peacekeepers arrive in Nagorno-Karabakh after the 2020 war. Photo © Scout Tufankjian.
9. "Dear Shusha" poster of Azerbaijani President Aliyev, 2022. Photo © Gabriel Gavin.
10. Captured Armenian materiel of the 2020 war in Azerbaijan, 2022. Photo © Gabriel Gavin.

LIST OF ILLUSTRATIONS

11. Armenian house shelled by Azerbaijan in the 2022 Two Day War. Photo © Gabriel Gavin.
12. Armenian paramilitary & civilian training after the Two Day War. Photo © Gabriel Gavin.
13. Anti-Russian protests in Yerevan, September 2022. Photo © Gabriel Gavin.
14. The author interviews Armenian Prime Minister Pashinyan, September 2023. Photo © Gabriel Gavin.
15. Protests in Yerevan against the fall of Nagorno-Karabakh, 2023. Photo © Gabriel Gavin.
16. Karabakh Armenians seek shelter at the Russian peacekeeper base, 2023. Photo: Associated Press / Alamy Stock Photo (Russian Defense Ministry Press Service via AP).
17. Mass exodus from Nagorno-Karabakh, 2023. Photo courtesy of the photographer (author's source, cannot be named).
18. "My legs!"—the Kornidzor checkpoint amid the exodus, 2023. Photo © Gabriel Gavin.
19. A Karabakh Armenian boy's last look at the mountains, 2023. Photo © Gabriel Gavin.

NOTES

INTRODUCTION

1. John F. Baddeley, *The Russian Conquest of the Caucasus*, London: Longmans, 1908, p. xxi.
2. CIA World Factbook: Armenia.
3. The All-Union Population Census of the Soviet Union, 1979 and 1989.
4. Vladislav M. Zubok, *Collapse: The Fall of the Soviet Union*, New Haven: Yale University Press, 2021, pp. 54–6.
5. Bridget Coggins, *Power Politics and State Formation in the Twentieth Century*, Cambridge: Cambridge University Press, 2014, p. 164.
6. Thomas Goltz, *Azerbaijan Diary*, Armonk: M.E. Sharpe, 1998, p. ix.
7. Levon Ter-Petrosyan, "War or Peace? Time for Thoughtfulness," *Hayastani Hanrapetutiun*, 1 November 1997, pp. 59–71.
8. Population of the Republic of Azerbaijan, Azerbaijani President's Office, 2024; Population Census, Statistical Committee of the Republic of Armenia, 2022.
9. Vasily Grossman, *An Armenian Sketchbook*, New York: New York Review of Books, 2013, p. 60.

1. THE BEGINNING OF THE END

1. "Artsakh shoots down 4 Azeri attacking helicopters, 15 UAVs, 10 tanks and armored vehicles," Armenpress, 27 September 2020.
2. Pashinyan's televised address to the nation on 27 September 2020.
3. Karabakh Armenian officials routinely claimed their republic's population was around 130,000, while Azerbaijani sources insisted it was unlikely to be even half that. The events of September 2023 saw 100,400 people flee the region, but a sizeable population had already left the territory following the 2020 war or been trapped on the wrong side of the blockade.

4. Lara Rostomian et. al., "Effects of armed conflict on maternal and infant health: a mixed-methods study of Armenia and the 2020 Nagorno-Karabakh war," *British Medical Journal*, 2023, doi: 10.1136/bmjopen-2023-076171.
5. Statement by the Prime Minister of the Republic of Armenia, the President of the Republic of Azerbaijan and the President of the Russian Federation of 10 November 2020.
6. "Parliament Speaker Injured In Riots Over Karabakh Deal As Political Tensions Grow In Armenia," RFERL, November 2020.
7. "Why Armenia 'Velvet Revolution' won without a bullet fired," BBC News, 1 May 2018.
8. "'Privet, Rob' and other musings", *Armenian Weekly*, 12 March 2020.
9. Ministry of Finance of the Republic of Armenia, 2022.
10. Statement by the President of the Republic of Azerbaijan, the Prime Minister of the Republic of Armenia and the President of the Russian Federation, 10 November 2020.
11. Republic of Armenia Central Election Committee: Extraordinary National Assembly Elections, 2021 (in Armenian).
12. "Artsakh is Armenia, that's it, Arayik Harutyunyan says in inaugural address," Public Radio of Armenia, 21 May 2020.

2. FROM ONE WAR TO ANOTHER

1. Tom de Waal, *Black Garden*, New York: New York University Press, 2003, p. 171.
2. "The former Soviet Union," Human Rights Watch World Report, 1993.
3. "Armenian and Azerbaijani leaders embrace denialism," Eurasianet, 22 November 2019.
4. Goltz, *Azerbaijan Diary*, p. 237.
5. "Playing the 'Communal Card': Communal Violence and Human Rights," Human Rights Watch, April 1995.
6. "Conflict in the Soviet Union: Black January in Azerbaidzhan," Human Rights Watch, May 1991.
7. "Flame Towers, Baku," World Construction Network, 30 August 2012.
8. "Rise of Leader's Son Sharpens Azerbaijan's Identity Crisis," *The Washington Post*, 9 August 2003.
9. "Election Guide: Azerbaijani Presidency 2003," International Foundation for Electoral Systems.
10. "Azerbaijanism," Open Democracy, 2 August 2016.
11. "Azerbaijanism," Open Democracy, 2 August 2016.
12. "Former Armenian President Sarkisian's Office Does Not Deny Authenticity Of Leaked Audio," Radio Free Europe/Radio Liberty, 8 December 2020.

13. "Belarus Leader: Armenia Resisted Russian Push for Karabakh Peacekeeping," USC Dorsnife, Institute of Armenian Studies, 18 December 2018.
14. "Pashinyan calls for unification between Armenia and Karabakh," Eurasianet, 6 August 2019.
15. "Azerbaijan escalates punctuation war with Armenia," Eurasianet, 7 October 2019.
16. Aliyev's televised address to the nation of 27 September 2020.
17. UN Resolutions 822, 853, 874 and 884, all 1993.
18. "Artsakh President: The strike on Ganja was a warning," Mediamax, 4 October 2020.
19. Hikmet Hajiyev's statement on Twitter, 11 October 2020.
20. "Armenia: Unlawful Rocket, Missile Strikes on Azerbaijan," Human Rights Watch, 11 December 2020.
21. Aliyev's televised address to the nation of 10 November 2020.
22. "List of the fallen shehids in the Patriotic War," Ministry of Defense of the Republic of Azerbaijan, 2021.
23. "Aliyev admits Azerbaijan started the Second Nagorno-Karabakh War," OC Media, 9 November 2022.

3. "IT'S STARTED"

1. Pashinyan's appearance before parliament on 14 September 2022.
2. "Pashinyan assures no document has been signed," Armenpress, 14 September 2022.
3. "Armenia raises number of dead, missing to 207," CivilNet, 19 September 2022.
4. "Azerbaijan's casualties in tensions on Armenian border rise to 80—ministry," TASS, 17 September 2022.
5. State Department Press Briefing, 13 September 2022.
6. Borrell's appearance before the European Parliament, 4 October 2022.
7. "Turkey backs Azerbaijan, says Armenia 'should cease provocations'," Reuters, 13 September 2022.
8. "Russian-Led Bloc To Send Fact-Finding Mission To Armenia," Azatutyun, 14 September 2022.
9. Extraordinary session of the CSTO Collective Security Council, 28 October 2022.
10. "Russia Will Be One-Third Muslim in 15 Years, Chief Mufti Predicts," *The Moscow Times*, 5 March 2019.
11. "OSCE Rapporteur's Report under the Moscow Mechanism on Alleged Human Rights Violations related to the Presidential Elections of 9 August 2020 in Belarus," Organization for Security and Co-operation in Europe, 5 November 2020.

12. Aliyev's speech at the thirtieth anniversary of the founding of the New Azerbaijan Party, 21 November 2022.
13. "Pashinyan refuses to sign CSTO document on joint assistance measures for Armenia," Interfax, 23 November 2022.
14. "Hawkish Russian broadcaster Simonyan says she has been banned from Armenia," Reuters, 26 October 2022.
15. "Russian media coverage of MH17 leaves no room for dissenting voices," The Conversation, 21 July 2014; "Three men found guilty of murdering 298 people in shooting down of MH17," *The Guardian*, 17 November 2022; Margarita Simonyan on Twitter, 17 April 2022.
16. "Court Rejects Appeal Against Kocharian's Arrest," RFERL, 20 December 2019; "Armenian ex-president acquitted," Eurasianet, 6 April 2021.
17. "Armenian PM responds to comments of Russia Today editor-in-chief Margarita Simonyan," Armenpress, 28 July 2020.
18. "What Armenia's UN Votes Tell Us About Its Foreign Policy," EVN Report, 23 March 2023.
19. "Nikol Pashinyan Answers Parliamentary Assembly Delegates' Questions at PACE Plenary Session," Office of the Prime Minister of Armenia, 11 April 2019.
20. "Nagorno-Karabakh on the Crimean Referendum," CivilNet, 17 March 2014.
21. Margarita Simonyan on Twitter, 10 November 2020.
22. "Caucasus Barometer: Armenia," National Endowment for Democracy and CRRC Armenia, June 2022.
23. Aliyev's press conference with local media, 10 January 2023.
24. Aram Torosyan on Twitter, 15 August 2023.
25. European Union Mission in Armenia on Twitter, 15 August 2023—now deleted.
26. "WATCH: EU monitor takes cover in Armenian trench during Azerbaijani shooting," Armenpress, 15 August 2023.
27. European Union Mission in Armenia on Twitter, 15 August 2023.
28. "Markus Ritter—The European Union Mission in Armenia, Episode 322," Armenian News Network on YouTube, 29 March 2024.
29. "Results of the 2011 population census of the Republic of Armenia," ARMSTAT.
30. "Azerbaijan President Calls for Return to 'Historic Lands' in Armenia," Eurasianet, 13 February 2018.

4. JERUSALEM OF THE CAUCASUS

1. "Azerbaijan reveals number of people moving to Shusha by end of 2040," Trend.az, 20 October 2023.

2. Richard G. Hovannisian, *The Republic of Armenia, Volume Three*, Berkeley: University of California Press, 1996, p. 152.
3. "Caviar Diplomacy—How Azerbaijan silenced the Council of Europe," European Stability Initiative, 24 May 2012.
4. "During 2022, visits of around 200 foreign journalists organized to Azerbaijan's liberated territories," Azertag, 30 December 2022; "Annual Press Release," 2023, Azerbaijani Ministry of Foreign Affairs.
5. "Will Karabakh's Dadivank remain under Armenian control?" CivilNet, 13 November 2020.
6. Mubariz Gurbanli's comments to journalists, 2 May 2023.
7. "Illegal reconstruction of the Surb Ghazanchetsots church in Shushi," Monument Watch, 15 May 2021.
8. "Silent Erasure: A Satellite Investigation of the Destruction of Armenian Cultural Heritage in Nakhchivan, Azerbaijan," Caucasus Heritage Watch, September 2022.

5. A TALE OF TWO ARMENIAS

1. "Turkey's earthquake and the growing anger towards Erdogan," *The Spectator*, 12 February 2023; "Earthquake death toll surpasses 50,000 in Turkey and Syria," Reuters, 24 February 2023.
2. "800,000 Armenians counted destroyed," *New York Times*, 7 October 1915.
3. Henry Morgenthau, "Shall Armenia Perish?" *The Independent*, 28 February 1920.
4. Louis Dalrymple, *John Bull's Dilemma*, 1895.
5. Adolf Hitler, The Obersalzberg Speech, 22 August 1939.
6. "Countries that Recognise the Armenian Genocide," Armenian National Institute; Statement by President Joe Biden on Armenian Remembrance Day, The White House, 24 April 2021.
7. "The Armenian Allegation of Genocide: The issue and the facts," Ministry of Foreign Affairs of the Republic of Turkey.
8. "Why Foreign Minister Çavuşoğlu's Hand Signal Threatens Turkey's Minorities," Middle East Democracy Center, 13 May 2022. A video of the incident was posed on Twitter by Vicky Sheklian on 23 April 2022. At the time of writing, the video could still be viewed at: https://x.com/vickysheklian/status/1517946967229231104
9. "Extremist Groups: Grey Wolves," Counter Extremism Project.
10. "Uruguay President criticizes Cavusoglu's gesture to Armenian protesters," Public Radio of Armenia, 25 April 2022.
11. Eric Bogosian, *Operation Nemesis*, New York: Back Bay Books, 2017, pp. 200–212.

12. "The Armenian Secret Army for the Liberation of Armenia: A Continuing International Threat," CIA Directorate of Intelligence, declassified 11 January 2010.
13. Erdoğan's coronavirus briefing of 4 May 2020.
14. Interviewed for documentary *Screamers* (dir. Carla Garapedian), 2006.
15. Chamber judgement, Dink vs Turkey, 14 September 2010, European Court of Human Rights.
16. "France brings Armenian genocide bill one step closer to law," *The Christian Science Monitor*, 24 January 2012.
17. "Hrant Dink: an openDemocracy tribute," Open Democracy, 19 January 2007.
18. Tuba Tarcan Çandar, *Hrant Dink: An Armenian Voice of the Voiceless in Turkey*, Routledge, 2016.
19. Robert Fisk, "Award-winning writer shot by assassin in Istanbul street," *The Independent*, 20 January 2007.
20. Benjamin Harvey, "Mass protest at editor's funeral," *The Guardian*, 24 January 2007.
21. "Ruben Vardanyan renounces Russian citizenship, moves to Artsakh," Mediamax, 1 September 2022.
22. "The Troika Laundromat," Organized Crime and Corruption Reporting Project, 4 March 2019.
23. "Putin Accountability Act," H.R. 6422, 117th Congress, introduced 19 January 2022.
24. Vardanyan's interview with *Kommersant* of 9 November 2022.
25. "Ilham Aliyev received delegation led by Special Envoy of European Union for Eastern Partnership," Office of the President of the Republic of Azerbaijan, 17 November 2022.
26. Bayramov's press conference at ADA University, 24 November 2022.
27. "New Nagorno-Karabakh standoff as Azerbaijani officials temporarily block key road," Eurasianet, 3 December 2022.
28. "Unprecedented tax revenue growth recorded in Artsakh in 2017," Armenpress, 15 February 2018.
29. Caliber.Az on Telegram, 30 November 2022.

6. BLOCKADE

1. "Prime Minister Nikol Pashinyan's speech at the National Assembly during the discussion of the performance report of the Government Action Plan for 2021," Office of the Prime Minister of the Republic of Armenia, 13 April 2022.
2. "Nagorno-Karabakh: Armenia accuses Azerbaijan of using phosphorus bombs," France24, 19 November 2020; "Baku denies reports on use of white phosphorus munitions in Nagorno-Karabakh," TASS, 31 October 2020.

NOTES

3. Joint statement of the Armenian Armed Forces, 25 February 2021.
4. "Armenian National Assembly 2021 General," International Foundation for Electoral Systems.
5. "Greenwashing a blockade," OC Media, 1 March 2023.
6. Aliyev's press conference with local media, 10 January 2023.
7. "Who really are Azerbaijan's 'environmental activists' blockading Karabakh?," CivilNet, 14 December 2022.
8. "Azerbaijani 'environmentalist' chokes 'peace' dove during rally at Karabakh's Lachin Corridor," News.am, 15 December 2022.
9. "Karabakh accuses Azerbaijan of again cutting off gas supplies," Eurasianet, 22 March 2022.
10. "Armenia detains anti-Russia protesters as anger grows over Karabakh blockade," Eurasianet, 9 January 2023.
11. "Russian soldier jailed for life for killing Armenian family," BBC News, 23 August 2016.
12. "Armenia: After Landmine Deaths, Questions About Russian Army Base," Institute for War and Peace Reporting, 25 April 2013.
13. "Gyumri: How a Russian base destroyed local residents," *Kavkazskiy Uzel*, 25 April 2017 (in Russian).
14. Pashinyan's statement during a government session on 29 December 2022.
15. Toivo Klaar on Twitter, 22 January 2003.
16. "EU 'Not Considering' Sanctions Against Baku Over Karabakh Blockade," Azatutyun, 1 February 2023.
17. Application of the International Convention on the Elimination of All Forms of Racial Discrimination, Armenia v. Azerbaijan, International Court of Justice, 22 February 2023.
18. State Department readout following Blinken's Call with Azerbaijani President Aliyev, 21 March 2023.
19. "Aliyev Rejects U.S. Calls For Lifting Of Karabakh Road Blockade," RFERL, 21 March 2023.
20. Press statement: "Actions on the Lachin Corridor," US State Department, 23 April 2023.
21. "Azerbaijani activists end Nagorno-Karabakh sit-in as Baku tightens grip on region," POLITICO, 28 April 2023.
22. "Azerbaijani guard wounded by gunfire on the border," Daily Sabah, 15 June 2023.
23. Hikmet Hajiyev on Twitter, 24 June 2023.
24. "With Tightening Of Blockade, Azerbaijan Presents Karabakh Armenians With A Choice: Surrender Or Starve," RFERL, 31 July 2023.
25. Elchin Amirbayov's interview to Deutsche Welle, aired 7 September 2023.

26. "Azerbaijan blocks Red Cross access to Nagorno-Karabakh," OC Media, 11 July 2023.
27. "Azerbaijan arrests Nagorno-Karabakh resident during medical evacuation for 'war crime'," Eurasianet, 31 July 2023.
28. "Karabakh mother mourns the death of her two children," CivilNet, 20 July 2023.
29. "Azerbaijan/Armenia: Sides must reach 'humanitarian consensus' to ease suffering," International Committee of the Red Cross, 25 July 2023.
30. "The need to recognise the Nagorno-Karabakh Republic," French Senate Legislative File No. 145, 2020–2021 (in French).
31. "Samvel Shahramanyan was elected president of Artsakh," Radar Armenia, 9 September 2023.
32. "Armenia-Azerbaijan: Crucial to have 'unimpeded passage' of aid through Lachin Corridor, Security Council hears," United Nations, 16 August 2023.
33. "UK leads with larger investment in Azerbaijan, says Energy Minister," Azernews, 8 July 2024.
34. "Nagorno-Karabakh receives first aid in months, but route to Armenia remains closed," Eurasianet, 13 September 2023.
35. "Armenia MoD provides information on health condition of 2 soldiers wounded in Azerbaijan shooting," News.am, 4 September 2023.
36. "Defense Minister: Decisive retaliatory measures taken by the Azerbaijan Army have been highly appreciated by the Commander-in-Chief," Azertag, 24 September 2022.
37. "Commentary on the allegations made by Nikol Pashinyan, Prime Minister of Armenia, during his speech at the government meeting dated September 7," Republic of Azerbaijan Ministry of Foreign Affairs, 8 September 2023.
38. "Medvedev resorts to hate speech, saying wants all Ukrainians 'gone'," Ukrinform, 7 June 2022.
39. "Dmitry Medvedev: 'Guess what fate awaits him'," MediaMax, 19 September 2023.
40. "Eagle Partner Exercise Builds Upon Longstanding US-Armenian Security Cooperation," US Embassy in Armenia, 15 September 2023.
41. "Israeli weapons quietly helped Azerbaijan retake Nagorno-Karabakh—sources, data," *The Times of Israel*, 5 October 2023.
42. "Situation in Ukraine: ICC judges issue arrest warrants against Vladimir Vladimirovich Putin and Maria Alekseyevna Lvova-Belova," International Criminal Court, 17 March 2023; "Missing Ukrainian child traced to Putin ally," BBC News, 23 November 2023.

7. EXODUS

1. Statement by Azerbaijan's Ministry of Defense, 19 September 2023 (1.22pm).

2. Statement by Azerbaijan's Ministry of Defense, 19 September 2023 (2.25pm).
3. "The battle for battle position N32 in the defense of Martuni," CivilNet, 1 December 2023 (in Armenian).
4. Statement from the office of the Presidency of the Nagorno-Karabakh Republic, 20 September 2023.
5. Russian Ministry of Defence statement, 20 September 2023.
6. "Aliyev apologizes over death of Russian peacekeepers in Nagorno-Karabakh—Kremlin," TASS, 21 September 2023.
7. "President: The process of withdrawal of illegal Armenian armed units from their positions has already begun," Azertag, 20 September 2023.
8. "192 Azerbaijani servicemen martyred during local anti-terrorist measures, identity of 11 servicemen have not been identified," APA, 27 September 2023.
9. "Nagorno-Karabakh catastrophe fires anger against Armenia's leader," POLITICO, 20 September 2023.
10. Nikol Pashinyan's address to the nation, 19 September 2023.
11. "Nagorno-Karabakh denies reports on Azeri troops entering Stepanakert," Armenpress, 21 September 2023.
12. Statement of Azerbaijani negotiating team to local media, 21 September 2023.
13. Babayan's interview with Reuters, 25 September 2023.
14. "Prime Minister Nikol Pashinyan's message about independence," Office of the Prime Minister of the Republic of Armenia, 24 September 2023.
15. "218 Confirmed Dead In Karabakh Fuel Depot Blast," RFERL, 22 December 2023.

8. THE WORLD WATCHES ON

1. "Europe's energy crisis is Putin's problem now," POLITICO, 1 June 2023.
2. Memorandum of Understanding on Strategic Partnership in the field of energy between the European Union and Azerbaijan, 18 July 2022.
3. Statement by President von der Leyen with Azerbaijani President Aliyev, 18 July 2022.
4. "By choosing Azerbaijan as a gas supplier, Ursula von der Leyen weakens the European Union," Le Monde, 29 July 2022.
5. "Moscow sees persistent attempts by EU to intervene in agreements between Armenia, Azerbaijan, Russia," News.am, 25 May 2022.
6. "EU to host Armenia-Azerbaijan peace talks," POLITICO, 8 May 2023.
7. "Azerbaijan: Armenian POWs Abused in Custody," Human Rights Watch, 19 March 2021.
8. "Sofa, so bad: Turkish seating snafu hits von der Leyen, Michel," POLITICO, 7 April 2021.

9. Martin Schulz on Twitter, 2 July 2019.
10. "The scandal hanging over Ursula von der Leyen," POLITICO, 15 July 2019.
11. "Germany's offer to Ukraine of 5,000 helmets is 'joke', says Vitali Klitschko," *The Guardian*, 26 January 2022.
12. "EU, Russia and US held secret talks days before Nagorno-Karabakh blitz," POLITICO, 4 October 2023.
13. Charles Michel on Twitter, 20 September 2023.
14. Josep Borrell on Twitter, 21 September 2023.
15. European Parliament Resolution P8_TA (2015) 0316: Azerbaijan.
16. "Joint motion for a resolution on the situation in Nagorno-Karabakh after Azerbaijan's attack and the continuing threats against Armenia," European Parliament, 4 October 2023.
17. "Azerbaijani Parliament issues protest statement regarding European Parliament's resolution," APA, 16 March 2023.
18. Vaqif Sadiqov on Twitter, 22 June 2023.
19. "Ambassador of Azerbaijan to EU receives a warning for threats against MEPs who visited Armenia," Armenpress, 11 July 2023.
20. "Azerbaijan leader: 'France would be responsible' for any new conflict with Armenia," POLITICO, 8 October 2023.
21. "Karabakh Leadership Chides US Envoy," RFERL, 5 July 2023.
22. Senate Foreign Relations Committee meeting, 14 September 2023.
23. "Blinken warned lawmakers Azerbaijan may invade Armenia in coming weeks," POLITICO, 13 November 2023.
24. "As Azerbaijan claims final victory in Nagorno Karabakh, arms trade with Israel comes under scrutiny," CNN, 4 October 2023.
25. "Azerbaijan buys $1.2b Israel Aerospace Barak missile system," Aze.media, 14 November 2023.
26. "Israel-Azerbaijan Energy Deal Strengthens Strategic Partnership," Forbes, 13 November 2023.
27. "The unprecedented destruction of housing in Gaza hasn't been seen since World War II, the UN says," AP, 3 May 2024.
28. "Israeli envoy: Hamas 'animals' must be destroyed," POLITICO, 12 October 2023.
29. Erdoğan's speech to the Turkish parliament, 15 November 2023.
30. Israel Katz on Twitter, 12 January 2024.
31. "Life in an age of hyperinflation," *The Spectator*, 24 May 2022.
32. "Azerbaijan's Russian gas deal raises uncomfortable questions for Europe," Eurasianet, 22 November 2022.
33. Gubad Ibadoğlu and Ibad Bayramov, "An Assessment of the Potential of EU-Azerbaijan Energy Cooperation and its Impact on EU Gas Dependence on Russia,", *Foreign Policy Review* 6 (1), July 2023, pp. 91–108.

NOTES pp. [244–259]

34. Kartapolov, quoted by Russian newswire TASS, 19 September 2023.
35. "Ukrainian officials support Azerbaijan in blockade of Karabakh," Eurasianet, 25 January 2023.
36. "Azeris in Iran," Minority Rights Group, last updated December 2017.
37. Gohar Iskandaryan, "The Armenian community in Iran: issues and emigration," *Global Campus Human Rights Journal* 127–140, 2019.
38. "Iran Is Filling Armenia's Power Vacuum," *Foreign Policy*, 1 December 2022.
39. Khamenei speaking during a meeting with Erdoğan in Tehran, 19 July 2022.
40. "3rd day of IRGC military drill in Iran's Aras region," Mehr News Agency, 19 October 2022.
41. "Via official media, Iran and Azerbaijan issue escalating threats," Eurasianet, 9 November 2022.
42. "Indian migrants reshape Armenia's labor market," Eurasianet, 21 February 2024.

9. A NATION UNITED

1. "Azerbaijan: Prominent Opposition Figure Arrested," Human Rights Watch, 19 December 2023.
2. Details from interviews with Ibadoğlu's family members following his arrest in 2023 and 2024; "Azerbaijan: Opposition Leader Arrested," Human Rights Watch, 25 July 2023.
3. Gubad Ibadoğlu and Ibad Bayramov, "An Assessment of the Potential of EU-Azerbaijan Energy Cooperation and its Impact on EU Gas Dependence on Russia," *Foreign Policy Review* 6 (1), July 2023, pp. 91–108.
4. "Estimation of transparency and accountability of the budget funds spent for 'restoration and reconstruction of territories liberated from occupation'," Economic Research Center, 8 September 2023.
5. "Azerbaijani Authorities Crack Down on Eco Protests," Institute for War and Peace Reporting, 10 July 2023; "Crackdown on environmental protest in Azerbaijan sparks outrage," Eurasianet, 23 June 2023; "Aliyevs' Secret Mining Empire," OCCRP, 4 April 2016.
6. "The fight against the population of a village with tear gas. What happened in Soyudlu?" JAM News, 21 June 2023.
7. "Ilham Aliyev has chaired a meeting dedicated to the socio-economic performance of six months of 2023," Office of the President of the Republic of Azerbaijan, 11 July 2023.
8. Markar Melkonian, *My Brother's Road: An American's Fateful Journey to Armenia*, London: I.B. Tauris, 2005, p. 212.
9. Ilham Aliyev's address to the nation, 20 October 2020.

10. Ilham Aliyev's address to the nation, 15 October 2023.
11. Ilham Aliyev on Twitter, 19 March 2024.
12. Azerbaijani Presidency 2024, International Foundation for Electoral Systems.
13. "Karasin: Elections in Azerbaijan can become model for presidential elections in Russia," Report.az, 7 February 2024.
14. "Lack of genuine political alternatives in a restricted environment characterized Azerbaijan's presidential election, international observers say," OSCE, 8 February 2024.
15. "Freedom in the world 2024: Azerbaijan," Freedom House.
16. Charles Michel on Twitter, 8 February 2024.
17. "Azerbaijani state budget allots $3.8 bln for defense, national security in 2024," Interfax, 26 December 2023.
18. Aliyev on social media, 20 November 2012.
19. "Prime Minister Pashinyan presents the 'Crossroads of Peace' project and its principles at the Tbilisi International Forum," Office of the Prime Minister of the Republic of Armenia, 26 October 2023.
20. Parliamentary Assembly of the Council of Europe, "Challenge, on substantive grounds, of the still unratified credentials of the parliamentary delegation of Azerbaijan," 24 January 2024.
21. "Azerbaijan releases 32 Armenian soldiers in prisoner swap," Anadolu Agency, 13 December 2023; "Armenia backs Azerbaijan to host COP29 climate conference," Reuters, 8 December 2023.
22. "Good COP, bad COP: Azerbaijan's climate charm offensive is backfiring," POLITICO, 8 May 2024.
23. Office of the President of the Republic of Azerbaijan, "Ilham Aliyev met with residents who moved to city of Fuzuli and members of general public of the district on Fuzuli City Day," 17 October 2023.

10. A NATION NO MORE

1. CivilNet on Telegram, 27 June 2024 (in Armenian).
2. "Yerkrapah Volunteers Union of Armenia reports about volunteer soldier who died Monday," News.am, 13 February 2024.
3. "Armenia's Pashinyan: I should have said in 2018 that Karabakh should be part of Azerbaijan," News.am, 12 June 2024.
4. "Between State and Fatherland: A Tale of Two Mountains," EVN Report, 19 February 2024.
5. "Azerbaijani president says in case of 'serious threat' his country will take 'serious measures'," Anadolu Agency, 23 April 2024.
6. "Union of Russian Armenians condemns Armenian authorities' policy of unilateral concessions," Alpha News, 22 April 2024.

7. "Armenian Riot Police Formally Allowed To Use 'Deadly' Stun Grenades," Azatutyun, 10 July 2024.
8. Press conference given by Bagrat Galstanyan, 7 June 2024.

SELECT BIBLIOGRAPHY

Introduction

Broers, L. (2019), *Armenia and Azerbaijan: Anatomy of a Rivalry*. Edinburgh: Edinburgh University Press.

De Waal, T. (2013), *Black Garden: Armenia and Azerbaijan Through Peace and War*. New York: New York University Press.

Goff, K.A. (2021), *Nested Nationalism: Making and Unmaking Nations in the Soviet Caucasus*. Ithica: Cornell University Press.

Goltz, T. (1998), *Azerbaijan Diary: A Rogue Reporter's Adventures in an Oil-Rich, War-Torn, Post-Soviet Republic*. Armonk: M.E. Sharpe.

Grossman, V.S. (2014), *An Armenian Sketchbook*. London: MacLehose Press.

Ter-Petrosyan, L. (1997), "War or Peace? Time for Thoughtfulness," *Hayastani Hanrapetutiun*, 1 November, pp. 59–71.

Zubok, V.M. (2021), *Collapse: The Fall of the Soviet Union*. New Haven: Yale University Press.

Chapter 1: The Beginning of the End

Broers, L. and Ohanyan, A. (2020), *Armenia's Velvet Revolution: Authoritarian Decline and Civil Resistance in a Multipolar World*. London: I.B. Tauris.

Hakobyan, T. (2021), *The Valley of Death: 44-Day Catastrophe, September 27–November 10; War Diary*. Lusakn.

SELECT BIBLIOGRAPHY

Human Rights Watch (2020), "Azerbaijan: Unlawful strikes in Nagorno-Karabakh." 11 December.

Chapter 2: From One War to Another

Altstadt, A.L. (2017), *Frustrated Democracy in Post-Soviet Azerbaijan*. Washington, D.C.: Woodrow Wilson Centre Press.

———(2017), *The Politics of Culture in Soviet Azerbaijan, 1920–40*. London: Routledge/Taylor & Francis Group.

Cartner, H. and Human Rights Watch (1997), "Response to Armenian Government Letter on the town of Khojaly, Nagorno-Karabakh." 23 March.

De Waal, T. (2018), *The Caucasus: An Introduction*. Oxford: Oxford University Press.

Galichian, R. (2012), *Clash of Histories in the South Caucasus: Redrawing the Map of Azerbaijan, Armenia and Iran*. London: Bennett & Bloom.

Goltz, T. (1998), *Azerbaijan Diary: A Rogue Reporter's Adventures in an Oil-Rich, War-Torn, Post-Soviet Republic*. Armonk: M.E. Sharpe.

Mammadova, S. (2024), *Who Should Write National History?* Baku: Baku Research Institute.

Shafiyev, F. (2018), *Resettling the Borderlands: State Relocations and Ethnic Conflict in the South Caucasus*. Montreal: McGill-Queen's University Press.

Chapter 3: "It's Started"

Gavin, G. (2022), "On the Front Lines of Europe's Newest War," *The Spectator*, 15 September.

Gavin, G. (2022), "Putin's 'Cold War Alliance' gets frosty reception in Armenia," POLITICO, 23 November.

International Crisis Group (2023), "Averting a New War between Armenia and Azerbaijan." Europe Report No. 266.

Landgraf, W. and Seferian, N. (2024), "A 'frozen conflict' boils over: Nagorno-Karabakh in 2023 and future implications," Foreign Policy Research Institute, 18 January.

Chapter 4: Jerusalem of the Caucasus

European Stability Initiative (2012), "Caviar Diplomacy: How Azerbaijan silenced the Council of Europe." 24 May.

SELECT BIBLIOGRAPHY

Gavin, G. (2022), "Battle over Shusha highlights Armenian-Azerbaijani tensions." *TIME Magazine*, 12 September.

Hess, M.R. and Nabiyev, R. (2023), *Shusha's Legacy: The History and Development of Azerbaijan's Cultural Capital*. Berlin: Gulandot Verlag.

Hovannisian, R.G. (1996), *The Republic of Armenia, Vol 3*. Berkeley: University of California Press.

Chapter 5: A Tale of Two Armenias

Bogosian, E. (2017), *Operation Nemesis: The Assassination Plot that Avenged the Armenian Genocide*. New York: Back Bay Books.

Candar, T.T., Freely, M. and Libaridian, G. (2017), *Hrant Dink: An Armenian Voice of the Voiceless in Turkey*. Abingdon: Routledge.

Dédéyan, G., Demirdjian, A. and Saleh, N. (2023), *The Righteous and People of Conscience of the Armenian Genocide*. London: Hurst.

Poulton, H. (1997), *The Top Hat, the Grey Wolf and the Crescent: Turkish Nationalism and the Turkish Republic*. New York: New York University Press.

Suny, R.G. (2017), *They Can Live in the Desert but Nowhere Else: A History of the Armenian Genocide*. Princeton: Princeton University Press.

Chapter 6: Blockade

Crisis Group (2023), "Responding to the humanitarian catastrophe in Nagorno-Karabakh." 29 September.

Derluguian, G. and Hovhannisyan, R. (2022), "The Post-Soviet Revolution in Armenia: Victory, Defeat, and Possible Future," in Jack A. Goldstone, Leonid Grinn and Andrey Korotayev (eds), *Handbook of Revolutions in the 21st Century*. Springer, pp. 899–922.

Gavin, G. (2023), "Europe watches on as humanitarian crisis unfolds in Nagorno-Karabakh," POLITICO, 7 January.

Karapetyan, A. (2023), "Education second, life first." EVN Report, 4 September.

Koolaee, E. and Rashidi, A. (2024), "The Zangezur Corridor and Threats to the Interests of the Islamic Republic of Iran in the South Caucasus," *Caucasus Analytical Digest*, 136, pp. 3–6.

Office of the Prime Minister of Armenia (2023), "Prime Minister Nikol

SELECT BIBLIOGRAPHY

Pashinyan's interview to POLITICO Europe." 13 September. Available at: https://www.primeminister.am/en/interviews-and-press-conferences/item/2023/09/13/Nikol-Pashinyan-Interview-POLITICO-Europe/ (last accessed 15 August 2024).

Chapter 7: Exodus

Amnesty International (2023), "Azerbaijan: As Azerbaijani forces assume full control over Nagorno-Karabakh, it must respect and protect the rights of local ethnic Armenians." 29 September.

Gavin, G. (2023), "Azerbaijan launches attack in Nagorno-Karabakh, announces 'evacuation' of Armenian population." POLITICO. 19 September.

Gavin, G. (2023), "Azerbaijan declares victory in lightning Nagorno-Karabakh offensive." POLITICO. 20 September.

Gavin, G. and Melkozerova, V. (2023), "Russia reports peacekeepers killed in Nagorno-Karabakh fighting." POLITICO. 20 September.

Sauer, P. (2023), "'It's a ghost town': UN arrives in Nagorno-Karabakh to find ethnic Armenians have fled." *The Guardian*, 2 October.

Chapter 8: The World Watches On

Assenova, M. and Shiriyev, Z. (eds) (2015), *Azerbaijan and the New Energy Geopolitics of Southeastern Europe*. Washington, D.C.: The Jamestown Foundation.

Azerbaijani Ministry of Foreign Affairs, *Relations between Azerbaijan and European Union*. Available at: https://mfa.gov.az/en/category/regional-organisations/relations-between-azerbaijan-and-european-union (last accessed 15 August 2024).

Delanoë, I. (2021), "Israel—Azerbaijan: An alliance in search of renewal." Fondation Méditerranéenne d'Études Stratégiques, 29 July.

Gavin, G. (2022), "Azerbaijan stands to win big in Europe's energy crisis." *Foreign Policy*, 27 May.

Gavin, G. (2022), "Iran is filling Armenia's power vacuum." *Foreign Policy*, 1 December.

Global Witness (2023), "Oil firms bankroll Azerbaijan's warring regime with billions in fossil fuel money." 8 November.

SELECT BIBLIOGRAPHY

Tokmajyan, A. (2024), "'No People, No Problems': The Growing Appeal of Authoritarian Conflict Management." *Carnegie Middle East Center*, 31 January.

Chapter 9: A Nation United

Alstadt, A. (2017), *Frustrated Democracy in Post-Soviet Azerbaijan*. New York: Columbia University Press and Woodrow Wilson Centre Press.

Freedom House (2023), "Nations in Transit: Azerbaijan." Available at: https://freedomhouse.org/country/azerbaijan/nations-transit/2023 (last accessed 15 August 2024).

LaPorte, J. (2015), "Hidden in plain sight: political opposition and hegemonic authoritarianism in Azerbaijan." *Post Soviet Affairs*, Volume 31, Issue 4.

Levitsky, S. and Way, L. (2010), *Competitive Authoritarianism: Hybrid Regimes After the Cold War*. Cambridge: Cambridge University Press.

Mammadova, S. (2023), "Deconstructing Narratives of Pain: Speaking and Writing National History in Modern Azerbaijan." Baku Research Institute, 14 October.

Veliyev, T. (2022), "Azerbaijan's role in natural gas supplies to Europe." Baku Research Institute, 7 November.

Chapter 10: A Nation No More

Papazian, T. (2022), "Armenia and the West: Reassessing the Relationship." EVN Report, 22 July.

Zolyan, M. (2023), "Defeated Armenia Looks to a New, Post-Russia Foreign Policy." Carnegie Endowment for International Peace, 27 November.

INDEX

Abdullayeva, Leyla, 76
Abkhazia, 22
Absalamova, Nargiz, 253
Adamyan, Azat, 25–7, 28, 36–8, 194, 272, 291
Adygea, 4
Afghanistan, 239
Agababyan, Parkev, 214–15
Ağalı smart village, Karabakh, 113–14
Aghabekalanj, Karabakh, 174
Aghajanyan, Anush, 214
Aghavno, Karabakh, 45–6, 104
Aghdam, Karabakh, 12, 47, 57, 68, 69, 112
   blockade crisis (2022–3), 172, 174, 179, 180–81
   First War (1988–94), 12, 50, 51–2, 54, 69, 241
   Qarabağ FC, 115–16
   reopening of roads (2023), 205
   Second War (2020), 47, 68

Agos, 139, 141
agriculture, 39–40, 168
Akhundov, Sabir, 64
Albanians, 63, 119, 123, 178
alcohol, 102, 119, 246
Aleppo, Syria, 13, 131
Ali ibn Abi Talib, 6
Aliyev, Heydar, 15–16, 31, 32, 58–61, 64, 69, 290
Aliyev, Ilham, 31, 61–5, 107, 114, 124, 147, 253–4, 260–64, 290
   blockade crisis (2022–3), 155, 167, 179–80
   'crossroads of peace' plan (2023), 267–8
   economy and, 263–4
   environmental protests (2023), 254–5
   Erdoğan's visit (2021), 109
   EU, relations with, 223–30, 234, 244, 254, 261–2
   Iran, relations with, 248

INDEX

Israel, relations with, 241
joint statement (2023), 269–70
One Day War (2023), 198, 199, 259–61
presidential election (2024), 260, 261
purge (2023–4), 253–4, 265
returnees and, 265, 266, 277
Russia, relations with, 243–4
Second War (2020), 259
Syunik, views on, 103
Two Day War (2022), 68–70, 86, 87, 96, 98
United States, relations with, 238
Von der Leyen's visit (2022), 223–6
Allahverdiyev, Ilham, 57
Alma-Ata Protocols (1991), 13, 99
Amaras Monastery, Karabakh, 41, 63
American University of Armenia, 152
Amirbayov, Elchin, 172
Amnesty International, 253
Anglo-Asian Mining, 255
Ankara airport bombing (1982), 138
apples, 100
Arabs, 4, 140
Aras River, 114, 131, 248
Argentina, 5
Armenia; Armenians, 1–3, 4–5
Christianity, 41, 63, 118–24, 250

diaspora, 5, 13, 46, 131, 281, 288
genocide (1915–17), *see* Armenian genocide
in India, 250
in Iran, 246
khachkars, 63
languages, 63
names, 5
Republic, First (1918–20), 7, 136
Republic, Second (1991–present) *see* Republic of Armenia, Second
Russian Armenia (1828–1917), 4, 5, 7
Soviet Socialist Republic (1920–91), 7–11, 108, 123
Armenia and Azerbaijan (Broers), 16
Armenian Apostolic Church, 41, 121
Armenian genocide (1915–17), 5, 82, 92, 127–42, 143, 219, 240, 285
Turkish denial of, 134–6, 140, 256–7, 268
Armenian Revolutionary Federation, 128, 137–8
Armenian Secret Army, 138
Armenian Sketchbook, An (Grossman), 18
Artsakh, 19, 40, 42
see also Republic of Artsakh
Artsakh Football Federation, 272

INDEX

Askeran, Karabakh, 214–15
Assyrians, 131, 140
atheism, 8, 41, 119, 120
Aurora Prize for Awakening
  Humanity, 143
Avars, 6
Avetisyan family, 162–3
Aygestan, Karabakh, 214
Azerbaijan SSR (1920–91), 6, 7–
  11, 49–50, 56, 108, 123
  Nakhchivan emigration, 123
  religion in, 8, 41, 119, 120
Azerbaijan; Azeris, 3, 4, 5, 6
  Democratic Republic (1918–20),
    7, 55, 107–8
  in Iran, 246, 248
  Islam in, 6, 119–20, 246
  language, 29, 49
  March Days (1918), 55, 63, 91
  names, 6
  Republic (1991–present), see
    Republic of Azerbaijan
  Russian Azerbaijan (1828–
    1917), 4, 6, 7
  Soviet Socialist Republic (1920–
    91), see Azerbaijan SSR
Azerbaijan Youth Foundation, 155
Azerbaijani National Front, 57
Azerbaijani Popular Front, 51
Azeri language, 29, 49
Aznavour, Charles, 175

Babali, Hafiz, 253
Babayan, Davit, 205, 215
Babayan, Samvel, 177

Baddeley, John, 4
Baghdad, Iraq, 131
Baku, Azerbaijan, 8, 55, 58, 112
  Black January (1990), 56–8, 91,
    290
  graves in, 57–8, 69–70, 275
  Martyrs' Lane, 55, 57, 114, 275
Balladur, Édouard, 175
Baltic nations, 9
Barak MX missile system, 239
Barda, Karabakh, 67
Bardak, Stepanakert, 25, 29, 36–8,
  48, 66, 109, 194, 272, 291
Bartholomew, Saint, 133
Başlıbel, Karabakh, 49–50, 54, 71
Battle of Sarikamish (1915), 128
Battle of Shusha (1992), 52–3
Batumi, Georgia, 125
Baybalayev, Natiq, 252
Bayraktar TB-2 drones, 30, 185,
  242
Bayramov, Jeyhun, 147
Bedouins, 130
Beglaryan, Artak, 44–5, 145, 156,
  165, 172, 177, 203, 278
Beirut, Lebanon, 131
Belarus, 9, 86, 87, 90
Belgium, 5
Berdashen, Karabakh, 207
Bern Convention, 165
Biden, Joseph, 88, 134, 217, 236
Black Garden (De Waal), 16
Black January (1990), 56–8, 91,
  290
Black Sea, 21, 125, 130, 243

INDEX

black soil, 9–10, 38, 168
Blinken, Antony, 86, 168, 237
blockade (2022–3), 154–81, 199–201, 206–7, 212, 232, 235, 278
   food supplies and 156–7, 163, 165, 170, 172–81, 206–7
   famine and, 178–81, 199–200
   healthcare and, 156, 173, 174
blood feuds, 7
Blue Mosque, Yerevan, 120
Bolsheviks, 7, 55, 108, 129, 136
Bono, Louis, 232
border guards, Russian, 13, 86, 94, 98, 242
Borrell, Josep, 86, 164, 232
Bosnian War (1992–5), 230
Brazil, 178
bridal kidnappings, 7
British Petroleum, 59
Broers, Laurence, 16
Buenos Aires, Argentina, 131
Bulbul, 115
Bulgarians, 140
Bush, George Walker, 239

Calcutta, Bengal, 131
Caliber, 149
California, United States, 5
Canada, 286, 288
cannabis, 80
Caspian Sea, 56, 58, 59, 262
Caucasus Heritage Watch, 123
Çavuşoğlu, Mevlüt, 135
Central Asia, 6, 7, 9, 21, 62, 290

Chartar, Karabakh, 208
Chechnya; Chechens, 4, 7
China, 21, 88, 179, 236
Christianity, 4–5, 41, 63, 87, 118–24
Christmas, 151
circumcision, 85
Civil Contract, 153
civil society organisations, 265–6
Cleveland Clinic, 60
Collective Security Treaty Organization (CSTO), 86–7, 89, 90, 91, 94, 97, 183, 187, 189, 288
Committee to Protect Journalists, 253
consumerism, 85
COP29 (2024), 269
copper, 39
Cornell University, 123
corruption, 9, 33, 34, 40–41, 43, 65, 153, 281
Council of Europe, 93, 111, 165, 177, 268
Country to Live In, A, 145
Covid-19 pandemic (2019–23), 30, 104, 170
Crimea, 92, 93, 223–4, 245
'crossroads of peace' plan (2023), 267–8
cuisine, *see* food

Dadivank, Karabakh, 118, 208
Dagestan, 4
Dashnaktsutyun, 128, 137–8

INDEX

Dayton Accords (1995), 230
De Waal, Tom 16
Deir ez-Zor, Syria, 130
democracy
  in Armenia, 35, 65, 87, 89, 93, 245, 246, 278, 282, 284, 289
  in Artsakh, 44, 107, 260
  in Azerbaijan, 62, 65, 234, 235, 245, 253, 262–4, 265
  in European Union, 112
  in Turkey, 139
depopulation, 40, 55, 84, 113
dialects, 41
Dilijan, Armenia, 143
Dink, Hrant, 139–41, 256–7
Dixon, Rodney, 166–7
Diyarbakır, Turkey, 126, 128, 131
Djemal Pasha, 137, 138
drones, 2, 28, 30, 185, 194, 242
dual citizenship, 277
Dubai, United Arab Emirates, 58, 269

Eagle Partner, 184–5, 233
earthquake (2023), 126
Economic Research Center, 254
Ekmekjian family, 5
Elchibey, Abulfaz, 51, 58
electricity, 50, 198, 206, 269
energy
  fossil fuels, *see* fossil fuels
  green energy, 225, 261, 262
Enver Pasha, 128, 137
environmentalism, 149, 155, 165–6, 170, 254–5

Equinor, 59
Erdoğan, Recep Tayyip, 109, 126–7, 138, 230–31, 236, 240, 242
Erzincan, Turkey, 128, 137
Erzurum, Turkey, 128, 136
Escudero, Stanley, 61
Eshoo, Anna, 89
Estonia, 9
ethnic cleansing, 10, 44, 52, 54, 56–8, 205, 218
Europe Hotel, Stepanakert, 36, 46
European Commission, 223–6, 230–31, 232
European Council, 226, 230, 261
European Court of Human Rights, 268
European External Action Service (EEAS), 95, 230
European Parliament, 111, 164–5, 234, 235, 261
European Political Community, 236
European Stability Initiative, 111
European Union (EU), 21, 86, 95–8, 111, 223–36, 261–2, 286–7, 289
  Armenia, relations with, 284–5
  Artsakh election (2023), 177
  Azerbaijan election (2024), 261
  Azerbaijan energy deal (2022), 223–6, 230, 244, 254, 261
  blockade crisis (2022–3), 164–5
  monitoring mission (2022–3), 95–8, 188
  peace talks, 227–36

321

INDEX

Western Azerbaijan Community and, 266
Eurovision Junior Song Contest, 158

Fagot anti-tank launchers, 196
famine (2023), 178–81, 199–200, 206–7
Fedayi, 129
First War (1988–94), 11–13, 16, 38, 44, 257–8, 262, 279–80
  1988 outbreak, 10, 52, 108, 195
  1990 Black January, 56–8, 91, 290
  1991 blackouts, 50; referendum, 11, 245; Operation Ring, 11, 162; Meşəli massacre, 251–3
  1992 Khojaly massacre, 51–2, 53, 69, 257; Battle of Shushi, 52–3; Azerbaijani offensive, 53
  1993 Huseynov mutiny, 58; looting of Aghdam, 69; Zangilan campaign, 114
  1994 Kyrgyzstan talks, 59; ceasefire, 12–13, 59–60, 123–4, 227
First World War (1914–18), 128
Fisk, Robert, 141
Flame Towers, Baku, 58, 114
food
  blockade (2022–3), *see under* blockade
  khorovats, 27, 101, 180, 214
  lavash, 27, 100, 180

menemen, 125
refugee crisis (2023), 211
stolichniy, 115
tolma, 95
zhingyalov hats, 38, 156
football, 115–16, 272
fossil fuels, 58, 59, 66, 82, 109, 112, 239, 261–2
  EU-Azerbaijan deal (2022), 223–6, 230, 244, 254, 261
France, 5, 21, 82, 131, 134, 138, 140, 231, 285
blockade crisis (2022–3), 175, 179, 180, 204
EU-Azerbaijan energy deal (2022), 225–6
Freedom Support Act (US, 1992), 239
Friendship of Peoples restaurant, Baku, 56
FSB, 13, 78–9
fuel station explosion (2023), 209–10

Gabon, 178
Galstanyan, Bagrat, 285–8
Gambar, Isa, 61
gampr, 273
Gandzasar monastery, Karabakh, 145
Ganja, Azerbaijan, 67, 197
gas industry, 58, 66, 82, 109, 112, 223–6, 230, 254, 261–2
Gasparyan, Onik, 153–4
Gaza, 239–40

INDEX

Gazanchi Church, Shusha, 121
Gazprom, 94
genocide, 218
   Armenian genocide (1915–17),
      see Armenian genocide
   Gaza (2023–present), 240–41
   Holocaust (1941–5), 134, 135,
      142
   see also ethnic cleansing; war
      crimes
Georgia, 4, 5, 7, 22, 94, 120, 125, 226, 242, 247, 261
Germany, 134, 135, 142, 224, 231
Ghana, 178
Ghazanchetsots Cathedral, Shushi, 31, 105, 121–2, 124
ghost towns, 55, 84
Ghukasyan, Arkady, 215
Ghukasyan, Julieta, 162
glasnost and *perestroika* (1985–91), 9
Glendale, Los Angeles, 131
Goff, Krista, 8
gold, 39, 132, 142, 149, 255
Goltz, Thomas, 12, 53
Google Maps, 118
Gorbachev, Mikhail, 9, 56–7
Goris, Armenia, 1, 20, 75, 79, 95, 102, 143, 157–8, 160, 206
   One Day War (2023), 201–2, 204
   refugee crisis (2023), 210, 212, 214, 216, 219
Granada Summit (2023), 236
graves, 57–8, 151, 275

Great Terror (1936–8), 7
Greece, 285
Greeks, 130, 140
Green Chapel, Shushi, 105, 122
green energy, 225, 261, 262
Gregory the Illuminator, 41
Grey Wolves, 135, 141, 155
Grossman, Vasily, 18
Gurbanli, Mubariz, 119
Gyumri, Armenia, 162–3, 242

Hadrut, Karabakh, 35, 36, 67, 258
Hagopjanyan, Armen, 103–4
Hajiyev, Hikmet, 171–2, 180, 182, 193, 215
Hakari Bridge checkpoint
   blockade (2022–3), 154–81, 200, 201, 206–7, 212, 232, 235
   exodus (2023), 271
   Khachatryan arrest (2023), 251
   reopening (2023), 201, 204–5, 208
   skirmish (2023), 170–72
Hakari River, 46, 169
Hakobyan, Anna, 184
Hamas, 239
Hamidian massacres (1894–7), 128
Harris, Kamala, 88
Harutyunyan, Arayik, 43–5, 65, 106, 118, 165, 176, 215, 253
Hasanli, Ulvi, 253
healthcare, 156, 173, 174
Hidalgo, Anne, 175
Hin Shen, Karabakh, 170

323

INDEX

Hitler, Adolf, 134, 224
Holocaust (1941–5), 134, 135, 142
homosexuality, 85
horses, 107
Hotel Mirhav, Yerevan, 95, 159
Hotel Moscow, Baku, 58
Hovannisian, Richard, 108
Hovhannisyan, Hovhannes, 118
Human Rights Watch, 52, 53, 253
Hungary, 231, 234, 284
Huseynov, Maharram, 50, 53–4, 71
Huseynov, Rusif, 163, 234
Huseynov, Surat, 58
hydroelectricity, 168, 269

Ibadoğlu, Gubad, 254, 261–2
Iğdır, Turkey, 135
Ijevan, Armenia, 34
Imanov, Araz, 159
Independent, 133
India, 21, 50, 63, 249–50, 285
Ingushetia; Ingush, 4
International Court of Justice, 166, 178, 179, 240
International Criminal Court, 166, 186
Iran, 4, 6, 9, 21, 107
  Islamic Republic (1979–present), *see* Islamic Republic of Iran
Iraq, 21, 131, 288
Islam, 6, 63, 85, 101, 119–20, 123–4, 128, 249
Islamic Republic of Iran, 62, 70, 94, 102, 114, 120, 164, 167

Armenia, relations with, 246–9
Armenians in, 246
Azerbaijan, relations with, 246–9, 267
Lachin Corridor incident (2022), 147–8
Turkey, relations with, 247, 248
Israel, 21, 66, 112, 120, 185, 239–41
Istanbul
  Armenian community, 138–9
  Armenian genocide (1915–17), 130
  Dink assassination (2007), 141
  İstiklal Avenue bombing (2022), 126
  peace talks (2023), 232
  Young Turk trials (1919–20), 137
Istiglal sniper rifles, 235
İstiklal Avenue bombing (2022), 126
Italy, 231, 234, 261
İzmir, Turkey, 130

Jabrayil, Azerbaijan, 67
Jalavyan, Karen, 37
Japan, 178
Jermuk, Armenia, 75, 84–5, 148, 186, 233
Jerusalem, 5
Jewish people, 6, 17, 57, 119, 134
joint statement (2023), 269–70
journalists, 84
Junior Eurovision Song Contest, 158

INDEX

Kabardino-Balkaria, 4
Kafyan, Karina, 213–14
Kalbajar, Karabakh, 47, 54, 58, 68, 70, 118, 145, 241
Kalmyks, 7
Kapan, Armenia, 102, 103, 247–8
Karabakh, 9, 19, 228
Karabakh Clan, 33, 42
Karabakh Committee, 14, 15
Karabakh horses, 107
Karabakh Khanate (1748–1822), 107
Karachays, 7
Karasin, Grigory, 261
Kardashian family, 5
Kariuki, James, 179
Kartapolov, Andrey, 244
Kashmir, 249
Kazakhstan, 9, 21, 86, 244, 263
Kazan, Russia, 162
Kazimov, Anar, 116
Kekalov, Mahammad, 253
KGB, 13, 14, 18, 58, 59
Khachatryan, Vagif, 173, 174, 251–3
khachkars, 63
Khalapyan, Valera and Razmela, 29
Khamenei, Ali, 247
Khankendi, Karabakh, 51, 229, 260, 275
  see also Stepanakert
Khaza, Mirza, 57
Khodorkovsky, Mikhail, 14
Khojaly, Karabakh, 51–2, 53, 69, 162, 257

khorovats, 27, 101, 180, 214
Khovaev, Igor, 232
Khudavang, Karabakh, 119
Kim, Yuri, 237
Kirov, Sergey, 56
kılıç artığı, 138
Kılıçdaroğlu, Kemal, 127
Klaar, Toivo, 164, 227–8, 231, 233, 234
Kocharyan, Robert, 15, 33, 34, 42, 92, 154
Komitas, 130, 219
Kommersant, 145
Kornidzor, Armenia, 46, 161, 169
  blockade (2022–3), 201, 234, 237
  EU parliamentarians' visit (2023), 235
  One Day War (2023), 201, 205, 206, 207, 275
  Power's visit (2023), 217
  refugee crisis (2023), 210, 211, 213, 217, 219, 234
Kosovo, 22, 112, 213
Kovgan, Ivan, 198
Krasnodar, Russia, 131
Krasukha, 194
Krkjan, Karabakh, 197
Kulakov, Kirill, 162
Kurdistan Workers' Party, 126
Kurds, 6, 126–7, 131–2, 140
Kvien, Kristina, 237
Kyrgyzstan, 59, 86

Lachin Corridor, 31, 47, 68, 70, 83, 110, 118, 147–9, 267

INDEX

blockade (2022–3), 154–81, 200, 201, 206–7, 212, 232, 235
   refugee crisis (2023), 212, 214, 215, 278
   reopening (2023), 204–5
Lachin, Karabakh, 31, 47, 68, 214, 264–5
Lake Sevan, 25, 76, 180
Lake Van, 125
landmines, 44, 113, 115, 148, 163, 191
Latvia, 9
lavash, 27, 100, 180
Lavrov, Sergey, 97
Lebanon, 5, 46, 131
Lentsov, Alexander, 162
Lernadzor, Armenia, 102
Lezgins, 6
liberalism, 35
Life and Fate (Grossman), 18
Lion, Joel, 241
Lisagor, Karabakh, 170
Lithuania, 9
London School of Economics, 254
Los Angeles, California, 131
LPG (liquefied petroleum gas), 2
Lukashenko, Alexander, 14, 64–5, 87
Lvova-Belova, Maria, 186–7

Macaulay, Thomas Babington, 274
Macron, Emmanuel, 175, 236
Magnitsky, Sergey, 14
Maléna, 158

Malta, 178
Manukyan, Davit, 215
March Days (1918), 55, 63, 91
markets, 38, 40
Marriott Hotel, Yerevan, 88
Marseilles, France, 131
marshrutka, 2
Martakert, Karabakh, 36, 54, 58, 174, 195, 196
Martirosyan, Sergey, 202
Martuni, Karabakh, 36, 41, 195, 196, 217
Martyrs' Lane, Baku, 55, 57, 114, 275
Medvedev, Dmitry, 184
Meghri, Armenia, 102, 167, 247
Mehraliyev, Cherkaz, 253
Melkonian, Markar, 257
Melkonian, Monte, 241
Melkumyan, David, 202
menemen, 125
Meşəli massacre (1991), 251–3
Mets Shen, Karabakh, 170
Mets Taghlar, Karabakh, 123
MGIMO, 61
Mgrditichian, Harutian, 137–8
MH17 shootdown (2014), 92
Michel, Charles, 226–36, 261
middle class, 39
mining industry, 39
Minsk Group, 226
Mirzoyan, Ararat, 32–3
Mnatsakanyan, Levon, 215
mobile phones, 196
Modi, Narendra, 249

INDEX

Mohammed, Prophet of Islam, 6
Moldova, 22, 244, 263
Molotov-Ribbentrop Pact (1939), 9
Mongol Empire (1206–1368), 4
Montreux Convention, 243
Moscow, Russia, 131
mosques, 122, 123–4
Mount Ararat, 136, 142–3, 152, 282–3
Mountain Jews, 6, 57
Mustafayev, Adalat, 122

Nagorno-Karabakh conflict
1988 outbreak of First War, 10, 16, 52, 108, 195
1990 Black January, 56–8, 91, 290
1991 blackouts, 50; referendum, 11, 245; Operation Ring, 11, 162
1992 Khojaly massacre, 51–2, 53, 69, 257; Battle of Shushi, 52–3; Azerbaijani offensive, 53
1993 Huseynov mutiny, 58; Zangilan campaign, 114
1994 Kyrgyzstan talks, 59; ceasefire, 12–13, 59–60, 123–4, 227
2016 Azerbaijani offensive, 28–30, 37
2020 border clashes, 65; Second War, *see* Second War; ceasefire agreement, 31–2, 35–6, 45, 68–71, 76, 117–19, 144
2022 border clashes, 2; Operation Revenge, 116–17; Two Day War, 16, 76–99, 103, 148, 172, 229, 247; EU mission deployed, 95–6; Lachin Corridor affair, 148–9, 154–5; blockade begins, 155–6
2023 EU peace talks, 227–36; border clashes, 97; Hakari Bridge skirmish, 170–72; border clashes, 182; One Day War, 3, 16, 191–203, 235–6, 259–61, 271–6; refugee crisis, 203–19, 232, 237, 256, 271–3
Nagorno-Karabakh region, 9–10, 21
  agriculture, 39–40
  cuisine, 27, 38
  depopulation, 40
  dialect, 41
  middle class, 39
  mining industry, 39
Nagorny Park, Baku, 55
Nakhchivan, Azerbaijan, 15, 70, 101, 103, 109, 123
Narimanyan, Vera, 174
National Olympic Committee, 61
Nazi Germany (1933–45), 134, 135, 142, 224
Neftçi FC, 116
Nerkin Hand, Armenia, 98
Nersesyan, Alvina, 105–7, 110, 122
Nersisyan, Gurgen, 165, 177
Nested Nationalism (Goff), 8

INDEX

Netanyahu, Benjamin, 240
New Year holidays, 39, 158
New York Times, 133
Nord Stream pipelines, 224
North Atlantic Treaty Organisation (NATO), 12–13, 67, 87, 184, 185, 230, 242, 247
North Korea, 92
Northern Ireland, 17
Norway, 59
Nowruz, 260
Nrnadzor, Armenia, 98

Ocampo, Luis Moreno, 166
oil industry, 58, 59, 66, 82, 112, 224, 239, 254
Oil Rocks, 59
Olympic Games, 61
One Day War (2023), 3, 16, 191–203, 235–6, 259–61, 271–6
Operation Iron Fist (2020), 66
Operation Nemesis (1920–22), 137–8, 268
Operation Revenge (2022), 116–17
Operation Ring (1991), 11, 162
Orly airport bombing (1983), 138
OSCE, 226, 261
Osmanbey, Istanbul, 141
Ottoman Empire (1299–1922), 4, 5, 55, 127, 136
  Armenian genocide (1915–17), 5, 92, 127–42, 143, 219, 240, 268
  Hamidian massacres (1894–7), 128

Young Turk Revolution (1908), 137

Pakistan, 249
Palestine, 112, 136, 239–40
Pallone, Frank, 89
Paris, France, 131, 138
Pashinyan, Nikol, 27, 31, 32–5, 40, 42, 43, 53, 91, 153, 181, 184, 290
  Artsakh visit (2018), 65, 67, 109, 281
  blockade crisis (2022–3), 167
  'crossroads of peace' plan (2023), 268
  Eagle Partner (2023), 184–5, 233
  EU peace talks (2023), 227–8
  interview (2023), 181, 187–90
  joint statement (2023), 269–70
  local elections (2023), 233
  military reforms, 185–6
  Mount Ararat dispute, 282–3
  One Day War (2023), 200–201, 203, 204
  parliamentary election (2021), 154
  protests (2023), 200–201, 204, 278
  protests (2024), 285–9
  Putin's visit (2022), 91
  refugee crisis (2023), 205
  reunification, statement on (2024), 280–82
  Rome Statute ratification (2023), 186–7

INDEX

Russia, relations with, 90–95, 162–3, 184–7, 189
Russian peacekeepers, views on, 163
Second War (2020), 70, 153–4
Shushi visit (2018), 65, 67, 109, 281
Tavush handover (2024), 285–8
territorial integrity, statement on (2023), 167
Two Day War (2022), 80–81, 86, 98, 99
Ukraine, relations with, 184, 189
Velvet Revolution (2018), 33, 40, 43, 44, 87, 89, 93, 204, 281
Pashinyan, Vova, 181
Pashonyan, Hovhannes, 128, 131–2
Pelosi, Nancy, 88–90, 101, 237
Permyakov, Valery, 162–3
Persia, *see* Iran
Peskov, Dmitry, 187, 227
petrol, 207, 209–10
Petrosyan, Aram, 196
Petrosyan, Ruben, 191–2, 207, 211, 272, 276, 291
Petrosyan, Sarhat, 118
Poghosyan, Narek, 182
Polyanskiy, Dmitry, 179
Power, Samantha, 217–18
PR (public relations) firms, 112
Price, Ned, 86
prisoners of war, 36, 68, 229

Problem from Hell, A (Power), 218
Puck, 134
Putin, Vladimir, 14, 31, 64, 65, 68, 89, 144, 186–7, 216, 250
  Armenia visit (2022), 90–91
  presidential election (2024), 261
  rules-based order, views on, 245

Qarabağ FC, 115–16
Qu'ran, 63

Radio Free Europe, 57
railways, 94
Red Cross
  blockade (2022–3), 156, 160, 163, 171, 173, 178, 180, 204, 229
  refugee crisis (2023), 211, 213, 217, 219
refugees
  First War (1988–94), 100, 104, 113, 114, 264–5, 279–80, 291
  One Day War (2023), 203–19, 232, 237, 256, 271–80, 284
  Second War (2020), 40, 104
religion, 8, 41, 118–24
Republic Medical Centre, Stepanakert, 209
Republic of Armenia, First (1918–20), 7, 136
Republic of Armenia, Second (1991–present)
  Alma-Ata Protocols (1991), 13, 99
  Artsakh refugees in, 276–80

329

INDEX

corruption, 33, 34, 40–41, 153, 281
'crossroads of peace' plan (2023), 267–8
dual citizenship in, 277
Eagle Partner, 184–5, 233
Eurovision Junior Song Contest (2022), 158
GDP per capita, 263
Gyumri base, 162–3, 242
India, relations with, 249–50
international journalists in, 84
Iran, relations with, 246–9
joint statement (2023), 269–70
Kocharyan Presidency (1998–2008), 33, 42
military, 185–6
Mount Ararat dispute, 282–3
Nagorno-Karabakh conflict, see Nagorno-Karabakh
New Year holidays, 39, 158
Pakistan, relations with, 249
parliamentary election (2021), 154
Pashinyan Premiership (2018–present), 32–5, 40, 43, 65, 91, 153, 181, 184
Pelosi's visit (2022), 87–90, 101, 237
protests (2023), 200–201, 204, 278
protests (2024), 285–9
Putin's visit (2022), 90–91
railways in, 94
Rome Statute ratification (2023), 186–7
Russia, relations with, see Russo-Armenian relations
Russian migration to, 183
Sargsyan Presidency (2008–18), 33, 42, 64–5, 92, 163
Tavush handover (2024), 285–8
Ter-Petrosyan Presidency (1991–8), 13–15, 33, 290
Ukraine, relations with, 184, 189, 245
Velvet Revolution (2018), 33, 40, 43, 44, 87, 89, 93, 204, 281
Republic of Artsakh (1991–2023), 40, 42–8, 65, 145, 271–85
Azerbaijan, wars with, see Nagorno-Karabakh conflict
blockade (2022–3), 156–81, 200, 201, 206–7, 212, 235
evacuation (2023), 205–19, 232, 271–80, 284
famine (2023), 177–81, 199–200
flag, 259, 276
fuel station explosion (2023), 209–10
general election (2020), 43–4
Ghazanchetsots, symbolism of, 121
parliament, 65, 106, 176, 260–61
presidential election (2023), 104, 176–7
Russia, relations with, 143–7, 216, 284
surrender (2023), 197, 202–3

INDEX

Vardanyan's move to (2022), 143–7
Republic of Azerbaijan (1991–present)
Alma-Ata Protocols (1991), 13, 99
Black January (1990), 56–8, 91, 290
'caviar diplomacy', 111
Christian communities, 119
civil society organisations, 265–6
'crossroads of peace' plan (2023), 267–8
Elchibey Presidency (1992–3), 51, 58
energy industry, 58, 59, 82, 109, 112, 224–6, 239, 243–4, 254, 261–2
environmental protests (2023), 254–5
GDP per capita, 263
Heydar Presidency (1993–2003), 15–16, 31, 32, 58–61, 64, 290
Huseynov mutiny (1993), 58
Ilham Presidency (2003–present), see Aliyev, Ilham
India, relations with, 249–50
Iran, relations with, 246–9, 267
Islam in, 119, 246
Israel, relations with, 66, 120, 185, 239–41
Jewish community, 119
joint statement (2023), 269–70
Khachatryan trial (2023), 251–3
military spending, 264
Nagorno-Karabakh conflict, see Nagorno-Karabakh
Pakistan, relations with, 249
parliamentary elections (2005), 62
presidential election (2003), 61–2
presidential election (2024), 260, 261
prison system, 37
purge (2023–4), 253–4, 265
Russia, relations with, 64, 243–4
secularism in, 119, 246, 256
Tavush handover (2024), 285–8
Ukraine, relations with, 245
United Kingdom, relations with, 179
United States, relations with, 237–9
Von der Leyen's visit (2022), 223–6
Zangezur Corridor, 10, 101, 103, 109, 164, 167, 178, 225, 247, 267
Republic Square, Yerevan, 88, 154, 158, 181, 200
returnees, 109, 264–5, 277, 291
Ritter, Markus, 96
Rome Statute, 186–7
Rostov-on-Don, Russia, 131
Russian Civil War (1917–23), 7, 55–6, 108, 129, 136

INDEX

Russian Empire (1721–1917), 4, 5, 6–7, 63, 120, 128, 129, 136
Russian Federation (1991–present), 12–13, 14, 21, 62, 64, 104, 110
   Alma-Ata Protocols (1991), 13
   Armenia, relations with, *see* Russo-Armenian relations
   Artsakh refugees in, 280
   blockade crisis (2022–3), 156, 160, 161–3, 179–80
   border guards, 13, 86, 94, 98, 242
   COP29 vetoes (2023), 269
   Crimea annexation (2014), 92, 93, 223–4, 245
   Gyumri base, 162–3, 242
   Istanbul peace talks (2023), 232
   One Day War (2023) and, 191, 193, 197, 198
   peacekeepers, *see* Russian peacekeepers
   presidential election (2024), 261
   refugee crisis (2023) and, 205, 216, 233
   Second War (2020) and, 31–2, 36, 68, 117, 118, 144
   Turkey, relations with, 242–3
   Two Day War (2022) and, 78–9, 86–95, 97–9
   Ukraine War (2022–present), *see* Russo-Ukrainian War
   Valdai Discussion Club, 65
Russian language, 8, 29
Russian Peacekeeper (cocktail), 36
Russian peacekeepers, 31–2, 46, 68, 86, 101, 109–10, 144, 146, 147, 154, 244–5, 267
   blockade crisis (2022–3), 156, 160, 161–3, 169, 170, 171
   Dadivank, guarding of, 118–19
   One Day War (2023), 191, 193, 197, 198
   Operation Revenge (2022), 117
   refugee crisis (2023), 205, 216, 233, 272
Russian Revolution (1917), 7, 129
Russo-Armenian relations, 13, 90–95, 104, 184–7, 189, 216, 242, 244–5, 283–5, 287–90
   Gyumri base and, 162–3, 242
   Pashinyan's statement (2024), 282
   Putin's visit (2022), 90–91
   Tavush handover protests (2024), 287–8
Russo-Ukrainian War (2022–present), 9, 20, 84, 88–90, 144, 182–3, 185, 189–90, 226, 237, 250
   abductions of children, 186–7
   Armenia and, 242, 245, 289–90
   Azerbaijan and, 232, 234, 243, 245
   buildup to, 182–3, 228
   energy and, 223–5, 243–4
   Germany and, 231
   Turkey and, 88, 242–3
   Western aid, 231
   'Z' symbol, 182

INDEX

Sadiqov, Vaqif, 96, 111, 235
Sahakyan, Bako, 43–4, 215
Samadov, Mohubbet, 113–14
Sargsyan, Serzh, 33, 42, 64–5, 92, 163
Sarsang reservoir, 168
Sasna Tsrer, 287
Sberbank, 142
Scholz, Olaf, 236
Schulz, Martin, 231
Scud missiles, 67
Seaman's Silence prison, Moscow, 14
Second War (2020), 3, 16, 27–31, 35–6, 42, 65–8, 226, 247, 259
    Armenian military and, 185–6
    casualties, 151–3
    ceasefire agreement, 31–2, 35–6, 45, 68–71, 76, 117–19, 144, 267
    refugees, 40, 106
Second World War (1939–45), 224
secularism, 119, 246, 256
Seljuk Empire (1037–1194), 4, 6, 102
Serbia, 112
shahid, 3
Shahramanyan, Berta, 211
Shahramanyan, Samvel, 177, 193, 197, 205, 278
Shahverdyan, Nina, 45
Shia Islam, 6, 120, 246
Shushi/Shusha, Karabakh, 30–31, 35, 42, 47, 105–17
    Azerbaijani redevelopment (2021–4), 110
    Erdoğan's visit (2021), 109
    First War (1988–94), 52–3, 108
    Ghazanchetsots Cathedral, 31, 105, 121–2, 124
    Green Chapel, 105, 122
    Ilham's visit (2020), 68–9
    One Day War (2023), 196, 261, 273
    parliament move plans, 196, 261
    Pashinyan's visit (2019), 65, 67, 109
    pogrom (1920), 108, 121
    Second War (2020), 65, 67–9, 80, 255
    Turkic capital of culture (2023), 110
    Upper Mosque, 122, 124
Silk Road, 3, 21
Simonyan, Alen, 89–90, 201
Simonyan, Margarita, 92, 93–4
Simson, Kadri, 261
Sisian, Armenia, 103–4
Smerch missiles, 67
Smyrna, 130
SOCAR, 61
solar power, 225
Sotk, Armenia, 26, 54, 76–9, 82, 83, 97, 99–101, 148, 182, 233
South Africa, 187, 240
Soviet Union (1922–91), 1, 2, 6, 7–11, 12, 19, 56, 63, 120, 131
    atheism, 8, 41, 119, 120
    Crimea transfer (1954), 92
    dissolution (1991), 11, 19, 39, 46, 56, 59

INDEX

glasnost and *perestroika* (1985–91), 9
Great Terror (1936–8), 7, 92
Operation Ring (1991), 11, 162
Söyüdlü, Azerbaijan, 255
Speier, Jackie, 89
St. Bartholomew Monastery, Van, 133
Stalin, Josef, 7, 9, 56, 63, 92, 131
Statoil, 59
Stepanakert, Karabakh, 12, 25, 229, 291
    Bardak pub, 25, 29, 36–8, 48, 66, 109, 194, 272, 291
    blockade crisis (2022–3), 156–7, 176, 200, 206–7
    central market, 38, 156, 291
    Europe Hotel, 36, 46
    One Day War (2023), 194, 195, 197, 198, 259–60, 271–3
    Republic Medical Centre, 209
    University, 105, 110
    Vardanyan's move to (2022), 143–7
    We Are Our Mountains sculpture, 41, 259, 276, 291
    see also Khankendi
Stepanyan, Gegham, 117
stolichniy, 115
Sumgait FC, 116
Sumgait pogrom (1988), 10, 52
Sunni Islam, 119–20
Switzerland, 178
Syria, 5, 13, 21, 46, 63, 92, 126, 129, 131, 136, 162, 288

Syunik, Armenia, 15, 70, 79, 101–4, 167, 233, 247, 280

Tabriz, Iran, 248
Taiwan, 22, 88
Tajikistan, 9, 86, 263
Talaat Pasha, 137–8
Talaatpasha, Istanbul, 139
Talish, Karabakh, 29, 67
Talysh people, 6
Tatars, 6
Tatev, Armenia, 102, 143
Tatik and Papik, 41, 259, 276, 291
Tats, 6
Tavush handover (2024), 285–9
Tbilisi, Georgia, 94, 242
Tehlirian, Soghomon, 137–8
Telegram, 35, 80
Ter-Petrosyan, Levon, 13–15, 33, 64, 290
Thomas-Greenfield, Linda, 179
TikTok, 195
Tiridates III, King of Armenia, 5
tolma, 95
Topchubashov Centre, 163, 234
Torosyan, Aram, 97
tourism, 26, 250
Trabzon, Turkey, 130
Transnistria, 22
Troika Dialog, 142, 144
Tsitsernakaberd, Yerevan, 285
Tufenkjian family, 5
Turkey, 12, 21, 67, 90, 94, 119, 125–42, 154, 242–3, 247
    Ankara airport bombing (1982), 138

INDEX

Armenian community, 138–42
Armenian genocide denial, 134–6, 140, 256–7, 268
'crossroads of peace' plan (2023), 267–8
Dink assassination (2007), 141
earthquake (2023), 126
elections (2023), 126, 127
Erdoğan's Shusha visit (2021), 109
Iran, relations with, 247, 248
Israel, relations with, 240
Istanbul trials (1919–20), 137
Mount Ararat dispute, 282–3
national identity, 140
NATO membership, 12, 67, 86, 88, 185, 242
Russia, relations with, 242–3
Ukraine War (2022–) and, 242–3
Turkic peoples, 4, 6, 9, 21, 63
Turkmen tribes, 4
Turkmenistan, 56
Twelver Shi'ism, 120
Two Day War (2022), 16, 76–99, 103, 148, 172, 247

Udi people, 119
Ukraine
  Azerbaijan relations with, 245
  Crimea annexation (2014), 92, 93, 223–4, 245
  Maidan Revolution (2014), 93
  MH17 shootdown (2014), 92
  Russian War (2022–present), see Russo-Ukrainian War

Union of Russian Armenians, 287
United Arab Emirates, 58, 269
United Kingdom, 21, 64, 82, 177, 179, 180, 202, 254
United Nations (UN), 13, 64, 66, 93, 178, 269
United States, 21, 64, 144, 230, 236–9, 289
  Armenian diaspora in, 131, 288
  Armenian genocide, recognition of, 82, 134
  blockade crisis (2022–3) and, 168, 169, 179
  Eagle Partner, 184–5, 233
  Istanbul peace talks (2023), 232
  peace negotiations (2023), 232, 236–9
  Pelosi's Armenia visit (2022), 87–90, 101, 237
  refugee crisis (2023) and, 217–18
  Two Day War (2022) and, 86, 88–90
  War on Terror (2001–present), 239
United World Colleges, 143
Upper Mosque, Shusha, 122, 124
uranium, 102
Uruguay, 135
USAID, 217
Uzbekistan, 9

Vagifgizi, Sevinj, 253
Vakhtang, Prince, 119
Valdai Discussion Club, 65

INDEX

Van, Turkey, 125–32, 141–2, 143
Vardanyan, Ruben, 142–7, 156, 165, 168, 176, 215, 253
Velvet Revolution (2018), 33, 40, 43, 44, 87, 89, 93, 204, 281
vodka, 40, 100, 208
Volkov, Andrey, 146, 162
Von der Leyen, Ursula, 223–6, 230–31, 232, 234, 244

Wahhabism, 120
walkie talkies, 196
war crimes, 12, 29, 251–3, 256
War on Terror (2001–present), 239
We Are Our Mountains sculpture, 41, 259, 276, 291
weddings, 180
Western Armenians, 5, 13, 46, 131, 140
Western Azerbaijan Community, 266
Wilson, Woodrow, 136
Wilsonian Armenia, 136, 138
wind power, 225, 262
Wings of Tatev, 143
Wosornu, Edem, 178

Yagublu, Tofig, 253
Yamal pipeline, 224
Yazidis, 7
Yeghnikner, 37

Yeghtsahogh, Karabakh, 170
Yerablur cemetery, Yerevan, 151–2, 257, 275
Yerevan, Armenia, 1, 8
  Blue Mosque, 120
  Eurovision Junior Song Contest (2022), 158
  protests (2023), 200–201, 204
  Republic Square, 88, 154, 158, 181, 200
  Tsitsernakaberd, 285
  Yerablur cemetery, 151–2, 257, 275
Yevlakh, Azerbaijan, 197, 203
Yılmazer, Ali Fuat, 141
Young Turk movement (1908–18), 137–8
Yugoslav Wars (1991–2001), 213, 230

Zabukh, Karabakh, 46, 104
Zakharova, Maria, 227
Zangezur Corridor, 10, 101, 103, 109, 164, 167, 178, 225, 247, 267
Zangilan, Karabakh, 113–14
Zas, Stanislav, 87
Zelenskyy, Volodymyr, 245
zhingyalov hats, 38, 40, 156
Zubok, Vladislav, 10